Hiring the Best and the Brightest

Hiring the Best and the Brightest

A Roadmap to MBA Recruiting

Sherrie Gong Taguchi

AMACOM

American Management Association

Atlanta • Brussels • Buenos Aires • Chicago • London • Mexico City • New York • San Francisco

Shanghai • Tokyo • Toronto • Washington, D.C.

This is dedicated to the hundreds of hiring managers who were my customers when I was VP of University Recruiting at Bank of America and Director of Corporate HR for Dole Packaged Foods and Mervyn's Department Stores. Also, a debt of gratitude to the 1400+ executives with whom I have worked in the diversity of companies that annually recruit our Stanford MBAs. You all are an amazing source of inspiration. Cheers!

Library of Congress Cataloging-in-Publication Data

Taguchi, Sherrie Gong, 1961–
    Hiring the best and the brightest : a roadmap to MBA recruiting / Sherrie Gong Taguchi.
        p.   cm.
    Includes index.
    ISBN 0-8144-0635-1
    1. Employees—Recruiting.   2. Employee selection.   I. Title.

HF5549.5.R44   T28   2002
658.3'11—dc21

2001041231

Printing number

10 9 8 7 6 5 4 3 2 1

WHETHER WORKING WITH EXECUTIVES IN old or new companies—a Fortune 500, a start-up, a venture capital firm, an investment banking or management consulting firm, or a high tech, entertainment, consumer products, or manufacturing company—one of the top challenges I hear over and over is: *How do we recruit, develop, and keep the best talent?* The refrain is the same in both boom years and down times. This challenge is especially on organizations' radar screens for MBAs and experienced talent.

Whatever the state of the economy, whether vigorously growing or decidedly slowing, the best and the brightest employees are always in strong demand by great companies or by those aspiring to be so. It takes strategy, imagination, and execution to recruit, develop, and keep this talent—whether new MBA recruits or your current employees. The past few years have seen an intensely competitive and complex market. The rules have changed. Power has shifted from the companies to the candidates and back to the companies. There are new players competing in what some still call a war for talent. There are old players trying new things. The lessons that we learned, and are still learning, are incredibly useful.

Now is an ideal time to reflect, to reinvigorate your thinking, and to build strengths in effective recruiting, developing, and keeping the best talent.

Whatever your level of recruiting experience or success, I hope this book will give you the inspiration, insight, and ideas to help you on many fronts:

- To build an MBA recruiting program from the ground up—from determining your hiring needs to researching and evaluating schools to creating a winning presence on your chosen campuses

- To improve significantly, or expand strategically, an existing recruiting program
- To gain insight on best practices across industries in interviewing, interviewer training, the callback process, compensation/offers, and job descriptions
- To add to your repertoire, your "toolkit"—as a manager of people or as an HR professional—retention strategies, recruiting on-the-fly when there's no time for planning, and top employment related web sites, among other critical knowledge and skills
- To benefit from the advice of a diversity of frontline managers—a CFO, COO, VPs of HR, marketing, and engineering, among others—on what works for them, their philosophies and approaches, and their proven ideas

I hope to offer some valuable strategies and advice, best practices, lessons learned, tips, and tools whatever your organization's size, industry, arena (profit or nonprofit), and capabilities. This includes encouraging you to reinvigorate some of your business fundamentals, get back to basics, as well as to try some new ideas. Although the focus of the book's first half is MBA recruitment, much of what is shared in this book has broader application to recruiting in general and to retaining ordinary or extraordinary talent already *in* your organization.

My perspective is threefold: as a recruiter, as a manager of small to large teams, and as an MBA/business school insider.

For many of you, I've walked in your shoes and am familiar with your realities. That's why I hope your reading this book is more like our having a conversation, bouncing ideas back and forth, discussing strategy with practical applications, and being creative.

Like some of you, I started up a college/MBA recruiting program the month before we were to launch it, while under intense time pressure, budget constraints, and simultaneous with major layoffs. As a hiring manager myself or an HR coach for other managers, I know what you go through. I too have had to deal with 170+ open reqs, lots of TBHs on the org charts from many different groups, all needing the ideal candidates yesterday.

I've also shared the experience of trying to keep all the great talent once it is recruited in. This has involved soup to nuts, from developing orientation programs to succession planning and what's in between (building morale, keeping people energized, performance management, career development . . .). I know it's a lot harder than it looks, but when you do it, what a critical result for your team and organization.

As head of Stanford's MBA Career Management Center, I've worked with our MBAs, alumni, and business school colleagues, both here and internationally. The coaching and advising have given me insights not only on what effective companies do to achieve recruiting success but also on what is most important to students in considering organizations and jobs, and later as alumni, what keeps them in their companies versus becoming tempted by that next big thing in another company or industry.

I hope you take away many things from this book; that the ideas stimulate you into action; that the strategies and frameworks help make you a more effective recruiter or manager; that the lessons learned are guiding food for thought. Most important, I hope that what is said resonates and that you come away more inspired and confident, with new tools, skills, and knowledge to achieve what you want for yourself professionally and for your organization.

ACKNOWLEDGMENTS

This book would not have been possible without the involvement of literally hundreds of people. I would especially like to thank my deans at the Stanford Graduate School of Business: Bob Joss, George Parker, and Dan Rudolph, and my incredible team and colleagues, particularly Liliane Baxter, Charlotte Carter, Cathy Castillo, Uta Kremer, and Becky Scott, for their belief in me and this project.

A debt of gratitude to the thirty-eight executives who contributed their quotes, advice, and lessons learned in the book.

The organizations represented include Goldman Sachs & Co., McKinsey & Co., Bain & Co., Booz Allen & Hamilton, Kleiner Perkins Caufield & Byers, Metro-Goldwyn-Mayer Studios, Enron North America Corp., YuniNetworks Inc., Charles Schwab & Co., General Mills, Korn/Ferry International, Del Monte Foods, MarketFirst, Maple Optical Systems, Hewlett-Packard, The Tech Museum of Innovation, The San Mateo City Library, Catholic Charities, idealab!, Capital Partners, Eli Lilly & Company, Seneca Capital, Marketocracy, Netergy Networks, Computer Motion, Brecker & Merryman, the Saratoga Institute, iQuantic, DialPad Communications, GED Global—Hong Kong, the Graduate Management Admissions Council, WetFeet, Global Workplace, CruelWorld, a Spencer Stuart Talent Network group, L'Oréal USA, Bertelsmann, Exxon Mobil Corporation, and Yahoo!

To my nineteen business school career management center director colleagues: My appreciation for sharing your in-depth knowledge about your MBA programs and your insights on effectively recruiting your students.

To my remarkable AMACOM editors, Adrienne Hickey, Charles Levine, Jim Bessent, and Andy Ambraziejus: Many thanks for your good humor, wisdom, and experienced guidance. Your late-night e-mails, valuable input to the manuscript, and smooth shepherding of the book through the process made this project a reality.

To my husband, Mark: Thank you for being my most trusted adviser. Your loving support, patience in bouncing ideas back and forth, and IT expertise made all the difference in this writing endeavor. To my mom, Magen Gong Jensen: I am eternally grateful for your example of using what gifts you have to help others, the courage you instilled in me to follow my heart, and your boldness in leading an inspired life.

Thank you all for playing a part in this adventure with me.

Hiring the Best and
the Brightest

MBA Recruiting at a Glance

WHATEVER YOUR EXPERIENCE OR SPECIFIC organization, this book can help you discover imaginative and productive ways to effectively recruit and keep MBAs and other great talent.

- Are you starting up or trying to reenergize an MBA recruiting program as a key resource for new talent in your company, or responding to a call-to-action from a senior manager?
- Whether in a for-profit or nonprofit company, do you want to hear insights and lessons learned from front-line managers from such companies as Bain and Co., Bertelsmann, Computer Motion, Del Monte Foods, General Mills, Goldman Sachs, Hewlett-Packard, Korn/Ferry International, McKinsey and Co., The Tech Museum of Innovation, and Yahoo!?
- Beyond MBA recruiting, are you interested in an eclectic mix of resources and advice for recruiting on the fly and tapping into the best of what the Internet offers?
- Are you new to recruiting, or an experienced HR manager who wants to broaden your knowledge and skills?
- Are you an executive or manager who plays a key role in recruitment for your company or leads and develops top talent, including MBAs?

- Are you just interested in adding recruitment and retention strategies to your toolkit?
- Are you a global, established company that started out in the old economy and needs to figure out new strategies and approaches to compete for talent in Act II of the new economy?
- Are you part of a Net start-up with ample capital, great ideas, and a compelling business model, but with a critical need for smart, capable people?

Do any of the following scenarios sound familiar? You're new in HR and you've been given the mandate of starting up or revving up MBA recruiting. The new CEO and VPs of Marketing and Finance are MBAs who think your company should be doing a better job of MBA recruiting, and they want you to get results quickly. You're a star performer and the firm wants *you* to lead recruiting activities, realizing that competition is tougher than ever and you can "save the day." You're in a large, global company that is world class in HR, but MBA recruiting can be much improved. You need to build the pipeline and bring in fresh, new talent, especially as you continue expanding globally, developing new business and products.

WHY COMPANIES RECRUIT MBAs

Dr. Karen Dowd, of Brecker & Merryman, an Empower Group Company, and an expert on MBA recruiting trends, is on point when she says:

I think what the current economy is showing us is that the MBA degree is alive and well. Whatever new industry is hot, there seems to be a key role for MBAs in shaping the industry and helping companies to compete successfully within the industry. Examples of this are real estate in the mid-eighties, consulting and investment banking in the eighties through the present, and now the dot-com world. Each of these industries found ways to utilize the skills and capabilities offered by MBAs, and MBAs were instrumental in helping these industries move forward at the time.

Companies of all sizes, across a diversity of industries and countries, have recruited MBAs since the 1980s—and for good reason. During times of recession, boom, and steady-does-it, the underlying premise is: People are important. Talent is what sets a company apart from the rest. The human capital, the human resources, is your competitive advantage and most valuable asset.

When you look at exempt-level openings in your own company,* there are several core sources for candidates to fill those openings: (1) executive recruiters who charge up to one-third of the first year's compensation; (2) your in-house or contract recruiters or HR groups who use a range of recruitment alternatives, including independent contractors or consultants who must fulfill those tricky I-9 immigration requirements, undergraduate college recruiting, online or newspaper ads and Web sites, and employee referral programs.

There are many compelling reasons companies engage in MBA recruiting. Some of the most popular ones are:

- Your competitive landscape has changed enormously—new entrants, new rules, new economics. Some of the best minds out there in the MBA marketplace could help your seasoned management create an even more formidable mix of brainpower and leadership for your future.
- You need some analytical horsepower and new energy for certain areas, such as strategy, finance, marketing, operations, or business development.
- You need the unique mix of skills, knowledge, and abilities that MBAs can bring to the table: the analytical horsepower, intellectual firepower, strategic sense, ability to lead others and to work in teams, resilience to learn quickly and be flexible, and interpersonal and communication skills.
- You have a huge number of openings, and MBA recruiting is a viable source that is also a relatively good value for the money.
- You are a high-growth company or start-up and A-list talent attracts more A-list talent, so you need to shoot for the best and the brightest.
- There are some gaps in experience and skills in your company and MBAs can come in, or be developed, more quickly to fill those gaps.
- You're looking ahead and realize that once many of your top executives leave the company, you don't have enough bench strength. You need to build potential successors. MBA recruiting can prove to be powerful for you too.

*Exempt employees are not paid by the hour and do not qualify for overtime.

WHAT IS MBA RECRUITING?

When I tell people I do MBA recruiting, I often get a huge smile with a "Wow. NBA recruiting. Professional sports. How exciting." Well, it is exciting, but I should learn to pronounce better: "em-bee-ay" recruiting.

But I'll try to stick with the sports metaphor for a moment: NBA draft, free agents, utility players, specialists; superstars who have fantastic track records and up-and-comers who may be a bit undervalued, but the quality is there; intense competition for the best talent around; compensation important but intangibles like the coaches, other team members, the team's reputation, and amount of playing time even more important. The process of recruiting is crucial because everyone understands that one of *the* keys to winning the playoffs and titles is getting the most talented players you can and developing them into a cohesive team with the help of great leadership and a winning strategy.

That's about where the metaphor with the NBA ends. Put simply, MBA recruiting means recruiting degree candidates for the Master of Business Administration. MBA recruitment differs from other types of recruitment in the following ways:

- **Phasing and length of the interviews.** You will typically conduct preliminary interviews on campus, with second rounds on site in your office. There are four phases to MBA recruitment. Refer to Figure 2-1.

- **Experience and expectations of the candidates.** MBAs typically have more years of experience than undergraduates, but fewer years than executive search candidates in your specific industry. MBAs possess the added repertoire that MBA experience and education can bring. This includes a strong foundation in all the core functional areas of business, a strategic general management perspective, and a distinguished network of colleagues.

- **Level of intensity.** Although effective MBA recruiting requires year-round effort, for the most part MBA recruiting has a season, in which activities are intense and focused. When the season starts, your strategy and plan need to get set in motion quickly with exceptional execution. You'll be vying for the limited supply of top MBA talent with a formidable group of competitors—diverse industries and companies of all sizes, locations, and reputations.

- **Highly relationship-based, not transactional.** For many companies, it can take several years of consistent work before results are seen.
- **Extensive legwork.** You usually do the majority of the work for MBA recruiting on behalf of your company and are involved throughout. It requires a substantial investment of time and energy. In contrast, when working with an executive recruiter, the recruiter will work on your behalf and do the legwork from start to close: the research for sourcing candidates, preliminary screening and evaluation, even the reference checks. The cost for a recruiter depends on whether you use a premier global firm, such as Korn/Ferry International*; a boutique firm that focuses on a certain industry or kind of company; or a contract recruiter. The in-house cost-per-hire figure for an MBA could commonly be $5,000 to $25,000, while an executive recruiting fee is up to one-third of the total first-year compensation.
- **Compensation.** The base median salary for MBAs from top schools is around $90,000. Add in some of the usual other compensation components—such as signing bonuses, year-end bonuses, stock, or options—and the total compensation package out of the gate can easily top $150,000. Most companies recruiting MBAs say it's excellent value for the money, given the skills, abilities, knowledge, and expected level of contribution MBAs bring to the table. This is one of the most compelling reasons that many companies recruit year after year, most stepping up their efforts when they are in growth mode.

All said, MBA recruiting does not replace all other viable options for recruiting top talent, but it is a powerful resource that can be well worth the effort. MBA recruiting is not for everyone, not for every company, especially the faint of heart. It's a tough market, with intense competition and demanding "customers," and it can be a roller coaster ride of wins and losses. Ultimately, though, it is an adventure that can bring some of the best talent into your organization to meet many of your most critical needs.

MARKET SNAPSHOT: TRENDS, THEMES, REALITIES

Dr. Jac Fitz-enz, founder and chairman of Saratoga Institute and renowned HR visionary, notes:

---

*See www.kornferry.com.

The shortfall of talent will continue into the foreseeable future no matter how the economy reacts in the near term. The demographics of growth in the U.S. gross domestic product and decline in the birth rates makes this inevitable. Accordingly, Saratoga Institute projects that the cost of hiring will increase approximately 40 percent over the next five years and the time to fill jobs will parallel it. [For example,] the time to fill those jobs will exceed 100 days on average. [Additionally, employers with openings will experience] significant increases in operating costs while at the same time a decrease in productivity as jobs go unfilled.

In general, this is a competitive and complex market for MBAs and A-list talent. Even with the cooling economy and company downsizings, the demand for MBAs continues strong.

Look in your Sunday paper at the job openings; go to the theater and see the catchy recruiting ads; note the number of job fairs and networking events, such as company-hosted open houses or the Brassring Career Events or Fast Company's TalentLabs coming to a city near you. Visit any of the estimated 2,500 employment-related Web sites. Close-to-home, note how many people your company needs.and the challenges you face recruiting and keeping the best talent. Great employees, especially those with managerial or executive talent, are still a great source of envy among companies.

What else are we seeing in this market? Established companies vying for talent with emerging growth companies; candidates with multiple offers; capital and ideas in significant amounts, albeit declining from the peak of the venture capital investments and dot-com frenzy of 2000. The constant is that people continue to be the scarce resource. Companies are also realizing that investing to keep their people is a smart decision.

To give you two pronounced examples: At Stanford in 2000, a record number (1,170 companies) recruited our 720 MBAs. This was a 34 percent increase over 1999, and in 1999 we had seen a 100 percent increase in the number of companies over a 5-year period. For 2001, although it's a tougher job market, more than 1,000 companies recruited our MBA students. A recent discussion with career management center directors at top-tier business schools confirmed that demand for their MBA talent from companies continues at a high level, even against the backdrop of a cooling economy.

When chatting with colleagues—whether in a Silicon Valley start-up or a mature global company based in Austin, Atlanta, Chicago, New York,

London, São Paulo, or Hong Kong—I hear that it is common for their in-house HR departments and recruiters to have 50 to 500 exempt (versus nonexempt or independent contractor) openings to fill at any point in time.

Many companies spend lots of money trying to attract and recruit top talent. Some numbers are in the stratosphere. When a valued employee leaves, a lot walks out the door.

Cost-per-hire figures for managers and executives range from a low of $500 (an employee referral) to well over $100,000 (the fee paid an executive search firm for a senior VP opening). Costs, including opportunity costs, add up quickly. Costs include items like print or Internet advertising for the opening, creating any special Web sites for open jobs or using online resources, the use of in-house and outside recruiters, participation in job fairs or other events, interim consultants doing the work while you search to replace a manager who has left, lost productivity and knowledge, the impact on customer relationships, and time for the replacement to come up to speed and begin to produce.

Some companies pay handsomely for employee referrals for their job openings—commonly $500, $1,000, $1,500, $2,500, $5,000, or even $10,000. They give away digital cameras and even Porsche Carreras to encourage their employees to bring in potential new recruits. Others spend big bucks to hire premier retained search firms such as Korn/Ferry International or Heidrick Struggles. My colleagues in the executive search firms and boutique shops tell me they are still deluged with business. Jana Rich, a respected San Francisco–based managing director of Software and Emerging Technology for Korn/Ferry International, estimates that top executive search firms charge one-third of the total first-year compensation, which includes the base salary and an estimate of year-end bonus and any signing bonus. For pre-IPO companies, most search firms also require equity. Many searches can take three to six months or longer to fill.

Although these fees may be worth it, all of these numbers are daunting, and think about it: These figures are just for attracting the talent, not the actual offers of compensation or the investment by the company in the new hires once they are on board.

In general, the in-house MBA cost per hire could range from $5,000 to $25,000 and is trending up while acceptance rates and yields have been trending down over the past few years.

Most companies will say that while it's costing more on average to hire a top MBA, their acceptance rates and yields on offers are mostly down, although there may be some "blip" years. This translates into having either to attract more qualified candidates in order to get the number of hires you need or to improve the yield rate on offers by proving more effective up front in attracting, interviewing or evaluating candidates, and getting them to accept your offers.

Established and mature companies have been shaking things up to compete with start-up or emerging growth companies.

Top investment banking firms began offering perks to their employees, which look a lot like what emerging growth companies offer: concierge services, fruit and beverages all day, and casual dress days. Some big manufacturing companies now offer co-investing (the ability for an individual employee to invest in a portfolio of companies, like a fund, that otherwise would be off limits because of minimum individual investment requirements) or have their own internal groups dedicated to investing in or hatching e-commerce initiatives and businesses.

Start-ups in Silicon Valley may have established the baseline for these newfangled perks to keep their employees motivated and happy, but, increasingly, established companies have adapted quickly to leverage the best of what they can learn from the new economy companies while also adeptly capitalizing on their own strengths and the fact that they are not-coms, which for many is considered a good thing these days.

The key industries that attract MBA talent remain strong, but new ones are making inroads. Investment banking, management consulting, and high technology have tended to be the biggest winners in MBA hiring overall. They remain the top industries of choice by MBAs. The successful group includes consulting firms like McKinsey and Co., investment banking firms like Goldman Sachs, and high-technology companies like Cisco Systems.

Newer to MBA recruiting success are venture capital firms such as KPCB (Kleiner Perkins Caulfield and Byers) and Mayfield Fund, as well as emerging growth companies such as eBay and Openwave Systems.

Time and time again, our MBA students and alumni tell us that a company has to make a dollar offer in the ballpark, but it's a giant ballpark. Repeatedly, they tell us that more important to them are the intangibles—such as colleagues, learning new skills, exciting work, the company culture, their boss, and the CEO. These are the deal breakers. In a recent story on compensation in the new economy for our Stanford MBA alumni magazine, the overriding sentiment from those interviewed—from executive search and venture capital partners to company executives who hire and manage highly sought-after MBAs to the MBAs themselves—was that compensation may have won out in the past, but nowadays it takes a whole lot more to attract and keep top talent.

Companies are casting wider nets for top candidates. In the past, companies may have looked for specific backgrounds and experience in their industries or recruited in a small subset of places for their talent. For years consulting firms and investment banks have recruited MBAs, and the smart ones have considered candidates with nontraditional backgrounds. For example, a consulting firm may hire an MBA who has been a professional ballerina for her impressive discipline, creativity, ability to teach others, and esprit de corps. An investment bank may hire an MBA who has been an entrepreneur in a failed start-up for his risk taking, experience with funding options, and ability to build a team. They have recruited some great talent this way, and once in the firm these MBAs, who did not fit the traditional profile, have proven to perform as successfully as those with prior experience in the same industry or function. There's the premise these days that if candidates made it into a top MBA school, their experience and knowledge are transferable across different industries. Anything they don't know, they can learn fast.

Other companies have been adopting this approach. We see more companies casting wider nets for candidates within the MBA programs. We also see companies who look in other places on campuses—beyond the MBA programs—for some great talent. It's common for many of the top companies who have sizeable needs for talent to come to meet with me, then visit with my counterparts in the schools of law, education, or engineering to discuss recruiting their students as well. In this war for talent, the companies that are effective are those with a thoughtful strategy and plan, spirited imagination, and focused execution. Sounds simple, but we know there is so much behind it. It just looks effortless when it's done well. Where do you start?

PROGRAMS WORLDWIDE

MBA programs come in all shapes and sizes. In an e-mail interview with me, David Wilson, CEO of GMAC (the Graduate Management Admissions Council), notes that currently there are more than 1,500 MBA programs around the world, with about 900 in the United States. Most of these require the GMAT (Graduate Management Admissions Test), the standardized entrance exam, like the MCAT for medical school and LSAT for law school. The accrediting body for the top schools is the AACSB, the American Association of Colleges and Schools of Business.

Some of these 1,500 programs include, in addition to their full-time MBA programs, doctoral programs; specialized masters programs in areas such as international management and taxation; and part-time programs for executives (EMBAs) or midcareer executives. For example, a midcareer executive may enroll in a full-time 1-year compressed program for high-potential managers with on average 8 to 15 years' experience. These managers are often sponsored by their companies and are expected to return to apply all they have learned in the program. Graduate schools of business also offer short-course, nondegree programs for executives. These are executive education programs, which are 1- to 3-week courses focused on specific interests and needs, such as managing high-growth companies, supply chain management, HR, strategic management, e-commerce, or finance.

According to Wilson, in the United States there are approximately 100,000 MBA graduates each year, with this number trending up. However, gathering information on MBA graduates from countries other than the United States is less simple. Many countries do not consistently collect numbers for the programs they offer. Anecdotally, we know there are some excellent programs abroad. Among those most recognized are the European Institute of Business Administration (INSEAD) in France; London Business School in the United Kingdom; International Institute for Management Development (IMD) in Switzerland; IESE Business School in Spain; Australian Graduate School of Management (AGSM) in Australia; HEC-ISA (Hautes Études Commerciales–ISA) in Paris; Bocconi University School of Management in Italy; Hong Kong University of Science and Technology; and the National University of Singapore.

While the number of applications to MBA programs overall is increasing, the number of places at the highly selective schools remains steady, making it more competitive to get into these top schools.

For our purposes, we'll focus your recruiting on full-time MBA programs, where the most intense and opportunity-filled war for talent continues in full swing. The MBAs in these programs are the most sought after by companies around the globe that already rely on this top talent or want to start tapping into it for their management and executive recruitment needs.

The Four Phases of MBA Recruiting—Real Time

THIS CHAPTER PROVIDES A COMPREHENSIVE outline and timeline of the critical top ten to-dos and how-tos for developing a world-class, impactful MBA recruiting program. In the following chapters, each major action item comes with explanations and examples. I've also given the ideal months for these activities; however, realizing that situations are usually not ideal and many activities need to be done all at the same time or with shortened timeframes, in the drill-downs I've offered more general timing so you can at least understand the optimal sequencing.

RECRUITERS' TERMINOLOGY

Because there's no standard nomenclature to categorize MBA programs and recruiting, let's start by defining the key terms used throughout the book. Some companies have their internal vocabulary, like *corporate school* for those programs that yield top numbers of hires.

If you've ever heard people in Net start-ups talk with each other, it can sound like cyberbabble—"GUI"; "ARPU." In the retail business, you hear about comp store sales, SKUs, and inventory turn. In consulting, there are engagements and being on the beach, and in banking, dealflows and tomb-stones. In your own company, you probably also have your acronyms and special buzzwords. At Stanford, for example, our MTCs are "Meet the Company" presentations by recruiters for students, and OCR is short for "on campus recruiting."

Overall, MBA recruiting also has its own vocabulary. The MBA terminology is not particularly colorful; nevertheless, it is important to your success to understand what these key words and phrases mean so you can talk the talk and know what you're asking for and doing. Some of these are obvious but are included to make sure everyone is exposed to the fundamental language. The most important—the short list—and abbreviated definitions when needing explanation are included here.

MBA programs offer *concentrations* for their students. For example, MBAs can emphasize a specialized functional area such as marketing, finance, or operations. Some MBA programs such as Harvard's and Stanford's offer *general management degrees.*

Throughout your recruiting planning and efforts, your main contact at the school is with the *career management center* (CMC)—a.k.a. the placement office, career services, career planning and placement center, or career development center. These offices represent the team of professionals who provide expertise, resources, services, and programs for MBA students and the companies that recruit them. Companies view the CMC staff as advisers, partners, clients, brokers of sorts, or even as adjunct HR.

Other key influencers within the schools are the *dean,* a cadre of *associate* or *assistant deans,* and, of course, the faculty.

The students, or MBAs, as a group or class are called different names in different schools. For example, at Stanford the incoming class of students is usually referred to as *MBA1s* or first years, because they are in the first year of their 2-year program. The graduating class comprises the *MBA2s* or the second years. For ease, the class is referred to by the year it graduates, for example, the class of 2002.

Alumni are graduates of the MBA programs, but in some cases schools extend the alumni mantle to others, such as participants in their nondegree programs like the executive education courses.

The key sources of published information about the school and its recruiting are the career center's *recruiter guide,* which offers advice and information for on-campus recruiting or other ways to access the MBAs, and the *placement reports,* which detail student job choices (by industry, function, and location), compensation, and a list of recruiting companies.

Additional sources of information are the school's or career center's *Web site* and its corporate relations department. The best source of learning about the school, however, is meeting with key influencers, which will be discussed starting in the next chapter.

The recruiting process in brief comprises four phases: (1) the up-front work, (2) pre-recruitment, (3) interviews, and (4) second rounds and offers. (See Figures 2-1 and 2-2.)

While *up-front preparation* can cover all the work you do in-house ahead of time, *pre-recruitment activities* are what you do on-campus before interviews begin. These are activities designed to generate interest and build visibility for the company before your interviews begin. Chapter 4 covers pre-recruitment in depth, from brainstorming ideas to use on specific campuses, to best practices for hosting an employer information session, a pre-recruitment staple, to some of the best ideas being used by some very effective companies.

On-campus interviews are facilitated by the school's career centers. You request interview dates/number of interview schedules. The interviews get allocated to students through a bidding system or some other means. You may conduct the interviews on campus or in local offices or hotels close to the school.

An *interview schedule* is a set of interviews. For example, one interview schedule could have seven 1-hour interviews or fourteen 30-minute interviews, including breaks and lunch.

Figure 2-1. The Four Phases of MBA Recruiting.

Figure 2-2. Top Ten To-Dos and Time Lines for the Four Phases of MBA Recruiting in Real Time

Phase One: Up-Front Preparation

Time Line: June–November, Before You Recruit

Step 1.   Assess Your Organizational Needs and Enlist Internal Resources
Refine Your Purpose for MBA Recruiting
Estimate Number of Openings and Kinds of Jobs
Set the Stage for Internal Support
Decide on Hiring for Full-Time Openings and/or Summer Internships
Think about Budgets

Step 2.   Research, Evaluate, and Choose Schools and Programs
Do Some Digging
Establish Key Evaluation Dimensions
Select the Best Schools for Your Recruitment
Put Your Big Picture in Perspective

Step 3.   Cultivate Relationships with Key Influencers within the Schools
Identify Key Influencers—Faculty, Career Center Staff, Student
   Leaders
Initiate Partnerships
Get the Most from Your Campus Visit
Schedule Interview Dates

Step 4.   Formulate Your Communication Strategy and Key Messages
Keep It Simple and in Sync
Stay in the Loop
Overcommunicate
Mind the Internal PR and Marketing
Develop Compelling Job Descriptions
Tchotchkes, Anyone?

Phase Two: Best-in-Class Pre-Recruitment

Time Line: October–February, Before Interviewing

Step 5.   Plan and Execute Your Pre-Recruitment
Go on a Mission to Create Your Presence
Know Your Customers
Leverage the School's Offerings
Brainstorm Ideas for Specific Campuses
Choose the Best Mix to Pre-Recruit
Plan a Great Employer Information Session
Engage in Best Practices for Your Session
Sponsor Your Own More Focused Event(s)
Target and Communicate with Your MBA Candidates

Phase Three: Interviews

Time Line: October–April, After Pre-Recruitment

Step 6. Select and Train Your Interviewers
Enlist People to the Cause
Consider the Team Approach
Decide When to Use HR
Coordinate, Brief, and Train Your Interviewers
Target Your Candidates One More Time

Step 7. Leverage the Interviewing Process
Prepare for the Interviews and the Interview Questions
Make a Starter List of Interview Questions
Create a Taxonomy of an Interview
Evaluate Candidates and Follow up
Observe the Golden Rule

Phase Four: Second Rounds and Offers

Time Line: November–May, Within 2 to 6 Weeks After Interviews

Step 8. Plan and Execute On-Site Second Rounds
Design the Agenda
Orchestrate Like a Maestro
Be Shepherds and Timekeepers
Rate the Candidates and Decide on Offers

Step 9. Make Offers That Get Accepted
Do Your Homework
Make Offers—Sequentially, in Waves, or Open
Woo, Woo, and Woo
Make It Stick—No Buyer's Remorse

Step 10. Get Feedback, Give Thanks, Make Improvements, Start Over Again
Initiate Unabashed Feedback
Seek out Student Impressions
Debrief the Schools
Spread the Wealth
Refine Your Plans for Next Time

Open schedules are those for which students bid on interviews with points on the open market or sign up for interviews following their career center's guidelines. Companies do not get to select candidates based on any prescreening, such as reviewing student résumés ahead of time.

For *closed schedules* companies review student résumés and choose whom to invite for interviews, providing a closed invitation list to the career center. Schools offer variations on this theme. For example, a school may offer schedules that are 100 percent closed, 100 percent open, 75 percent closed/25 percent open, or 50 percent/50 percent.

The *bidding system* houses all of the on-campus recruiting information and is used to allocate interviews to students. Students are given a certain number of points for each quarter or semester during recruiting. For "open" interview slots, students are able to bid points for a place on a specific company's interview schedule. Places go to the highest bidders except when there are class conflicts. For "closed" slots, students do not have to bid points, since the company invited them. They do have to confirm their interest in the invitation and get assigned an interview time via the system. The number of students that a company ultimately gets to interview in a school can vary widely across schools, depending on such factors as number of students in the program (supply), level of interest, total number of interviews you are offering, when you are interviewing, what else is going on at that time, and student availability during nonclass hours.

Interviews can be for either *career positions* or *summer internships*. A career position is a full-time job available to an MBA who will be graduating. A summer internship is an 8- to 12-week program (formal or ad hoc) for students to work with a company during their summer break before their first and second years in their MBA programs. Developing a summer internship program is discussed in Chapter 9, as point 7 of the Best Practices section.

After the on-campus interviews, companies invite candidates back for *second rounds, final rounds,* or *callbacks on site.* These are discussed in Chapter 7.

Offers may be straightforward or complicated. These are highlighted in Chapter 8. Some firms make *exploding offers,* which are highly discouraged by the schools; these have a monetary incentive tied to making a decision fast. For example, I offer you a job with a $15,000 bonus, but for every hour that you have not accepted the job offer, I take away $1,000 until the $15,000 fully explodes and goes away. These offers, if used at all, come mostly from investment banks. If you are in the majority of companies that do not engage in this practice, you need to know whether the candidate to whom you are making an offer is under this time pressure, so you may choose to do something about it.

Most top schools have policies or guidelines on the *time for students to consider offers.* Companies are asked to give students a certain amount of time to consider their offers, 3 weeks or the end of January, whichever is later, or for a summer internship, 1 week or the end of March, whichever is later. The rationale behind the time is to recognize that the company is making a big investment in making an offer, as is the student in accepting it. Also, this gives students time to evaluate offers across industries, which recruit at different times in the year.

Sell weekends or *days* started out with investment banks and are becoming more popular with high-tech companies, consulting firms, and others. This focused event takes place after offers are made and lets the candidates experience the company more personally, while wooing them and letting them know the company really wants them. This is also a good time to help any spouses or significant others get to know the company and feel comfortable with a move to the area.

RESOURCES FOR RESEARCHING MBA PROGRAMS

Researching and evaluating MBA programs at your target schools is discussed in depth in Chapter 3, "Phase One: Up-Front Preparation." To get you started, a short list of online and offline resources for researching business schools and their MBA programs follows.

- *US News and World Report*, www.usnews.com/usnews/edu/eduhome. htm, provides a wealth of information on top graduate schools, including business, law, engineering, and Ph.D. programs. Its 2002 ranking of the top fifty U.S. business schools is based on dimensions such as reputation by academics (deans), by recruiters, the student average undergraduate G.P.A. and GMAT score, admission acceptance rate, average starting salary, the number of full-time MBA students, among others. This site also offers education news and trends and ranks the best part-time MBA programs in the United States.
- *Business Week*, http://origin.businessweek.com/bschools/00/, offers its 2000 ranking of top U.S. and international business schools, the schools' profiles, and timely stories and interviews on business education, specific school initiatives, etc.
- *Financial Times*, http://ftcareerpoint.ft.com/businesseducation/mba, is a global, integrated ranking of the world's top full-time MBA programs, including the United States, Europe, and Asia. It ranks the schools based on twenty criteria, such as value for money, career progress, women or international faculty and students, international mobility,

and placement success. A unique feature of its comprehensive information is the schools' dean profiles.

- www.bschool.com provides side-by-side comparisons of the best U.S. and international business schools. For U.S. schools, it lists specialty rankings such as *Computerworld*'s top twenty-five techno MBA programs, *Working Woman*'s best business schools for women, *Success Magazine*'s top entrepreneurial schools, and *Hispanic Business*'s top schools.

- The National Association of Colleges and Employers (NACE), www.naceweb.org, is the professional association for career services and HR professionals who recruit college graduates. It offers a monthly newsletter, links to career services offices, research, benchmarks, resources, and networking/educational events.

- For a sense for the MBA market—recruitment trends, what's on students' minds, specific industries' and companies' recruiting and compensation—the Wet Feet suite of services is particularly valuable.

  www.wetfeet.com/employer/home.asp

  www.wetfeet.com/corporate/CampusPulse.asp

  www.wetfeet.com/employer/research.asp

- For researching MBA recruiting, programs, and best practices, Brecker & Merryman, a part of The Empower Group at www.empowergrp.com, is helpful. For over 25 years Brecker & Merryman has helped organizations by aligning people with strategy. The Empower Group has practice areas in strategic resourcing and recruiting, talent management, organization effectiveness, strategic communications and survey diagnostics, and a specialty practice in campus and MBA recruiting. Brecker & Merryman also produces annual surveys on the recruiting outlook including "Snapshot" and "MBA Compensation."

- *The MBA Newsletter*, published by Dick Kwartler, is the only publication devoted exclusively to global coverage of graduate management education, including recruiting trends, placement, admissions, and new initiatives. To subscribe, call 516-488-2010, or visit www.thembanewsletter.com.

A theme you will discover when researching the MBA programs is that they vary widely in selectivity, student class size and demographics, faculty, curriculum, and level of demand for the students by recruiters and companies. You will need to choose the schools for your recruiting wisely and think about which will give you the best value back for the time and energy you'll expend.

WEB SITES FOR THIRTY OF THE TOP SCHOOLS

The URLs for thirty of the top MBA programs, both U.S. and international, are shown here. These thirty give you a broader base of schools than the top twenty picks discussed in Chapter 10.

School/Web Site: School Home Page	Web Site: Career Center (Direct)
Carnegie Mellon	
www.gsia.cmu.edu/	www.gsia.cmu.edu/afs/andrew/gsia/coc/
Chicago	
gsb.uchicago.edu/	gsb.uchicago.edu/dynamic.asp?nNodeID = 32361
Columbia	
www.columbia.edu/cu/business/	www.columbia.edu/cu/business/career/
Cornell (Johnson)	
www.johnson.cornell.edu/	www.johnson.cornell.edu/cservices.html
Dartmouth (Tuck)	
www.dartmouth.edu/tuck	www.dartmouth.edu/tuck/jobs/index.html
Duke (Fuqua)	
www.fuqua.duke.edu/	www.fuqua.duke.edu/admin/cso/
Emory (Goizueta)	
www.emory.edu/BUS/	www.emory.edu/BUS/recruiters/index.html
Georgetown (McDonough)	
www.msb.edu/	www.mba.georgetown.edu/mbacm/
Harvard	
www.hbs.edu/	www.hbs.edu/career_services/
IESE	
www.iese.edu	www.iese.edu/companies/index.html
Indiana	
www.kelley.indiana.edu/mba/	www.pacioli.bus.indiana.edu/gcs/
INSEAD	
www.insead.fr/mba/	www.insead.fr/mba/career1.htm
London Business School	
www.london.edu/	www.london.edu/recruiters
Michigan	
www.bus.umich.edu/	www.bus.umich.edu/companies/ocd/
MIT (Sloan)	
www.mitsloan.mit.edu/	—
Northwestern (Kellogg)	
www.kellogg.nwu.edu/	www.kellogg.nwu.edu/career/
NYU (Stern)	
www.stern.nyu.edu/	www.stern.nyu.edu/ocd/

School/Web Site: School Home Page	*Web Site: Career Center (Direct)*
Pennsylvania (Wharton)	
www.wharton.upenn.edu/	www.wharton.upenn.edu/actions/recruit.html
Purdue (Krannert)	
www.mgmt.purdue.edu/	www.mgmt.purdue.edu/programs/masters/mpo
Rochester (Simon)	
www.simon.rochester.edu/	www.simon.rochester.edu/corp/corp-shell.htm
Stanford	
www.gsb.stanford.edu/	www.wesley.stanford.edu/cmc/
Texas—Austin (McCombs)	
www.bus.utexas.edu/	www.cso.bus.utexas.edu/
UC Berkeley (Haas)	
haas.berkeley.edu/	www.haas.berkeley.edu/careercenter/
UCLA (Anderson)	
www.anderson.ucla.edu/	www.anderson.ucla.edu/resources/cmc/
UNC—Chapel Hill	
www.kenanflagler.unc.edu/	www.kenanflagler.unc.edu/programs/mba/career
USC (Marshall)	
www.marshall.usc.edu/	www.marshall.usc.edu/career/index.html
Vanderbilt (Owen)	
mba.vanderbilt.edu/external/	mba.vanderbilt.edu/external/corp_center.htm
Virginia (Darden)	
www.darden.virginia.edu/	www.darden.virginia.edu/career/
Washington University (Olin)	
www.olin.wustl.edu/	www.olin.wustl.edu/wcrc/employers/
Yale	
mba.yale.edu/	—

Phase One: Up-Front Preparation

DRILL-DOWN #1. ASSESS YOUR ORGANIZATIONAL NEEDS AND ENLIST INTERNAL RESOURCES

Time Line: June–November, Before You Recruit

Refine Your Purpose for MBA Recruiting

Why do you need or want to do MBA recruiting? What are you trying to achieve? What's the driving force that your people can rally behind? You want to enlist those whose support you need.

Clarifying your purpose doesn't have to take a long time. It could entail the program leader brainstorming with other interested colleagues, writing ideas on white board to see which one most resonates with everyone. Getting buy-in up front from those pushing for MBA recruiting and from the team who will be doing the bulk of the work will give you a common ground to work on and an energized purpose for starting your efforts.

Estimate Numbers of Openings and Kinds of Jobs

Try to estimate the number and kinds of opportunities within your company that could benefit from MBA recruiting. If you're in the recruiting area of HR, you know which groups have hiring needs and what kinds of talent they most need. Ask who can benefit the most from MBA recruiting. If you don't know, or to make sure you are inclusive, send an e-mail to managers in all of the departments that could use MBA talent. Talk with them, or invite them to come together for a quick powwow. You could also send a voicemail and ask them to reply, or distribute a short memo with some blanks to fill in for the number and kinds of opportunities and job titles they may be interested in recruiting for, and the names of who in the groups to involve in recruiting. This could be the basis for any follow-up.

The mission critical here is to get a good read so you know whether you're dealing with 1 potential need or job opening for an MBA, 10, or 110.

These are the basic elements to communicate to your colleagues:

- We've been asked to "start up" or "given the resources for" or "I think we need to rev up" MBA recruiting as one key part of our overall recruiting strategy.
- The compelling reasons for MBA recruiting are x and y.
- Your area is a key one in the company, and you have lots of people needs or critical special needs that I believe MBAs could meet.
- I am trying to get a sense of your level of interest and what kinds of job needs you have. Would you or others in your group commit to getting involved to help the company's efforts off to a great start?
- Give me an estimate of how many (#'s) and what kinds of openings you think you could use MBAs to fill.
- What are your ideal profiles for these candidates' backgrounds, including education, experience, skills, knowledge, and abilities? Required or preferred?
- Note that you are available and happy to discuss any of this to further flesh out their specific recruiting needs.

Set the Stage for Internal Support

Set the stage for involvement and support from your organization by doing some internal marketing that will help fuel the momentum of your recruiting program. Communicating with hiring managers and assessing their needs is a positive first step to engaging your colleagues and getting the word out about your starting up or re-energizing MBA recruiting. By asking people to get involved up front and by being interested in their input, you are laying the all-important foundation for working together later. Any enthusiasm and coordination now will make a substantial difference throughout all your recruiting efforts and to the cohesive, enthusiastic image you portray at your target schools.

Decide on Hiring for Full-Time Openings and/ or Summer Internships

Make your best decision about recruiting for your full-time openings (career positions), and whether you also want to hire summer interns, realizing that you can always change your mind later, even into the school year. This is a good topic to get advice on when you visit the career centers of the schools you are considering.

If you're starting out, it is better to go after the full-time jobs first, then to phase in summer internships the following year. Practically speaking, you'll already have full-time jobs open that MBA talent could fill, whereas summer internships may require your creating new openings that would take a lot of work to do well. By starting out with full-time jobs, you also then have MBA hires whom you can utilize as alumni for recruiting at their schools the next year.

To start off recruiting for both career and summer positions could be a lot to do and do well during your start-up or rev-up year.

Summer Intern Tradeoffs. If you can pull it off, offering a summer intern program can work to your advantage. It can be incredible viral marketing. You can engage your interns to help you with your recruiting the following year and to be your ambassadors on campus when they return to school. Additionally, positive word-of-mouth from a peer is priceless if your interns have had a terrific summer experience. Another benefit is that an internship usually lasts 8 to 10 weeks, which gives you a golden opportunity to test and evaluate the interns' abilities, while giving them the up-close and personal feel for who you are as a company and what it would be like to work with you. An additional positive is that you could easily conduct one set of interviews on campus. Many companies send interviewers who can recruit on behalf of all the groups that will take summer interns and do not conduct any follow-up interviews.

On the downside, internships can backfire and could actually hurt you and your reputation if they are done haphazardly. The core to a successful internship program is providing meaningful work and some structure. Although they can be fluid, they require advance planning. What makes a memorable summer internship experience for the MBA? What kinds of projects for the 8 to 10 weeks are attractive? What's an ideal internship program? Chapter 9 offers answers.

Think about Budgets

Money is usually not a hurdle to doing MBA recruiting, and most HR groups or people leading the efforts have the support of senior management and the dollars to go along with it. The more tricky resource to secure, I believe, is the right people in your organization to get involved. Their time and attention, and in some cases their patience, are things you build over time.

It makes sense that most MBA recruiting budgets are part of HR, but sometimes related expenses are charged back, prorated, to the groups that get the MBA hire(s), or all the groups that decide to do MBA recruiting divide up the costs evenly, or there is just a centralized pot of money.

My take is that since the recruiting budget is absorbed entirely within your company, spend the time on the recruiting substance and not on the internal nits and nats of allocating expenses. What matters is that, as one company altogether, you get a good return on your investment and that the $$$ you spend give you maximum impact.

You *will* want to formulate some metrics so your recruiting efforts can be evaluated vis-à-vis your goals and results. Sample MBA recruiting metrics, such as cost per hire and offer and yield rates along with their formulas, are in Appendixes A, B, and C. The cost-per-hire formula calls out what kinds of costs are involved in MBA recruiting, such as recruitment brochures, Internet strategies, career fairs, company information sessions including food and giveaways, interviewing expenses, and candidate flybacks.

DRILL-DOWN #2. RESEARCH, EVALUATE, AND DECIDE ON SCHOOLS

Time Line: Before Your Campus Visits

Do Some Digging

You'll want to research the schools and programs. Do some digging above and beyond what's readily available on the schools' Web sites and in their brochures. Due diligence is crucial so you can decide which schools are best for your needs, both short- and long-term. Some of the research can be done impersonally: You can review the school's Web site, read its hard-copy information, and peruse a directory of MBA programs. The best information can be gleaned only by meeting with or even speaking by phone with key people within the school. You'll think of questions unique to your needs, but here are some starters.

Fifteen Key Evaluation Dimensions

1. Program description, its mission, structure, and so forth.
2. What is the program known for? What is its reputation among students, peers, recruiters, media, and others in general?
3. What kinds of courses are offered? Do they all sound like the latest business jargon, or do research, depth, and continual innovation go into them?
4. Who are the faculty? Are their biographies or their research viewable on the Web site? Many schools have faculty directories, but you will need to ask for one.
5. Selectivity. How many applicants apply each year? How many make it in, and what's the class size?
6. Does the MBA program offer a general management focus or concentrations? If concentrations, in what areas? Review a course catalogue on the Web site or ask for a course schedule for the year.
7. Find out about the dean's background, management style, and vision and priorities for the school. This tells you a lot about the school, about what it values and how it is run, all of which will impact your interaction with its career services, corporate relations group, and the students it admits. This is not something you'll find from a book or a Web site. You'll need to find out in more personal ways, for example, in your preliminary meeting with key school administrators and opinion leaders.
8. Student demographics and profiles. What is the mix of genders, average years of work experience, range of and median ages, international and domestic breakout, top industries and functions the students come from, and their undergraduate colleges and universities and majors? Note that this is harder to find out about, but any information you can glean will be helpful: What are the students' preferences in general?

Where do they want to go to work? Which industries are their top choices? Which functional areas? What locations, internationally or within the United States? Do the students note what kinds of companies they want to work with—small, mid-size, or large? Or are there further delineations that will help you learn more about what they want—a start-up or a Fortune 500? For example, in 2001 Stanford launched a special Web site to help recruiters understand student preferences, as well as to aggregate demographics about the class—what industries and functions they came from, their educational backgrounds, language fluencies, and percentages of minorities and women.

9. Sources of these data include the career center's placement report or its Web site. Where did the MBAs go to work (industries, functions, locations)? Is there more information on where they went to work by size of company or type of company (i.e., a start-up with fewer than 25 people or a global company with 25,000 + employees)? Another good resource is the school's class résumé book, often available in hard copy and in a Web version. Prices range from $350 to $800 for bundled sets. These list students' preferences for industries, functions, locations, and types of companies. Otherwise, the career management director could supply this information. Schools usually also provide a recruiter's guidebook that is a quick source of valuable information. It will include a recruiting and academic calendar, options for on- and off-campus interviews, recruiting events, résumé book, order forms, and interview request forms.

10. List of student clubs and the officers. You can get a good feel for which clubs you want to target as well as what the students' interests are. For example, if you have finance opportunities, you may wish to do special outreach to students in the finance, investment management, or i-banking clubs. If diversity recruiting is a focus, you may want to do some targeted recruitment with the Women in Management, Asia, Latin America, or Europe Clubs or the Black Business Students Association.

11. What events are planned throughout the year? Is there a school calendar, hard copy or online, which lists programs such as a distinguished speaker series or conferences the school is hosting? Find out when key dates are: when recruiting starts and ends, when school starts and ends, when the breaks, holidays, and off-limit dates are. These can usually be found in the recruiter guide.

12. Who are the key people and their backgrounds in the career management center? What do they offer for current and potential recruiters? Do they offer special programs, such as a new recruiter briefing or special services via their Web site? Do they offer one-on-ones by telephone or in person? How accessible, helpful, and knowledgeable are they? Are they willing to work with you in partnership on your strategy and plans, but also tackle problems and issues? The important thing to remember is that while your company may be working with five to twenty-five schools, the career centers may be working with 300 to more than 1,000 different companies plus all of their MBA students, so it's the quality of their partnership and not quantity of time with you that counts.

13. Placement statistics. Where do the students go for their career positions (first jobs after graduation) and their summer internships? Which industries, functions, companies, cities, and countries? What's the compensation picture? Base compensation, median, average, range; total compensation (usually includes signing bonus and any guaranteed year-end bonus, excluding options or other nonmonetary compensation). Trends and what's behind them?

14. Which other companies recruit at the school? Which especially in your industry and space? Which of the companies are most successful at recruiting and why? What are the top industries and functions? How has this changed over the years and why?

15. How can you recruit alumni if you decide to do that?

Select the Best Schools for Your Recruitment

Decide on the schools that will best meet your needs. You can make the decision yourself, get others' input, or leave the decision to those who will be involved, including the CEO or other senior executives who are champions for MBA recruiting. The key to deciding on schools is choosing whatever fits your culture. Usually the more input you seek from others, within reason, the more buy-in and support you will have going forward. People will feel involved and a part of the action, with a stake in making your company's MBA recruiting a success.

If you're starting up and truly have not had much experience doing MBA or even undergraduate recruiting, it is better to start small, choosing fewer schools so you can focus, generate some early wins, and build on strong results with a good reputation—rather than taking on too much and later having to clean up any mistakes. You must keep in mind that MBAs make quick judgments given all the information and opportunities available to them. They have a heightened sense of information overload; they are bombarded not only from companies that want to recruit them but also by all the details related to their coursework and extracurriculars. Most MBAs, therefore, as a matter of survival and time management, use their skill at making fast decisions on what's important and what's not, blocking out the rest, fast and with laser focus. Initial bad impressions are difficult to turn around. One class of students may pass down to the next class their advice and perceptions of certain companies, creating an institutional memory about your company that you have to either live up to or fix.

Put Your Big Picture in Perspective

Think about your big picture: your overall hiring objectives, number of schools that should be on your target list, and the interviewing schedules you'll need overall to hit your hiring goals. You'll probably need to make initial assumptions about how many students you'll have to interview and the number of schools you'll visit. You can start by backing out these numbers, by starting with the target number you need, and then factoring in what you think your yield on offers will be. You can figure out from there approximately how many students you'll target to interview, call back, and make offers to.

For example, if you want to hire five MBAs and your yield on exempt managerial hires has been about 50 percent, that means you'll need to make offers to at least ten MBAs to get your five new hires. If you think you'll make offers only to one-quarter of your finalists, that means you may need to call back forty MBAs (after the on-campus interview). Realistically, if you are able to get one to two MBAs from each interview schedule to continue in your process, you'll need about twenty interviews scheduled (fully to partially full) on campus to create a pool of forty first-round candidates. You may want to start with five to ten schools. At different schools you will ask for different numbers of schedules. The numbers will be based on the competition and demand from other companies, anticipated level of student interest, and the size of each class.

The career center's director or recruiting assistant director can also give you some guidance on these issues when you meet and before you have to turn in the interview schedule and employer information request forms. The director will be able to help you customize your requests to that school's environment. For example, at one school it may be common for finance-related companies to garner lots of interest from students and thus lots of interview sign-ups. At another school, it may be more common for consulting firms and Internet start-ups to garner overflow interest. Depending on supply and demand at that school and student preferences, the amount of interest in your interviews will vary dramatically. This in turn affects the number you'll be able to bring in for further interviewing and ultimately your job acceptances. The career center staff can guide you. You can schedule interviews and information sessions now, so you have more of a chance of receiving the dates you think you would want. You can always change them later. If in doubt about timing or other issues, delay this until after you visit the schools, when you'll have a lot better information.

DRILL-DOWN #3. CULTIVATE RELATIONSHIPS WITH KEY INFLUENCERS WITHIN THE SCHOOLS

Time Line: Before Pre-Recruitment Begins

Identify Key Influencers—Faculty, Career Center Staff, Student Leaders

Call the career center director to schedule some meetings by phone if you cannot visit in person. You can get the clearest sense of the school by going there in person. Before you call, try to figure out whom among the core groups of influencers you want to meet, along with the career center director and assistant director of recruiting.

Ask alumni of the school who work in your company, or some of your executives who may be on a board of directors along with the dean or a professor at the school, to recommend particularly well-regarded, industry-friendly faculty or key career center staff.

Look at the school Web site or request a list of the student club leaders for additional information about key influencers. Review the faculty directory and research. Is there a professor who is doing some interesting research, for example, on supply chain management, e-commerce, or HR, that dovetails with something in your organization?

The dean's, faculty's, and student leaders' time is scarce. Although they may value recruiting and corporate relationships as a priority, meeting with company executives is not a high percentage of their daily activity. It never hurts to try to engage with some of these other influencers, but it will be rarer that you'll schedule time with them. See Chapter 9 on ideas for integrating into the educational process and getting to know the faculty.

If you are pressed for time, don't do any research about the key influencers on your own. Just fast forward to calling the career center director to schedule a visit. He or she can give you some specific names of others with whom to meet for your upcoming visit.

Most often, companies choose to develop a partnership with the students and the career center staff first, and as their recruiting efforts grow or become more defined, they broaden their relationships within the school.

Initiate Partnerships

There are really five core objectives for your first visit to the school; these will hopefully be the start of a long-term partnership:

- Research what you haven't been able to find out via reading and the school Web site to get a sense of the culture, personality, differences, and what will work there.
- Begin to develop relationships with key people in the school.
- Lay the basis for open communication and sharing of ideas and feedback.
- Ask for advice on questions important to you. Use the starter list of fifteen dimensions in Drill-Down #2.
- Clarify how you will work with them: the point person in your organization and the roles for those who will be involved in recruiting.

If possible, try to set meetings at the schools during their less busy times. Summers are less hectic since typically planning and development work for the next academic year are in process and students are not on campus.

Ideally, the people who should visit the school from your company include you or someone in your HR group who will be involved in recruiting, a senior manager, and the team captain if you've named one, who can talk more in depth about your business and the content of the work the MBAs would be doing.

Try to meet at least with the career center's directors and the recruiting assistant director. A quick hello to the rest of the staff to introduce yourself and put your face with your name is a nice touch. Other helpful people on the career center staff include whoever does the majority of student career advising (sometimes called career counseling or coaching) and whoever has responsibility for the resource center (Web site, "library" of industry research and company materials).

Get the Most from Your Campus Visit

Your visit can provide valuable information on the MBA program and help you begin a meaningful dialogue and partnership with the career center. Here are some tips for taking away the most from your initial and subsequent visits.

With the *director* get the lay of the land and the big picture. Ask broadly about the school's mission, values, culture; its program structure, applicants, and selectivity; the demographics of the individual classes (international vs. domestic students; women vs. men; industry and functional backgrounds; age range; and years of experience); and how they are different from other schools. Ask for a quick rundown of the staff, who does what and whom to contact for what; how recruitment fared last year (number of companies, key placement stats, new programs and initiatives for recruiters and students), and how it looks so far for this year; the director's take on student interests and what's on their minds now; when is the best time to recruit given your number and kind of openings and type of company; and what briefly are the options for on-campus recruiting, participating in other events or programs, and ideas for pre-recruitment activities.

Tick down the fifteen dimensions for evaluating schools (in Drill-Down #2 above) for any holes in your research; ask about the director's background, including length of stay and biggest challenges and frustrations; ask how you can best work together and how you can help the school. Give the director your information as well to make this a two-way communication. Talk about any shared connections you may have—alumni in your organization and how they are doing; your CEO who spoke to the School of Engineering last year; what you read in an interview the director gave and how the comments on X were particularly interesting. Talk about your organization and your business: your leadership, priorities, and team, your overall recruiting plans, and how you develop people.

With the *assistant director of recruiting* learn about the school's recruiting process and how it works with companies. Learn about the mechanics of requesting interview dates, the timing for full-time and summer internship opportunities, and the strategic opportunities for your company to get involved with the school. Get advice on how you can best work with them; on the outlook so far for companies recruiting—whether trending up or down, results of certain industries; on how interviews will get allocated to students; on who handles changes in the interview schedules and how they handle students who don't show up for interviews; on level of interest/interview sign-ups from students so far, factors that influence.

With a *career adviser* or *counselor* find out what is on students' minds these days. What are they most interested in and what are their preferences for industries, functions, companies, and locations? What's important to them in a company and in the content of a job? How has this changed over the years? How are they deciding on what companies to pursue? How do they evaluate offers? What skills are being focused on for the students in the career center's workshops or programs? What, in general, are the top issues on students' minds?

With the *manager of career resources* or *resource library* find out the most popular sources of information a student uses to research a company. Which companies have the best recruitment materials (ask to see some examples) and Web sites? Ask for a quick overview of the Web site and advice on how you can get the most out of it yourself. What other resources are there for recruiters? Which Web sites or resources (directories, reports, and books) are most popular with their students?

Although the career center staff is there to work with you and help make your recruiting experience as productive and enjoyable as possible, the staffs are usually small and their time is stretched responding to companies, students, and programming. Specifically, if every company recruiting at a school met with each of the key career center managers—let's say a low of 100 companies and a high of 700 companies at 30 minutes with each person—you can do the math. These career center managers would have little time for much else, so use the time wisely and maximize your takeaways from the people with whom you are meeting. It is not a must, only an ideal, that you meet with the key career center managers. It may be that one person will be very knowledgeable and well versed and able to answer most of your questions. Or perhaps ten minutes with one person, supplemented by your own research efforts, will be just fine for your being informed on the school's recruiting.

As someone who spends about one-third of my time meeting with new and current companies' recruiters, brainstorming ideas, advising on recruiting strategy, and working through myriad issues, I can say unequivocally that this is an energizing and rewarding part of my role. At the same time, it is extremely time consuming and needs to be balanced with student needs and programs, developing the team, participating in the MBA program's other dimensions, and day-to-day operations. Many of my colleagues and I are fortunate to have a talented team, any one of whom could answer the above questions as well. In addition, our Web sites and recruiter guides and other materials are designed with recruiters in mind: to give you the information foremost on your minds and to be the most helpful to you.

Also, remember, MBA recruiting is not a one-shot deal, so you do not have to do everything at once and establish an instant relationship. If you are truly building an enduring, mutual relationship and creating a partnership for the long term, there will be much interaction beyond the initial visit together. An ongoing dialogue should develop for airing any problems that arise, touching base, and keeping the career center updated on any big company events, announcements, plans, or changes. Essentially, you need to communicate often by e-mail, by phone, and in person.

Schedule Interview Dates

From your meetings, you will now know what you need to do to schedule interviews and your employer information session. If others in your group or company are handling scheduling, they can review "how to schedule interviews" on the school Web site's or in the recruiter guidebook. Scheduling dates for interviews and company information sessions will involve filling out a form noting the following: how many schedules you want and your preferences for dates; whether your jobs are full time or summer internships; the desired length of interviews (30 minutes, 30 minutes back-to-back, 45 minutes, 60 minutes); and the kind of interviews (all open or do you want to be able to preselect some of the schedule, i.e., closed interviews).

To preselect, you review student résumés and invite those you choose before your interviews become open to all others through bidding points. You'll also be asked to turn in job descriptions at that time or later, and to list any citizenship requirements and locations for your jobs. You'll be asked about your date preferences and AV and other requirements for your employer information session.

The career center will confirm your interview schedule and employer information session dates soon after your request, with other particulars such as when to send recruitment literature and the due dates for other deliverables.

DRILL-DOWN #4: FORMULATE YOUR COMMUNICATION STRATEGY AND KEY MESSAGES

Time Line: Before Pre-Recruitment and Starting to Interact with Students

Keep It Simple and in Sync

As a start, think about your organization from the standpoint of the McKinsey 7 S model. The McKinsey 7 Ss are strategy, structure, systems, staffing, style, skills, and superordinate goals. The model was established for use in strategy development, not per se for communication strategy, but I've used it often when coaching students to evaluate different companies and offers by identifying these seven dimensions. I've also used it with companies to help them define what they want to communicate about themselves to students.

Can you talk about your company in each of these dimensions? It's a useful exercise to think about how you would describe your company using each of these Ss. If you are not clear on these basics, then whatever you're saying on campus may at best be diluted and unpersuasive. In addition to thinking about your seven Ss, you need to define the key themes and core messages you are trying to convey to your target audience. How do you position yourself vis-à-vis other companies using the classical marketing five Ps: product, price, placement, promotion, and positioning (see Chapter 9, Best Practices #2)?

Once you achieve clarity on these sorts of questions, then you need to make everyone who is involved with your recruiting efforts aware of these important themes. You need to be unified in your messaging, and use every opportunity to reinforce these points with your customers at the schools.

Contextual considerations for your communication strategy include: Who is your audience? Who are your customers (students first, career center staff and others second)? What will resonate with them? How are they most likely to get what it is you're trying to say? What words should you use? How do you deliver your message? How frequently do you need to communicate?

Bottom line: Formulate a communication strategy, know the key messages and themes you want to convey at the schools, and ensure your recruiters are informed and in sync.

Stay in the Loop

It's also important that your communication strategy is 360 degrees. In other words, communication is integral all the way around: within your own company for your higher ups, your peers, and your customers—the ultimate recipients you've targeted the communication to. Keep your executives in the loop about your plans and how things are going overall. Let colleagues internally know too so they feel involved in your efforts. It is especially critical to keep those involved in recruiting and your team up to speed so there's seamless coordination. This will go a long way when you are on campus. Students, the career center staff, and others notice inconsistencies. For your audience of MBAs, make a concerted effort to let them know your broad-brush plans for the year for their class, and remind them about activities and key dates or deadlines as they approach. Inform them quickly of any changes in your plans.

Overcommunicate

I've never heard any complaints of overcommunication, but I cannot keep count of how many times I've heard of communication breakdowns. The most common breakdowns occur when companies don't call back or follow up when they say they will; when the interviewer or person speaking at a pre-recruitment event is not aware of overall company plans for the school, what jobs are being recruited for, or interviews; and when last-minute changes crop up in the dates, times, or places of events. Communication gaps can undermine the big wins and the positive impressions your company makes. I cannot overemphasize how important effective communication is.

Mind the Internal PR and Marketing

Let the in-house champions supportive of MBA recruiting, or who have shown interest along the way, know about your plans, who has been participating so far, and how they can become involved. Start to think about interviewers on campus and callbacks, and nip any naysayers with understanding and information; the individuals in your organization may be feeling like they are the have-nots versus the MBAs who will be the haves. Keep people in the loop and engaged. E-mails or updates in bigger meetings will do. Or you can evangelize and create excitement by doing something like a countdown to launch. "Guess who is going back to school to hire our MBAs." List the teams involved by the schools and campuses you'll visit. E-mail the staff and tell them about the special MBA recruiting Web site you've created. Ask for their feedback. Run a "name contest" for the site or a contest to create a headline or tagline phrase. Hold a weekly drawing (at your Friday night happy hour?) for a give-away sweatshirt and school banner from each of your schools. Or, if not too expensive, give every employee one of the tchotchkes you're using on the campuses. Be out and about in your company. Keep repeating the message about the importance of MBA recruiting as a critical complement, not a threat, to the talent you already have in your company.

Develop Compelling Job Descriptions

Those job descriptions are an integral part of your communication strategy. They seem mundane and arduous to develop, and too detailed to those not detail-inclined. You do not, however, want to underestimate their powers of persuasion. A job description could be one of the first bits of information an MBA gets about your company. Most MBAs determine their fit with and interest in you from job descriptions. As such, something that is really compelling, yet presents the job as realistically and intriguingly as possible, can powerfully influence the MBAs you're hoping to attract.

Good and quick sources for ideas and information about other companies' descriptions are the career sections of your local newspaper and the *Wall Street Journal, New York Times,* and *San José Mercury News* Sunday editions. You can also visit such Web sites as Fast Company's HotJobs, Cruel World, JobTrak, or WetFeet.com to learn about the competition. Your reconnaissance will net valuable data on what others are doing to help you decide how you can best differentiate and position your company to compete successfully.

Several "best of" job descriptions in media, banking, and consumer products are included in Appendix C. These job descriptions come from companies that have managed to create outstanding and impactful descriptions. They are clear, concise, and compelling—some of the best I have seen over the 14 years I've been doing MBA recruiting. These include:

- Bertelsmann: global junior executive group
- Charles Schwab & Co.: management associate program
- L'Oréal: marketing assistant

Job Description Pointers. A great job description will, in general, be brief and clear on what your company is and does, the core job responsibilities, and the ideal candidate's background. To resonate with the MBA candidates, it should sound fresh and current, incorporating words, phrases, and a writing style that grab the MBAs' attention and do not sound like everyone else's descriptions. A realistic representation of your company and the job is important as well, since it's better to let students self-select early on. At the same time, you will want to balance this approach with putting your best foot forward and marketing most effectively whatever strengths you have. Use your job descriptions to the fullest advantage.

What's in. Ideally, a job description will cover in one page, maximum, the following headlines:

- Job title, group name, and location.
- Company background: mission, products and services, and your strengths in the marketplace.
- Role and responsibilities. Make these exciting and interesting. Use action verbs and broad themes; don't bury them in minutiae. Use three to five bullet points maximum.
- Desired skills, experience, and knowledge.

What's out. Avoid the following:

- Outdated words and phrases, such as "job specifications," "requirements," "qualifications," and "personnel."
- Small fonts (less than 9 points) and dense text. Use bullet points and

make sure you have ample white space and "chunked up" text for easy reading.

- Hype and buzzwords. You want to point out your positives without using overstatements. Also, the latest buzzwords are overused and tired. They can make you sound like everyone else. For example, "Leading company is looking for dynamic, self-motivated talent" is a frequently used sentence, as are words like "top" and "high-growth."

Integration. Words are great for communicating, but actions, attitudes, and *how* you do things all combine to convey the overall impression of who you are. You've heard the saying "Actions speak louder than words." What you do and how you do it speak volumes—communicating a lot about who you are; the people you select to represent you; how you treat all the students, both those you are interested in and those you are not; how you work with the career center, student groups, and faculty; and how you handle any press crises that pop up unexpectedly. Examples of the latter include not meeting analysts' earnings projections, a layoff, your stock tanking, allegations of unfair labor practices in a third-world country, firing a CEO, and rumors of a merger or acquisition. These crises will test your mettle as a company, but they can set you apart for classy handling.

The content and style of how you communicate on your Web site and in your hard-copy recruitment materials are critical to your communication strategy. Develop a special Web site for MBA recruitment even if it's adding a few screens to what you generally have for recruitment. Ideas are discussed in depth in Chapter 14. Be daring within the comfort zone of your culture, so your hard-copy recruitment materials *pop*. Some that I've seen or created that work well include trifolds or one pagers in bright colors and different shapes and sizes of pages, when there's no time or money for a full-blown brochure. Interestingly packaged materials, when there's a lot to convey—many openings, multiple divisions recruiting—can also stand out. A few of the most imaginative ideas are recruitment materials encased in a Velcro-closed translucent folder (think iMac); in a tube; in a Japanese-inspired origamilike folder that looked more like a card; and on an oversized chocolate bar wrapper.

Many career centers also allow a company to send one binder of information for their on-site resource centers. These are best put to use if you make sure the contents are updated frequently, at least two to four times a year. Include information that students cannot easily find elsewhere. Don't rehash your Web site, recruitment brochures, or pre-recruitment handouts. Ideally, binders should contain a personal letter signed by the recruiting team with their contact information; a year-at-a-glance calendar of what you're doing on campus for each class; your company overview; top-line organization chart if available; job descriptions; select employee profiles (alumni or some of your stars and their résumés and highlighted career moves in your company); pictures of products; press releases; sample "day in the life of" schedules or diagrams for what it's like to work with you; and something fun like a company credo, a values wheel, or a picture of all the dogs that come into the office with their human companions. Make enough binders for every school plus extras for your campus teams and spare copies. Giving binders to your teams will keep your interviewers informed about what the schools are seeing about you. You may also want to get extra mileage from these materials by having some on hand in-house when candidates come in for interviewing.

You'll want to label both the spines and the fronts of your binders, since they will sit on bookshelves. And the rule of using a basic black-and-white binder does not apply here. You want to draw attention.

Tchotchkes, Anyone?

Giveaways don't have to be elaborate or even cost that much to make a lasting impression and reinforce your company image and communication strategy. The reality is that MBAs are being pursued from every direction, and clever tchotchkes can help you build visibility and create a buzz with the students. You do not have to spend a lot of money, however.

Giveaways can make a difference if they do something to help (1) set you apart from other companies; (2) leave a lasting, positive impression with the students; (3) create a positive buzz; (4) hit home on what you stand for as a company; and (5) familiarize the students with your products, services, or a key point of difference that they might not have otherwise been aware of.

I have seen many great examples over the years. Odwalla and Jamba Juice proudly gave away their juice drinks and smoothies at our Growth Company Career Fair. General Mills sends each of our staff a holiday basket full of its cereals, cake mixes, fruit roll-ups, and a picture calendar of its beautiful campus. At the International Career Forum, L'Oréal handed out its nail polishes and fragrances, Bertelsmann gave out its newest *Totally Hits* CD, and General Motors gave away toy cars. Cargill has given away yummy giant chocolate bars à la the commodities (cocoa) part of their business.

Companies that don't necessarily have givable products use tchotchkes like stress balls (those spongy, soft balls you can throw against a wall or squeeze in your hands), commuter mugs (we've seen some pretty original yet functional ones), baseball caps, t-shirts, water bottles, key chains, and pen-highlighter combos. Some of the more unique items are windbreakers that zip into their own pouches, company-logo toiletry bags, magnets with words or phrases, and rocks with "dream" or "joy" on them. When I recruited for Dole Packaged Foods, we gave away stuffed pineapples and pineapple-inspired aprons, and served the frozen sorbet desserts at the employer information session.

Phase Two: Best-in-Class Pre-Recruitment

SOME COMPANIES BELIEVE THEY CAN skip pre-recruitment and cut to the chase of interviews and then dash on to make offers. To the contrary, pre-recruitment is a paramount and strategic part of overall recruiting efforts: It is crucial for generating visibility and presence before the MBAs start signing up for interviews. Pre-recruitment, thus, is a key driver of interest among MBAs. This chapter is dedicated to discussing pre-recruitment in depth:

Why it is important not to fast-forward and skip over it

The five rules for ultimate success, including best practices for your employer information session

Examples from a diversity of companies that are remarkably effective in pre-recruitment

Notes on timing, invitations with flair, and what's in the crystal ball for pre-recruitment

For specific advice on pre-recruitment from the school's career center director of the top MBA programs, refer to Chapter 10.

DRILL-DOWN #5. DEVELOP AND ORCHESTRATE PRE-RECRUITMENT ACTIVITIES—BEFORE INTERVIEWING

Time Line: October–February, Before Interviewing

On a Mission to Create Your Presence

Pre-recruitment activities prior to your interviews are important in (1) building visibility for your company, (2) generating buzz about you and your opportunities, and (3) influencing interest in your interviews that follow that academic year or after. Gone are the days when a company could just show up for interviews and expect to have full schedules of candidates lined up. If you don't spend time up front on pre-recruitment, unless you are a fabulously recognized and popular company or have beginner's luck, you will receive disappointing interest in your company and interview sign-ups.

Additionally, by not doing pre-recruitment you miss out on a great opportunity to inform people, in a more personal way than you can through brochures or Web sites, about who you are, what you do, and what you have to offer. Consequently, without pre-recruitment the people who end up on your interview schedule may not be the best fits for your jobs, because they have been unable to gain an understanding of your company beyond the more superficial information on your Web site or in your recruitment materials.

Even the sexiest, most popular companies have to work at building visibility for themselves and generating interest in their interviews among the competition. In fact, pre-recruitment is one reason why those companies, which have been highly effective, were able to achieve those results.

Pre-Recruitment Trends. On MBA campuses over the past years, companies rolled out the standard fare of receptions and dinners, but spurred on by the dot-com frenzy and heightened war for talent, we've increasingly seen more innovative, personalized pre-recruitment ideas emerge. A few to note are a company hosting a golf tournament or taking eighteen students out to play; flying students out on the corporate jet for a day on the job as a brand manager; or launching a global "e-strategy marketing challenge" for students around the world. Effective pre-recruitment doesn't have to take a lot of money, however. An informal breakfast with the CEO when he's in town, a pizza party with recent MBA hires from the company, giving students the opportunity to come to your offices to talk to people and learn about something of interest on which you are an expert (investing or a new technology), or inviting them to participate in your community volunteer efforts or a bowling tournament can be just as compelling.

The Five Rules for Success. The rules for successful pre-recruiting activities are summarized and then explained in the following sections:

1. Know your customers and tailor your plans to each school.
2. Leverage what the school can offer, but brainstorm for each specific campus.
3. Choose wisely who will represent you—you are whom you send.
4. As a general rule, do a minimum of a company information session and one smaller, targeted event that you host.
5. Engage best practices in your company information session.

Know Your Customers

From your research and in-person meetings, you now have a better understanding of the MBA program's culture, personality, what may work best at the school, and the nuances of recruiting there. If you've come this far, you've covered a lot of ground and may be tempted to come to closure by developing generic plans and getting on with them versus tailoring for your target audience.

It may sound quite attractive just about now to decide to use the same pre-recruitment strategy and plan at all of your schools: a one size fits all. This can certainly be the easiest route—to use the same presentations, the same executives, and the same smaller event ideas—but you will want to resist this big time!

One of the enduring best practices we learn from companies across many industries is that they know their customers. In a business setting, a company that values its customers may not tailor actual products, but at least it will adapt product features and advertising to honor customers' differences. Related to pre-recruitment, this translates to refining and tailoring any overarching strategy and activities employed at all your schools to each individual school. For example, you may do an employer information session and use the same presentation format, slide show, handouts and giveaways, but you will choose a different set of people to represent you at each school and select the best timing within the school's total calendar. You may send one special recruitment brochure and binder for the resource center, and emphasize your MBA recruitment Web site at all your schools, but use a completely different mix of e-mail, in-person, and other communication for each school.

Knowing your customer means knowing what will best resonate with each school and adapting your plans accordingly. This is, of course, important throughout all of your MBA recruiting, but particularly crucial in pre-recruitment when you make your first foray in front of the students to build your identity, visibility, and reputation.

Leverage the School's Offerings

From your research and interactions with the schools, you will know the sum total of what options the schools are offering in addition to on-campus recruiting during the academic year. You'll want to take advantage of what the school offers, but also think about doing something on your own that's more targeted and personal. The questions you will need to answer are:

- What are my options for participating in something the school has to offer? What is the best use of our time and money, given our corporate strategy?
- What kinds of students will most likely be interested in each kind of program or event? Are they my target market?
- Does our participation in the school event fit the key themes we are trying to communicate about our company?

If you need a refresher, you can call the career center director or check out the school or career center Web site to find the recruiting and academic calendar or master list of events, conferences, and career fairs for the year. Beyond an employer information session that almost all schools offer, there are numerous opportunities for a company to pre-recruit by participating in events planned by the schools.

Brainstorm Ideas for Specific Campuses. Assessing the school-facilitated options, you can pick and choose which you'll do in concert with the school versus what you can do on your own. A good brainstorming session with those involved in recruiting at the school, including any recent alumni, will probably produce too many ideas that you'll need to pare down to work well. Remember, it takes 2 years or longer to build a successful recruiting program at a school, so you can save some ideas for the future.

When brainstorming ideas, former campus team captains can offer valuable perspectives about what's worked or not, the nuances of recruiting at a school, and the competitive landscape. Choosing the best mix of people for recruiting, including developing a team approach, is discussed in Chapter 5, in Drill-Down #6. Ideally the people you use for pre-recruitment constitute a subset of all your interviewers for the school, in addition to select senior executives and school alumni, if you have that luxury. This is the first time you are in front of the students, and you'll want to remember that to them, whom you send *is* the company.

Choose the Best Mix to Pre-Recruit

It is worth emphasizing here that when choosing personnel for pre-recruitment:

- Title is *not* the most important criterion. Bombarded with CEOs, presidents, and VPs, students can be jaded about titles. Sending people who enjoy what they do, are role models, and are engaging is what matters most to students.
- It is important to select people from your company who will best resonate with the school's personality, realizing that first impressions are made quickly.
- A good rule-of-thumb is to send to an event one person for every fifteen to twenty students you anticipate will participate.

Plan a Great Employer Information Session

When you are starting out at a school, it's advisable to do an employer information session (hereafter referred to as a session), a.k.a. a company or recruiter briefing, and at least one other pre-recruitment activity. You can plan more the next year as you build your repertoire and gain experience, or be excruciatingly discerning about adding on a few other events the first year if, for example, the school offers an event such as an entrepreneurs' conference or a global business summit that fits perfectly with your strategy. You can also make an exception if there is something opportunistic you want to jump on in a particular year: record sales numbers; a product launch that everyone is talking about; a new, hot CEO; a first to market; or a Nobel Prize winner in your midst. The employer session can serve as your broad event to generate overall visibility and buzz; then a second event can be smaller, more targeted, and more personal.

Most companies hold a session because (1) it generates a big impact for the time spent; (2) it's set up through the career center (you request it along with your interview dates); and (3) most students expect them and benefit from the amount of information they can learn in the 1-hour time slot. Additionally, it's easy for the students to drop by your session, because you are on campus and they are already there.

The school may also facilitate a speaking opportunity with a student club or in a class as the protagonist of a case study. You may also be able to sponsor student-led or school events. Career centers may also invite companies to help with their student programs, such as a career conference (with an industry and functional panels of experts), mock interviews, or advising students on their résumé writing.

Best Practices for Your Session

Companies that impress are those that pay attention to the execution of their plans and activities in addition to their substance. To show your best, prepare to handle details related to mechanics, logistics, and the flow. Your thoughtful care in these areas will make you stand out from all the worthy companies competing for student mindshare.

MECHANICS, LOGISTICS, AND FLOW

- Arrive at the school at least 30 minutes early, and drop by the career center for a barometer reading. How are things going so far in the season? How have other events been attended? How do they compare to last year? Is there anything going on with the students you should know or be aware of? Hot buttons? Concerns?

- Get into the room and set up and do not take anything for granted. Make sure the PowerPoint presentation is set to go. If showing a video, make sure it's queued up and that you know how to operate those persnickety controls. Make any handouts readily available.

- Make sure everyone from the company has met each other, that those who will talk know the order of speakers, and that you have clear understanding of who will kick off and close the session.

- Overall, think through and do what you need to in advance for smooth running while allowing spontaneity as you would normally.
- Keep the formal part of the presentation short, allowing ample time for questions.
- Use a senior executive who can speak broadly about the company and who is a skilled, dynamic, and engaging public speaker. Use someone who will resonate. A mix of people from your company from different functions and levels is recommended.
- Have a sign-in sheet so you know the names of students who participated.
- Introduce key or all your people from the company quickly.

TOPICS TO CONSIDER
- Who you are and what you do.
- Big picture recruiting plans, at all business schools and their school.
- Any noteworthy business results, news, or plans, such as a merger or an acquisition, new e-commerce initiatives, or expansion to new countries.
- How you are different from others vying for their attention.
- Why you value MBAs and top talent. How they can make a difference.
- For a recently hired MBA (2 to 5 years out): why the MBA joined the company, whether the experience has lived up to expectations, and what the employee learned from going through the recruiting process.
- For an HR head or someone who has responsibility for developing people: your company's commitment to career development, citing examples of career moves by MBAs in the company.
- If you are a consulting or investment banking firm: a recent high-profile deal or engagement described by a client who worked with you and whom you invite to speak.
- From an alumnus MBA who has since left your firm: the value of his experience with you and his leapfrogging to industry or a start-up senior role.
- Dates to remember for on-campus interviewing plans and callbacks.

FOLLOW UP
- Put your presentation on your Web site, including the names and faces of the people who spoke on campus with their contact information.
- Reach out to those who attended (e-mail or note) to let them know you

were glad they were at your session and to remind them about your interviews.

- Powwow with your team and discuss what worked and what didn't, so you can make midcourse corrections before using the presentation at your other schools.

Some ideas that worked for companies include:

- A top consulting firm giving a lively discussion on insights and advice for students going through case interviews. The session, called "Cracking the Case Consulting Workshop," was targeted to first-year students. Two firm managers offered a humorous but insightful dramatization playing interviewer and interviewee.
- A global cosmetics firm inviting their summer interns to talk about "how we spent our summers," the projects they worked on, and what they liked about the company.
- An investment bank bringing in the team of people that worked on one of the largest and most fascinating deals in their history.

The frustrating news is that an employer session alone can be quite ineffective. You need to market it beforehand, and you need to supplement it with at least one other activity if possible.

Sponsor Your Own More Focused Events

Most companies that excel in pre-recruitment utilize the information session as a broad activity to build visibility and generate overall interest in their companies. They then follow up by hosting a smaller, more targeted, more personal event.

Use your imagination in brainstorming to end up with an event or a program that speaks volumes about your culture, reinforces your communication strategy, and makes a positive impact. The following are some of the best-in-class examples that we have seen recently. Hopefully, these will provide some food for thought.

Goldman Sachs. Considered a class act and a world-class firm, Goldman Sachs hosted a study break for the first-year class the quarter before they started their summer intern interviews. It was informal, with chips, margaritas, and pan-Asian finger food. This allowed first years to interact with the recruiting team early on in the process, creating highly favorable impressions of the very "real," eclectic people they'd be working with side by side. It was also successful in increasing the number of MBAs who otherwise might not have been interested in investment banking but who wanted to learn more about the company and to talk frankly about some of the misperceptions. Most were pleasantly surprised.

Lauded as exemplary for its diversity efforts, for example with women on Wall Street, the firm sponsored a women's panel with the Women in Management Club. Substantive issues were discussed: the differences of working in fixed-income sales and trading, private client services, or corporate finance, co-mingled with straight-up, lively conversation about what it's like to be a woman in banking and work-life issues impacting both men and women today in the workplace. In line with their commitment to diversity, Goldman Sachs also sponsored the Stanford Business School women's conferences in New York and Palo Alto and a dinner for Harvard's gay MBA students. It took the employer information session to new heights when the team presented its prized economist, Abby Joseph Cohen, to a standing-room-only crowd at Kellogg. Its other campus presentations were also hits, especially those that included a description of its role in the eBay IPO.

What did Goldman Sachs accomplish? It strategically conveyed that its people are interesting, stimulating, and diverse, with all kinds of backgrounds but with the commonality of being exceptional in whatever they are or do; that it is world class in its business and execution, with a strong emphasis on people and relationships; that it is accessible and really cares about MBA recruiting; that it is an overall superb place to work.

Paul DiNardo, Managing Director, High Technology Group, Investment Banking Division, notes, "We stress creativity and imagination in everything we do. We pride ourselves on having pioneered many of the practices that have become standard in the industry. For several years, we have taken the approach of hosting or sponsoring several events prior to actual interviews, targeted both at the general student population and specific groups within the student body.

"We plan a calendar that includes a large firm-wide presentation and then drill down to smaller events that focus on the work of particular divisions. Our focus is on a broad and ongoing commitment to the business schools as an important source of talent."

L'Oréal. The "e-Strat Challenge" launched by L'Oréal this year was a first of its kind. A global Internet challenge for graduate students and students in their junior and senior years of undergraduate study, it included 400 teams of three students each from around the world. Each team operated in its own virtual world managing a portfolio of global brands over six consecutive 6-month periods and competing against virtual, traditional bricks-and-mortar competitors as well as new economy e-competitors in a Web-based, simulated cosmetics industry environment. Each team was evaluated on its final share price index, calculated on a combination of profits, brand market shares, number of registered customers, and level of customer relationship management. Teams from forty-two countries took part. The top three teams, from Spain, Turkey, and the U.S., were announced with great fanfare in April, flown to L'Oréal's Paris headquarters in May, and awarded as a grand prize an all-expense paid trip to London, Tokyo, or San Francisco.

Notes Martial Lalancette, Director of HR, Corporate Strategic Recruiting, "This is the perfect illustration of a L'Oréal initiative: ambitious and innovative projects on a worldwide level. The success of our e-Strat Challenge reinforces our strategic orientation, especially concerning e-recruitment."

L'Oréal achieved high-profile visibility, emphasizing its global reach and formidable marketing and strategy abilities.

Charles Schwab & Co. In an interview with Shelly Anderson, former VP of Corporate Staffing for Charles Schwab, she discussed the mix of innovative pre-recruitment activities that made the company a standout on MBA campuses that year. Schwab hosted half-day sessions on-site at its offices with the career center professionals from their schools so that they could learn more about Schwab's culture, services, and recruiting plans and could meet key people within the firm. Anderson notes, "This helps the career center professionals understand our business and culture so they can refer the best candidates for Schwab jobs." In a strategic move at several of its pre-recruiting events, Schwab used its CEO, Dave Pottruck, an impassioned speaker who resonates with students. At UC Berkeley, the firm put into action the idea of one of their summer marketing interns. The intern served as the student ambassador and helped the firm's Berkeley recruiting team host 175 students for an investment seminar. This proved to be a success in generating interest in both investing *and* employment opportunities at Schwab. Fourteen different investment clubs co-sponsored the event. To underscore its commitment to diversity, it sponsored a "Diversity in the Workplace Conference," which Anderson says "helped the firm dramatically increase the diversity of the candidate pool looking at Schwab on Bay Area campuses." The conference drew more than 100 student club presidents and officers. They were invited to Schwab for the day to discuss what diversity looks like in American business today, how to evaluate it in potential employers, and what questions can be asked. Sessions were led by the VP of diversity and the diversity task force.

What did Schwab accomplish? It convinced candidates that, in addition to its extraordinary reputation as an innovator in technology and a model in corporate philanthropy and community outreach, it takes time to build relationships with the career centers and students, and that it values its summer interns in recruiting effectively.

Eli Lilly and Company. The health care/pharmaceutical company provided a cool-looking cart offering international coffees, café lattes, biscotti, and functional, fun commuter mugs for Stanford's International Career Forum. The cart was at the entrance of the job fair and open to both MBA students and the fifty companies participating. Lilly successfully conveyed one of its core messages: Although based in the Midwest, it is a global company with an impressive international management team, and contrary to what some may perceive of health care/pharmaceutical firms, employees have fun and flair.

General Mills. The Stanford recruiting team hosted a breakfast of champions complete with its cereals and yogurts. The company set up a central meeting place for students in the courtyard, where the team could meet and greet interested students. This is a tradition at the school, and the students come away with positive impressions of the company's expanse of exciting products. The company also demonstrated in action its winning team approach to working together, the leadership it values in its people, and its organizational abilities.

Target and Communicate with Your MBA Candidates

Before you host your employer information session and other pre-recruitment activities, you will want to do some marketing communication to generate some intrigue and interest among students as well as to start building your presence. This is a perfect time to do some en masse communication to create visibility, and to target and communicate with the candidates you are interested in. Here are some tips:

- Find out how the career center already advertises or can help you to. It may list your events in a weekly update on its Web site, or it may post one of your flyers on its bulletin board.
- Think about announcements or invitations by e-mail with a "click here to add to your Outlook calendar" or as hard copy for distribution to student mailboxes.
- Create some cool posters that are catchy but not cute.
- Send special e-mails to targeted student clubs. Keep it short: key points, with dates for pre-recruitment and recruitment, or e-mail the whole class, if that option is available, or send something home (their résumés have their addresses).
- Take a look in the class résumé book or do some advance searching of the online database for the kinds of candidates who match your desired profiles. Communicate directly with this targeted subset. Personal phone calls can make an impression.
- Capitalize on the word of mouth by former employees who are now students, or ask a faculty member you know well to announce your events in class.

Companies have used the gamut for their marketing communication. A leading management consulting firm distributed a letter to student boxes signed by the recruitment team, heavy on alumni or at least MBAs from sister schools, with brief highlights of the recruiting plans for the year; key dates for summer events, career interviews, and pre-recruitment events; and contact information for each team member so that students could call on any one of them with questions.

A top investment bank convened a breakfast for former associates who were now at the business school to keep them informed on recruiting plans, to get their input, and to ask that they help get the word out.

An up-and-coming consulting firm gave the first-year class, right before their first midterm exams and way in advance of their interviewing, a care package including highlighters, aspirin, a deluxe street map of nearby San

Francisco, and movie passes. It printed on a Post-it pad the dates of its planned interview and pre-recruitment activities.

A Midwest manufacturing company sent out a three-part e-mail leading up to an invitation to its employer information session and to visit its table at an upcoming school-sponsored career fair. In part one of the e-mail, it emphasized some recent product innovations and business successes. In part two, it noted its recognition as one of the most admired companies to work for and other positives about its culture. In part three, it showed a humorous example of two houses side by side, illustrating what $200,000 could buy in the Midwest versus Silicon Valley.

You've Got Mail. E-mail can be one of the most effective mediums for marketing communication for the obvious reason that it is quick, efficient, and low cost. Effective recruiters make theirs grab attention by carefully crafting what goes in the subject line and including links and the "mail to" option for easy replying.

The Crystal Ball. In a brainstorming session with some recruiters who were on campus for a recruiter briefing, we discussed what we're seeing on the horizon for pre-recruitment. Although many companies still host dinners, receptions, and lunches, these are being de-emphasized in favor of smaller, more focused events. What's *in* for pre-recruitment activities? An alumni panel followed by an informal wine and cheese reception or champagne dessert buffet; a barbeque at an executive's house; light snacks at a billiards watering hole; cruises on the bay; a brunch or tea; a football game with a tailgating event before; small groups of seven to ten students hosted by company managers at a smattering of favorite local restaurants; a bowling or casino night; and business plan competitions.

Some activities on the horizon predicted to be hot and which someone, somewhere is probably already doing include a golf tournament, a scavenger hunt, a party, weekly online chats with a different manager in the company working on interesting stuff, renting out a movie theater. In addition to being pre-recruitment activities, most of these could also be used for callbacks or sell weekends.

Chapter 5

Phase Three: Interviews

DRILL-DOWN #6. SELECT AND TRAIN YOUR INTERVIEWERS

Time Line: October–April, After Pre-Recruitment

Enlist People to the Cause

Remember, from the students' perspective, the people you send to campus represent the company. The MBAs don't have the benefit of meeting every wonderful person in your company, so the ones involved in pre-recruitment activities and interviews *are* the company to them. That's why it's so important to choose wisely the people who will represent you for your campus recruiting. You've done your research at this point and you know the nuances of the school. Utilize your knowledge to make smart choices about the people who will resonate with the specific school and its MBAs. Involve those who will be impressive emissaries for you on campus.

Consider the Team Approach

Many companies use a team approach per school. They involve alumni of the school, when they have that luxury, and a senior manager who can be called on for high-profile efforts, such as performing as the lead relationship manager, speaking at the employer information session, building relationships with the dean and faculty, or closing the deal on the offers the company will make. Additional team members typically have recruiting experience, are role models and stars, or are enthusiastic and want to help.

You "are" the people you send to the schools, so choose your interviewers wisely, using these guidelines:

- Don't focus on titles; rather, choose those who are enthusiastic about working in the company, are good with people, and can be effective in marketing your organization.
- Use a mix of backgrounds, levels, functions, groups and departments, gender, ages, and ethnicities. Ideally, call on people who have MBAs or advanced degrees themselves.
- Select people who embody your culture and your company's personality and energy.
- Put your best foot forward. This is the time to call on your role models, stars, and those with interesting backgrounds and careers to date.
- Balance those who are experienced in recruiting with some up-and-comers who have ability and potential, thereby doing your succession planning and building bench strength for future recruiting leadership.
- Make sure to have at least one person from HR on each team. One could be assigned to a group of schools, for example five to ten schools on the East Coast. Ideally, one senior HR manager who is responsible for MBA recruiting (e.g., a VP or director of global MBA recruiting, campus recruiting, or university relations) could work up front with every team to develop a consistent strategy and integration across all teams, but could appoint a staff member to handle the day-to-day activities.

HR or whoever is driving MBA recruiting can name a school team captain, someone could volunteer to be the leader, or the team should choose amongst themselves—whatever works. A team captain who is chosen before the team members can be called on to recruit others.

If you are using a team approach, the people who do pre-recruitment (plus or minus a few) should also be involved in interviews. If it's not possible to have the same pre-recruiters and interviewers, then at minimum someone needs to be responsible for the hand-off of "intelligence" and progress to date so that your company's efforts are coordinated. In other words, someone needs to debrief on the pre-recruitment activities for the school and let the interviewers know how things went (level of participation, types of questions and issues that the students raised, and the competition and recruiting picture at the school).

When to Use HR

Although I have a deep respect for HR, individuals from HR should not as a general rule interview MBAs. There are two main reasons: (1) Typically, HR is either misunderstood or less respected by MBAs than the line-function executives who are central to the action of the business. (2) The students will want to interview with the managers (or ones like them) for whom they'd be working.

The exception for HR doing the interviews is when an interviewer cancels at the last minute and you need a knowledgeable replacement. The HR person does come from a line position as a banker or a consultant or a marketing director or has knowledge about the business.

Also, for summer intern interviews it may make the most sense for HR to conduct the interviews, especially if there will be only one interview and you need someone with broad knowledge of all your company's departments and groups that have intern openings. Someone from HR can recruit on behalf of all the managers who have openings.

A Sample of the Team Approach. When I was VP of corporate university relations at Bank of America, we invited the top seventeen executives (our CEO, COO, executive VPs) to be the relationship managers at our top seventeen (of fifty-two) schools. Based on a needs assessment, we knew we had about thirty different groups in the company with overall hiring needs of 350 to 425 undergraduates and MBAs. Although the bank was going through a major downsizing, the senior team had the vision and foresight to support and even strengthen campus recruiting efforts to keep building the pipeline of the best talent for the future.

Our HR group developed a short list of possible team captains—alumni from the school and our stars with really interesting careers. The senior relationship managers also had a say as to who was appointed team captain for the school. We had a kick-off with all the senior executives for those team captains, and then asked them to help recruit team members who would be involved on the campuses.

HR's Core Function. In this case, we, as HR, provided expertise to the teams in several ways: formulating overall strategy for campus recruiting; providing information and research on the schools; assisting in development of an individual action plan per school; making sure that all efforts and activities were integrated; managing the budget; briefing all who were involved on campuses so they were well-informed; and ensuring that all involved knew the big picture and had the tools, resources, and administrative help on the campuses that they needed.

We also took on all the operational activities so that the teams could focus on the personal interactions and critical activities at their schools. For example, we handled all the scheduling and logistics of the pre-recruitment events and interviews. This included developing invitations to events; choosing the venues and planning the menus and set-up for receptions; working with the hiring managers to write the job descriptions; ordering and distributing the school résumé books to the team; organizing the second rounds; developing the offers with input from the compensation group and hiring managers; all tracking and reporting by school (metrics and results vis-à-vis goals); managing the applicant tracking system and résumé database; and working through any issues between the schools and our recruiters or among different departments that wanted to pursue the same candidates.

Coordinate, Brief, and Train Your Interviewers

A training session or briefing for all those who'll participate in campus activities is a must for two reasons: (1) as a symbolic, team-building kick-off to energize people, and (2) so that everyone who will be representing the company will be as informed, knowledgeable, and coordinated as possible. A briefing can be jammed into an hour, if that's all that people can spare, but 2 to 3 hours or a half-day is best, so you have time to include interviewing training at the end. Live is best but videoconferencing or a presentation over your intranet will do if people are located in different locations.

Suggestions on what to cover include:

- Your CEO or a senior executive kicks things off with opening remarks about the importance of MBA recruiting to the company, followed by introduction of team members and their critical roles in this endeavor.
- The senior HR executive or someone with broad knowledge of all re-

cruiting activities paints the big picture: overall plans for recruiting, number of openings and groups within the company participating, schools selected, highlights of what's planned and when on the campuses; plans for second rounds, key themes you are trying to communicate at your schools, timing of when you'll get packets to them, and HR team members' roles and responsibilities.

- Q and A period.
- Interview training: what to expect on campus the day of the interviews; advice for conducting the interviews; sample questions; evaluation criteria (fit and job-specific), which can be discussed in broad terms if these are not defined; and the legal, illegal, and PC (politically correct) questions they should be aware of.
- Hands-on learning for those newer to interviewing:

  Role playing. One person plays interviewer, another interviewee, and a third an observer who gives feedback. Give each triad a job description and have them brainstorm interview questions. Rotate the three roles until each person has played each one.

  Dramatizations. Act out a good interview from start to finish, from greeting to close, and then a bad one. Discuss and evaluate.

  Bringing in an interviewing expert or organizing a panel discussion of your more seasoned interviewers to share lessons learned and give advice.

Handy Handouts. Handouts should be included in binders for the team members. The information you give them needs to be organized for ease of use. You can also put a copy of the handouts on your Web site for easy access and updating. If you really want to go the extra mile, your handouts for all the teams will include:

- Master time and action plan in chronological order for MBA recruiting.
- List of schools targeted.
- Target numbers and specific job titles being recruited for by each division and group, with copies of job descriptions.
- Interviewing team members' names and pictures (perhaps with school logo) and contact information.
- Recruitment materials, including anything the students will see, and your McKinsey 7 Ss or key themes and messages.

- Plans by school: key dates and names of pre-recruitment activities; on-campus interviews; and follow-up (i.e., when someone will get back to the candidates about next steps or with a rejection).
- Sketch for second-round plans on-site, with timing and a rough agenda.
- Sample interview questions, evaluation criteria, and a rating sheet (if you have them). There is a template in Appendix D.
- For each school team, add to the above school-specific research: Web site printouts; key people; the academic and recruiting calendar; any pertinent rules and policies; recent hires from the school and where they are now in your company (title and group); organizational chart for career center staff; recruiter guide; placement report; student club list; admissions information and the school annual report; and to go the extra mile, your written findings on the fifteen dimensions of the school from your research (see Chapter 3, Drill-Down #2).

Target Candidates One More Time

As a last push before your schedules become available for students to sign up, do some further outreach. Contact those who were at your employer information session or other pre-recruitment events; review the résumé book and target candidates from there; and ask former employees who are now in the school to help with word of mouth. Use the sign-up list from your employer information session to invite those students to a more personal activity, like a visit to your local office. Send e-mails to club leaders with some reminders about your interviews and ask them to pass these on to their members.

DRILL-DOWN #7: LEVERAGE THE INTERVIEW PROCESS

Time Line: Before, During, and After Interviewing

Prepare for the Interview and the Interview Questions

There are a myriad of books on interviewing. Refer to the Harvard Business School Press at www.hbsp.harvard.edu; Amazon.com at www. Amazon.com; Barnes and Noble at www.Barnesandnoble.com; and the

American Management Association at www.amanet.org. Other resources are your HR department; a colleague outside or inside your industry who has done a lot of interviewing; your local library, bookstore, or HR professional association, such as the Society for Human Resource Management (SHRM) at www.shrm.org.

Like many who have done a lot of interviewing, I am a believer in a behavioral approach based on the premise that past behavior or performance is the best predictor of future behavior or performance. Rather than asking candidates hypothethical questions (What would you do if?) or questions on traits, you ask about specific experiences the candidates hàve had in the past, when they exhibited specific behaviors you are trying to assess. The catch phrase is "Give me an example of a time when you _____." This blank could be filled in with actions, such as *used creativity, solved a complex problem, influenced a difficult group of people, dealt with a crisis, conceived an idea and quickly put it into action,* or *faced failure.*

For the preliminary on-campus interviews, behavioral questions related to job content and general cultural fit with the company are most commonly asked. Questions probing technical areas and qualifications can be focused on later, on site during the second rounds.

In Chapter 6, "Interview Lessons Learned," extraordinary managers from several companies share their broad and deep experience in recruiting MBAs and managerial and executive-level candidates, offering their favorite interview questions, approaches, and philosophies.

To refine your list of interview questions, review what you covered in your interviewer briefing; think about the questions you've been asked over the years from great interviewers; and consider what you are trying to evaluate and how you can best draw out that information. Interview questions are as different as interviewers. Some interviewers are more formal and have a set of questions they'll ask each candidate so they can calibrate the results. Others treat the interviews more like a conversation. There's no magic formula. Typically, since the on-campus interviews last 30 minutes, you will have time for both the more general behavioral and fit questions. The probing and technical questions are for the second rounds.

Starter List of On-Campus Interview Questions

The first ten questions are designed to gauge the MBA's motivations, ambition, and maturity; intentional versus haphazard choices in life; ability to communicate and think on his/her feet; self-awareness; and what the person values:

1. Why did you decide to get your MBA?
2. What have been the best and worst parts of the experience? What have you learned the most from your experience? Favorite class and why?
3. What do you consider special about yourself?
4. Tell me in 2 minutes or less what you're most proud of in each of the jobs you've had, and why you made the moves you did. (It will become evident quickly if this person can synthesize their 3 to 5 years of experience and decisively cut to the chase in prioritizing what to emphasize for you.)
5. What would your boss, peers, and staff tell me about you?
6. What are your top three work-life priorities?
7. If the applicant went to a school for undergraduate education that you are not familiar with, ask about the selectivity of the school: What was your GPA? What kinds of courses did you take and your class rank? You may also want to ask about GMAT scores, where the MBA ranked (percentile), and current grades. Note that this is off limits at some schools.
8. What do you think you want to be doing in the next 2 to 5 years?
9. What are your top three criteria for evaluating among your offers?
10. What's important to you in a company? Culture? Your job content? The people? The senior team? The products or services?

The second set of questions uses a behavioral approach designed to assess how the candidates have behaved, acted, and performed in the past, which is one of the best predictors of future performance:

11. Describe a time you failed. How did you handle it?
12. Tell me about a time when you had to influence people who did not report to you.
13. Give an example of a time when you took a risk.
14. Tell me about a time you had an idea and implemented it.
15. Give an example of a time when you had to become an expert overnight.

16. Give an example of a time you had to make a major decision with minimal information. What did you rely on to fill in the blanks?
17. Describe a time when you broke the rules or had to support a policy you did not agree with.

The last set of questions is for evaluating fit—fit with the job, with your company, level of interest:

18. What are your strengths and weaknesses?
19. Why do you want this job? Our company? What could you contribute?
20. What do you know about us that you like? That you don't like? Assess our recruiting efforts so far. How could we improve?

Taxonomy of an Interview

There are five distinct phases of an interview:

Phase I: Break the ice and put the candidate at ease.
Phase II: Confirm what job you're interviewing for.
Phase III: Ask questions, then circle back to cover areas you need more information on to evaluate.
Phase IV: Give the candidate a chance to ask you questions.
Phase V: Close, next steps, and thanks. If you know you want to pursue the candidate, do some soft selling. End on a positive note.

In Phase I, try to get the person to relax. Introduce yourself, extend your hand, make some small talk to put the candidate at ease.

In Phase II, reiterate the job title you're recruiting for and the group. You can add something warm like, "We're delighted to be here, and I am interested to find out more about you and your background."

In Phase III, ask your behavioral interview questions and take notes throughout for jogging your memory later. After the fifth interview, the candidates could begin to blur together. Be sure that after you've asked the candidate a question, if there is a silence, you do not try to fill the awkward void by talking. Give the candidate time to think.

It is useful to rank and prioritize the candidates continuously throughout. I attach my notes to the corresponding résumé and rank their order with the top candidate on top of my stack, continuing to rearrange the pile as I interview the other candidates.

In Phase IV, ask the candidate what questions he or she has for you. This is not a freebie, because you can tell a lot about a person by the questions asked. A well-researched, interested candidate, no matter how pursued by lots of companies, will have thoughtful and informed questions. This is an opportunity for the candidate to bring out how knowledgeable he or she is about what's going on in your market and industry, the differences among the players in your space, and any recent big events involving your company.

In Phase V, you'll need to quickly evaluate whether this is someone you want to pursue. If yes, do some soft selling: "I'm glad we had the chance to meet. We've been fortunate to speak with so many outstanding candidates, but you are especially impressive. I hope we can talk further."

Let each candidate know the next steps and *when* you'll be in touch next: that evening, within the next few days, or two weeks from then. Communicate *what* would be the next step, for example, that you'll be hosting second rounds in your New York and London offices during the week of ___.

Evaluate Candidates and Follow Up

After you've conducted the interviews, you'll need to evaluate which candidates to invite back for second rounds hosted on site. If you have multiple interview schedules and, therefore, multiple interviewers on campus on the same day, try to get everyone together to discuss the candidates at the end of each day (yes, a very long day) or soon after. Many companies just stay at the school, convene in one interview room, order in pizza or Chinese food, and talk about candidates while the information is freshest on their minds. Do whatever works for you to evaluate and decide on the candidates to invite back. Here's something that has worked for the managers I've advised and for my own interviewing:

• Do a quick go-round of the interviewing team and ask how many candidates each would like to invite back for second rounds. You want to know the for-sure yeses. If the total is around your goal for the school and is OK within your company's overall efforts, then you can trust each interviewer's judgment, asking them all to rank order the candidates' résumés. You can then call it a day. You have the list for second rounds.

- If you have too many candidates for follow-up, you'll then need to review them to decide to eliminate or hold for now. Most companies would love to be in this situation, and if you have some flexibility, inviting back a few more candidates than anticipated is a good thing. Across all schools, some will most definitely drop out between first and second rounds. Some will say no to your invitations for second rounds because of other companies' interviews and offers, or a change of heart.
- If you have too few candidates, you'll need to decide whether to just go with those, not trying to force fit, or whether to discuss a few of the candidates with question marks. It's also possible to conduct more interviews at a later date or to add some other schools to your recruiting.

If more than one interviewer talked to a candidate, they'll need time to come up with their yeses, maybes, and nos in concert before the discussion begins.

Observe the Golden Rule

Although investment banks and consulting firms amazingly call candidates the same night of the on-campus interviews, for most companies, it is OK to call within a few days to two weeks after the on-campus interviews. If you're going to be longer than that, at least let the candidates know that it's a difficult decision, that you need to get all the interviewer feedback, letting them know when you'll be back in touch.

The nicest gesture is to have the team captain or team members/interviewers call the candidates. HR can also make the calls. When you reach the candidates, you want to let them know either (1) that you're inviting them for second rounds and who will be in touch later about details (dates, schedule, travel arrangements, any preparation they will need to do, for example, prepare a presentation) or (2) that you have decided not to pursue them at this time. Thank them.

The golden rule is important here: You want to treat people as you'd wish to be treated, especially if you are turning down someone. How you say no to someone is just as important (at least on the student grapevine) as how you say yes. The reality too is that those very same candidates you are rejecting today may be your customers some day in the future, or even your boss.

Around this time, if you have not already made plans, you'll need to start preparing for your second rounds: the agenda, venues, people to involve, interviews to schedule, offers to develop in anticipation. The HR head of recruiting, with input from the school teams, usually drives this process. We cover Phase Four of the recruitment process, second rounds and offers, in detail in Chapter 7.

Interviewing Lessons Learned

PERHAPS MOST ILLUMINATING ON THE whole art of interviewing are the lessons learned from managers who have years of experience interviewing MBA, managerial, and executive talent. These executives have had stunning successes and are generous in sharing their knowledge and insights. In this chapter fifteen managers share their favorite interview questions, approaches, and philosophies.

Heather Killen, SVP of worldwide operations at Yahoo!. Killen has had a fascinating background herself: two undergraduate liberal arts degrees (studying modern languages, political science, economics and French communication theory); an MBA from Columbia Business School; and an eclectic portfolio of roles in corporate finance, journalism, media, and telecom. Killen believes that there is a renaissance of true generalists as managers, and that because you "can't be the master of all aspects of the business," to build a great organization you need to hire "people who are smarter than you in particular areas."

She treats each interview as a conversation. When interviewing candidates for senior level openings at Yahoo!, Killen tries to find out "who somebody really is. How their head works. Initiative, intellectual curiosity, personal authenticity, and a reasonably high tolerance for ambiguity are important characteristics." By the time candidates are extended offers, they will have interviewed with a lot of people within the company: in-house recruiters who do the preliminary screens; midlevel managers; and most of the people in the group with whom they'd be working. The last set of interviews will be with senior-level managers across different functional areas. "It's a collegial way of hiring. Some people think we overinterview, but this has been effective for us. It lets the candidates know as much as possible about us before making a decision, and we get the benefit of different perspectives on the candidates—one interviewer may pick up on something another has not."

Wes Smith, COO of Del Monte Foods. Smith doesn't ask the same questions from interview to interview. In his previous company, he led a highly successful MBA recruiting program as vice president of North American manufacturing. He was also a mentor for the MBAs' development once they joined the company. Wes looks for "where someone wants to go" in their careers, but also where they have been, not just in terms of recent jobs and education but what they have learned about life. To him, "It's incredible how many smart people with excellent credentials are really clueless about what it might take to get a few hundred or thousand people to work together. Personality and perception that a person could work well with others, no matter what their economic lot in life, counts for a lot. Any sign of elitism is the kiss of death."

John Helding, former senior director of worldwide recruitment for Booz, Allen, & Hamilton. Helding says,

> *My favorite and most frequently asked question of MBAs was 'What's the best practical joke you've pulled off and why?' In that question I am looking for a sense of creativity, a willingness to have fun, and, at a deeper level, an ease with others that's made evident by a willingness to joke around and take some risks. Moreover it breaks down some of the seriousness and tension in the interviewing room. And as a bonus I've gotten more than a few good ideas for my own practical joke endeavors!*
>
> *In a more general category, I like to get a sense for how MBAs deal with graphical representations of relationships. Simply put, can they understand, interpret, and, more important, convey the meaning and the "so what"*

of a chart? So much of what a manager or a consultant needs to do is to understand numerical relationships and then convey the key message to others. I'll place a relatively simple chart in front of first-years and ask them to explain it to me as though I was a client new to the concepts. Just that consistently does well in identifying individuals who are comfortable with analytical analysis and who can explain such relationships to others.

Erik Lassila, managing director of Clearstone Venture Partners. Lassila hires executives, including CEOs, for his portfolio companies, and was formerly with Mayfield Venture Capital after graduating from the Stanford Business School. His general philosophy of interviewing is great advice across industries:

I want to find out if this is the person who really made things happen in their prior positions. Sorting the doers from the posers might be the hardest task of interviewing. Also, I always ask why they want the position—not because there is a right answer, but because (1) I want to hire a person who will probably stay for a while; (2) if they are just kicking the tires, I know not to focus too much time and energy on the candidate; and (3) I want to know they are capable of making purposeful decisions. I am always open and honest about the pros and cons, risks, and rewards of a position. It's an incredible waste of time if someone leaves a job because it's not what they bargained for, and also this is fundamental to building a working relationship based on mutual trust and respect.

Ken Kam, president and CEO of Marketocracy. Kam has successfully started up three companies in Silicon Valley and was formerly founder and partner of the Firsthand Funds and co-manager of the $4.6 billion Technology Value Fund, Kam likes to ask people to tell about their history. How they got to where they are. What they want to do now. What they aspire to. In the course of the conversation, Kam listens for the major decisions they've made and he asks them to help him understand how they made those decisions. In general, he likes people who realized they were making a big decision and handled it with an appropriate level of serious effort. "People who won't put in the effort to make the right decisions for themselves will probably not be willing to do so for solving a company's problems either." He chooses people who actively seek out information on which to base their decisions over those who make decisions to please others, since in his view business decisions should be based on information.

David Stuart, VP of operations for Computer Motion. Stuart has managed people for 21 years and by all counts has an amazing ability to recruit, then motivate, all kinds of talent—from freshly minted undergraduates to MBAs and seasoned executives. He says,

> *My interviews do not seem like they are long, but they last at least two hours. I like to begin by getting the person to relax and trust me. Not an easy task. I make myself appear approachable and vulnerable. I do this by genuinely being approachable and vulnerable, and not afraid to share my fears and weaknesses. After a time, as I sense some openness beginning to emerge, I begin to invite sharing of experiences and philosophies and accounts or stories that represent examples of some difficult challenges overcome. After candidates feel good about sharing their strengths for a time, I wait for a moment when they might be comfortable with balancing the discussion by sharing what some of their weaknesses may be. I disarm their defenses by suggesting that I do not want to know what they think about themselves; rather, I want to know what other people might think of them, and I suggest that rarely would anyone agree necessarily with what others think. So I ask these three questions:*

1. What would your current boss say were your three greatest strengths?
2. What would your boss say are your three greatest opportunities for improvement?
3. How do people in your department view you? (Very open ended, and I expect a long answer.) In terms of the answers, I do not worry about the content of the answer, I look to understand how quick they are at answering questions, how sincere they seem, how articulate they are, and how comfortable they are with sharing their vulnerabilities.

Sara Boonin, partner at Seneca Capital and former global head of recruiting and training for the Equities Division of Goldman Sachs. Boonin helped to keep the firm a top employer by leading recruiting efforts on MBA campuses, leveraging her wit and willingness to share her experience and advice with MBAs considering investment banking or management. Boonin's favorite interviewing technique focuses on résumés.

I have found that candidates in general are pretty straightforward about their academic and professional credentials: If their résumé says they went to a certain school, received certain honors, and worked at a certain firm in a specific capacity, those things generally check out. Students from high-quality business schools particularly know that all of these details can and will be checked out, and thus are unlikely to embellish too much. However, the same is not true for the hobbies or personal interests category of the résumé. There, people tell all kinds of whoppers. For a long time, I ignored this section on the résumé, as I didn't really care whether or not someone skied or read poetry or whatever. Once I began to ask questions about this data, I got all kinds of interesting insights into the people I was interviewing.

To wit, many people put down reading as one of their hobbies. Would it surprise you to learn that when I asked these folks what they are reading or to name the last good book they read, many of them had no answer, or a really lame answer. I actually had one guy say The Catcher in the Rye *(mandatory ninth grade reading). Another guy couldn't come up with a book title at all. I told him that I thought he had misrepresented himself and that led to a very interesting conversation. I have also had people put down wine tasting and then explain that their favorite type is white. The list on this is endless. These cases made me question their judgment as well as their veracity. This is a silly little technique of mine, but time and time again, it has caught candidates unaware, and the way they handle the discussion often tells me much more about them than I would have learned from the standard questions about work.*

Louis Amory, partner, Bain & Co. An excellent recruiter and manager, Amory had this to say about his favorite question:

I enjoy what I call the "little sister" test for candidates with brilliant backgrounds—could be MBAs or Ph.D.'s, for example. I select one of the most specialized items on their résumés, e.g., their Ph.D. thesis title, and ask them to explain what it is as if I were their 6-year-old sister. It is a great way to test their ability to explain synthetically and simply very complex things. This skill is key in our business." In terms of the interview process, Amory says he tries "to have a clear assessment of the candidate by the end of the interview. Ten minutes before the end, I pause and ask myself "Am I clear?" and I then try to focus on identified issues. I am often very direct, saying something like "I still need to be convinced on dimension X." Good candidates turn around this tricky situation." Amory goes on to say, "The most difficult part of the interview for me is identifying the deep motivational drivers of the candidate. Bain does not have standard selling approaches. The best advice is in-depth and no bullshit and nothing to hide discussions. There is nothing worse than a candidate who discovers he or she made the wrong choice after joining. Also, a one-on-one dinner later on will reveal if the chemistry is there to go with the intellectual and personal qualities the individual has already proven to possess.

Terry Krivan, director of individual giving at the Tech Museum of Innovation. Krivan realizes there are unique challenges of attracting high-caliber candidates to her organization, even with its compelling value proposition and cachet, especially in an economy like this where top talent continues to be in high demand. Krivan has been effective in ferreting out candidates who not only have the experience and abilities but also are a strong fit with her organization. Krivan's list of probing questions includes:

What results are you particularly proud of producing?
Describe a difficult situation that you feel you handled well.
Describe a difficult situation that with 20/20 hindsight, you would have handled differently.
If hired, what do you think will be your greatest challenge in assuming this position?
Describe ways you have shown your support for your work team.
To what extent have you changed systems or procedures you work under?
Your current position?
Other than money, what rewards make you happiest at work?
What can management always count on you to do?

Diane Saign, CEO of Catholic Charities of Santa Clara County. Following her passion to become an executive in nonprofits for the last ten years, after a successful run in the for-profit world, Saign is known as some-one who can build cohesive, diverse teams. Saign says her interview philoso-phy is to "look and listen closely for values alignment." She continues, "try to dismantle any fantasies about working in this nonprofit sector and with the poor. Ask questions that are behavioral and don't allow for a lot of speculations about what someone might do in a situation, rather than what they have done. Overall, be creative, appeal to the heart and move quickly through the recruitment process."

K. G. Ouye, board chair of the Schools and Libraries Division, Universal Service Administrative Co., and city librarian, City of San Mateo. Ouye is the poster child for the Stanford Alumni Consulting Team, a volunteer group of alumni who work with nonprofits and government on a breadth of pressing issues and challenges. Ouye has managed to keep the alumni engaged even after the end of the formal project, in part because she is a visionary who can inspire belief in and enthusiasm for achieving even the toughest goals. For sourcing candidates, she leverages word of mouth, community visibility, and relationships, growing her own and building a pipeline. In the community and her day-to-day interactions, she is always marketing her organization even when not specifically recruiting for an opening. For her specific advice on interviewing, she notes that although she has participated in hundreds of interviews, mostly on the hiring side:

> *I believe there is value in being interviewed by others. Preferably, once a year, the résumé should be dusted off and one or two interviews should be attempted as a candidate. This is one of the best ways to test your own organization's interview techniques. I also invite candidates to have an informal interview, visit the work site and just chat before the formal process begins. I want to determine technical competence but most of all fit with the organization, with the team. We use an interview panel with a broad mixture of roles. At the San Mateo Library, the working teams interview candidates first. Then, as department head, I always interview a candidate recommended for hire. This is to affirm the team's selection, but primarily to lay out in my own words the goals and challenges of the library and my work style, and to give the candidate a chance to ask me anything.*
>
> *I prefer interview questions that are realistic and show me how a person thinks. I believe in probing follow-up questions. In a first screening*

interview, questions may arise that should be followed up specifically with the candidate in the "fit" interviews. Unless it is illegal, ask whatever you need to know. Don't leave the interview wondering about the candidate. Ask what a candidate would do about shoring up a weak area, such as writing or little experience in direct customer service.

Dr. Paul Ning, director of platform engineering at Netergy Networks. Ning interviews PhDs as well as others, in his senior role for his company. Having been hotly pursued himself as one of the youngest in his PhD program at Stanford, he has an HR savvy about people issues and knows what it takes to evaluate candidates for their interest as well as their technical and overall fit with Netergy.

I like to start interviews by introducing the company to the candidate, including our basic business model, market opportunities, and organization, narrowing in on the specific position and responsibilities. This puts them at ease, helps to sell the company, and allows me to gauge their interest and compatibility. Once the introduction is complete, I want to know if they can handle the technical aspects of the position. This means launching into a series of specific engineering problems that they are asked to work out on the whiteboard, easier ones first, and then harder ones if they get that far. These questions are predesigned and resemble what graduate students may see in qualifying exams. I only quiz them on their résumé if they list items of particular interest. Getting them to describe a previous project usually wastes too much time and doesn't allow direct comparison amongst candidates. Another time-saver is the short circuit: When we bring someone in we set aside slots with multiple people, but if any interviewer gives a thumbs down, we may end the visit early.

Paul DiNardo, Goldman Sachs managing director, High Technology Group, Investment Banking Division. He articulates:

. . . the underlying philosophy is that we select our people one by one. In a service business, we know that without the best people, we cannot be the best firm. Once you establish that a candidate has the necessary skills, it becomes a matter of assessing interest and fit. Our focus is on having candidates see a wide variety of interviewers. This approach provides both the

candidate and us with a diverse set of perspectives upon which to base a decision. Most importantly, it enables a candidate to get a great deal of insight into the culture and determine whether there is an appropriate fit.

As for favorite questions, there are as many as there are interviewers. I pay particular attention to a candidate's description of her or his developmental needs. Many candidates attempt to turn these into strengths or virtues (e.g., "I work too hard."), which can show a lack of thoughtfulness or self-awareness. Those candidates whose answers demonstrate that they are aware of their challenges and are open to addressing them help rather than hurt their candidacy.

Jim Beirne, director of recruiting, MBA programs and marketing, General Mills, and former Wharton director of career services. Beirne says:

While we use behavioral-based interviewing most of the time, I find that many applicants come in with too many prepared answers, sounding like politicians: No matter what question you ask them, they are going to give you a prepared answer. To get more to the core of the individual, I'll ask, "What motivates you to be as successful as you are?" Followed up by, "Can you walk me through how you set your goals?" These questions get to more of the essence of the individual.

The Killer Interview by a CFO. Andy Miller, SVP and CFO of MarketFirst and formerly VP of finance at Cadence Systems and Silicon Graphics, has had a gift for recruiting talent, including MBAs, for 12 years. He uses a behavioral-based interviewing style and a team approach for interviewing for his direct reports, including summer MBA interns. Here is a synopsis of his interview process step by step:

First, I consider the nature of the position and the resulting key behavioral attributes that I think are the success criteria. Then, I assemble an interview team, and each person on the team is assigned two to three behavioral areas to probe. With my direct reports, I generally will meet more than once, giving me the opportunity to directly probe more of the most important personal attributes. I typically probe the following areas:

- Strengths. *I probe pretty deeply here, asking for detailed examples of each one. I also probe in depth as to why others might consider this a strength—what examples would a peer or a boss give me to support a candidate's particular strength and why. I may probe the frequency with which they rely on this strength, the areas of weakness that this strength may compensate for, how important they feel this strength has been to accomplishing some of their most significant achievements, and the types of situations where they have found themselves relying on this strength recently. I get much more information from the follow-up questions than from the original question.*

- Weaknesses. *I usually probe this somewhat indirectly. One of the most effective ways I get at this is to ask the person how he has changed the most in the past 2 years—grown the most or focused his development the most. By focusing on examples of the situation in the past and examples of how he is now handling the situation, I get a pretty good understanding of a person's development needs in the recent past. Another way to probe weaknesses or development areas is to first probe for a few minutes about the most difficult person the candidate has worked with over the past few years, someone the person experienced some conflict with. After the interviewee gives you some background here, psychologically, they have somewhat invalidated what this person might have to say about him. Then, if you ask what this person would say are both the strengths and weaknesses of the interviewee, you are more likely to get a balanced response.*

- Accomplishments. *In probing this, I spend a good deal of time to understand why the person feels the accomplishment was significant; what was difficult about it; what obstacles had to be overcome; why, how, and by whom the objective was set in the first place; whom did he turn to for help and counsel, and what was the situation where he sought help; what were alternative solutions to the situation and why did he choose the path he took; etc. Essentially, here I try to understand the significance of the accomplishment, is the person a driver, is the person creative, self-motivated, committed, etc.*

- Motivation. *I generally will ask an interviewee what he thinks motivates him. I then probe the whys here in depth. I ask a few times what about this is motivating until I get a pretty deep answer. (Sometimes I will get the person thinking at a deeper level by asking him to explain*

*what motivates him the most: affiliation, achievement, or recognition.)
Here I try to understand the extent of the person's self-knowledge, and
whether he can give me examples that better explain what motivates
him. Later in the interview, I will often ask him to tell me about both
(1) a recent great day at work, so I can look for the alignment between
the situation he describes and what he said motivates him, and (2) a
recent frustrating day at work.*

- Stressful Situation. *I generally ask for the person to explain in detail
a very stressful situation in the past. I probe this in depth with lots of
why questions where I focus on what about the situation was causing
the stress.*

- Conflict. *I will usually ask the interviewee to describe a recent situation where the person felt there was significant conflict, and I will
probe this in depth. I tend not to do technical interviews. I can usually
tell the extent of the technical competencies indirectly as I probe other
areas. For example, in hiring in HR, if I am looking for someone with
depth in compensation, I may probe in depth an experience on his
résumé where he did a compensation project or where the person was
in a compensation department. Here, with an in-depth probe of the
work done, accomplishments, most difficult project, etc., I can generally
tell if the person has substance. In hiring a tax director, I probe the
technical competence through references. With sales managers and executives, I may probe how they are now managing their pipeline, how
they are assigning territories or quotas, etc. Essentially, I touch on a
technical area for the job that I know a little about, and I test whether
they can discuss it in depth, provide alternatives, etc.*

Chapter 7

Phase Four: Second Rounds and Offers

THE PURPOSE OF SECOND ROUNDS is three-pronged: (1) to give the candidates an up-close view of who you are and what it would be like to work for you; (2) to provide an opportunity for you to assess their backgrounds and their fit with the company and your jobs; and (3) to continue to build your reputation with candidates and your internal capability to recruit top talent into the company.

DRILL-DOWN #8, PLAN AND EXECUTE ON-SITE SECOND ROUNDS

Time Line: November–May, Within 2 to 6 Weeks After Your On-Campus Interviews

Second rounds require world-class execution and attention to details, along with a high-touch feel.

Design the Agenda

Depending on the number of candidates you're inviting back from all your MBA recruiting efforts, you can bring all the candidates back in one fell swoop, in groups (of ten to fifteen or smaller), or individually for one-of-a-kind jobs. The one fell swoop is best if you can pull it off, for several reasons:

- You can mobilize all your resources, including your own people, and give the second rounds your best shot with focused energy.
- It's easier to compare and calibrate candidates if you're seeing them at the same time, instead of spread out over months.
- It's a more efficient use of valuable time. You can ask key executives and those you'll involve to hold time on their calendars. In this way, you'll have available and participating the people you need to make the decisions.
- MBAs like to meet their colleagues from other schools as this gives them a good glimpse of those with whom they may be working, their new cohort class.
- Bigger can be better because you can generate more fun and fanfare with social events and meals when all the candidates come in at one time.

You can always do mini second rounds for the few candidates who cannot make the organized second rounds, but the longer things drag on, the more overextended your people will become. Note here as well that some firms conduct third (final) rounds, which are versions of second rounds except with a further winnowed down candidate finalist group.

CHECKLIST FOR SECOND ROUNDS
- Create your agenda of work and play—a time line with blocks of time for programs, interviews, activities, meals, and social events.
- Determine who will do what. In addition to the school team, who else will be involved for interview duties, to host a breakfast, or serve as an informal buddy? Ask those who'll be involved in second rounds to reserve time on their calendars. Time should be set aside for the interviews and participation in events, as well as for the discussions about the candidates *after* the second rounds are completed. It is best to hold the time now, but you'll still have a few who will have to give feedback by e-mail or phone.
- Refine your interview process. How many interviews for each candidate? One-on-one or a panel? Ask individual interviewers to each focus on evaluating a specific set of skills, abilities, and experiences, so you have all of them covered. This approach is preferable to every interviewer asking similar questions and covering the same ground.

- Keep in touch with the candidates. Send them a packet with an agenda, a map of the city, and any personalized touches to keep them interested and to let them know you are looking forward to their upcoming visit. You might include a baseball cap if you'll be taking them to a game, a ticket stub if you'll be going to a play, or a tropical drink umbrella if you'll be hosting a luau.
  -

An A+ Agenda. In general, callbacks take place during one night and the next full day. Some start on a Thursday evening and end the next Sunday midmorning. In setting the agenda, you'll need to consider how many candidates you're bringing in, how many interviews they'll go through, what you need to accomplish with them, how many events you want to host, and your budget.

An agenda usually incorporates these components:

- A definitive kick-off with welcome and remarks by the CEO or a senior executive.
- Meals and breaks.
- At least one main social event. This could be a reception and dinner, but could also be a theater outing, a sports event, or a theme party. You may host two events that the candidates may choose between.
- Interviews. These are the core activity.
- A tour of the campus, the trading floor, the plant, your fun room and award-winning cafeteria, and whatever you are proud of.
- Relaxed, unstructured time, for example, time for candidates to meet with recent hires and to get the straight scoop (could be during or after a meal).
- Time with HR to ask their questions and to hear about company benefits, such as for accompanying partners or spouses, housing in the area, career development, and timing for offers.
- A memorable last impression. Orchestrate an upbeat end to the second rounds with clear communication on when you will get back to them, the next steps, and your thanks for their interest.

At Dole Packaged Foods we always sent our top candidates a handwritten note and a basket (from Harry and David), which was waiting for them when they returned home from the second rounds. This was a big hit with candidates and one part of a total package that yielded 100 percent on offers.

Orchestrate Like a Maestro

For your second rounds, you still want to involve a mix of levels, functions, and personalities, but the emphasis is on interviewing with the people with whom the MBAs would most closely be working. As referenced in the checklist, it is also a good idea to divide and cover more ground. In other words, know the sum total of skills, abilities, and knowledge that you are looking for and assessing. Parcel out which interviewer(s) will probe which area(s), so that everyone does not ask the same questions, cover the same ground, try to evaluate the same one or two areas, which risks leaving gaps in the total evaluative picture of the candidate at the end of the day. I like to give an interviewer two areas to probe on and make sure that technical questions (are they able to do the job) and fit questions (will they fit with the team and culture and thrive here) are all covered.

Shepherds and Timekeepers

There's a flurry of activity and people throughout. While being careful not to stifle the energy, you will want to make sure you have shepherds appointed who can get your people and the candidates from place to place on time. For any events, speeches, interviews, and activities, you also need a designated timekeeper to keep people on track and moving. If someone is even 5 to 10 minutes late, the schedule can back up so that some candidates or interviewers won't be able to have their time. Shepherds and timekeepers need to be respected, organized, and firm.

Rate the Candidates and Decide on Offers

After all the callbacks, HR needs to coordinate getting feedback from all the interviewers, facilitating any discussions needed, ranking the candidates, and making final offers.

As a sample process, already have scheduled with interviewers a time for a powwow to discuss and evaluate the candidates. Ideally this will be the evening that the second rounds end or the next day. Bring everyone together and make sure to have a big flip chart or white board. Ask people to bring with them the candidate résumés, their interview notes, and any evaluation forms you had them fill out. Have all the names of the candidates listed on the board or page. Do a very quick go-around; ask the interviewers as you say the candidate's name to say yes, no, or maybe. At the end of this exercise, any unanimous nos don't have to be discussed further. If everyone also agreed on the yeses, you can put aside discussion on those too for now. The discussion can then focus on the maybes—their strengths, weaknesses, interviewers' general and specific impressions of them, and examples. This should not take any more than 15 minutes unless you have a huge number. As you discuss, it will become clear whether these maybes convert to either yeses or nos. If unclear, take a vote and the majority rules. The person with the pen is the tiebreaker.

From this point, you can discuss the yeses as needed and slot them into jobs/groups and/or rank them.

An Interview with General Mills, The Champion of Second Rounds

General Mills is successful in MBA recruiting overall and a model for their diversity efforts as well. In particular, they've been lauded for their thoughtful, high-touch, and quick-response second-round process by the MBAs going through it and the career center staffs who hear about it from their excited and impressed students when they return. What follows are excerpts from my interview questions and the insights from Jim Beirne, Director of Recruiting, MBA Programs and Marketing, General Mills, and former Director of the Career Management Center at the Wharton Business School.

Q: How would you describe your follow-up process after on-campus interviews? How do you handle your second rounds?

A: We have two types of second-round interviews: those which take place at our world headquarters in Minneapolis, and those which we do on a particular school campus within 10 days of our first rounds. We use the latter when it is essential for General Mills, or the students, to get an idea as to whether an offer will be forthcoming or not. Students love it because it gets them a rapid response, and they don't have to travel for a day and a half to get a decision. It is done on their campus.

If we invite candidates back to Minneapolis, we call them within 48 hours of their first-round interview and offer them a variety of dates which might meet their needs. Any given week usually has 2–3 days that they can choose from, so they can manage their academic schedule around their second (final) rounds.

In all cases we'll call students to let them know where they stand, whether they get an offer or not.

Q: What is the agenda like for second rounds at your headquarters?

A: In Minneapolis, we ask the candidates to arrive by dinner time to have a meal with a recent hire (who usually is from their school, and was in the same position 1–2 years before). The sponsor covers the process for the next day, updates them on the key company issues so they can really focus on the interviews, and has a schedule of the day and fills them in on the backgrounds of the interviewers.

Candidates stay in downtown Minneapolis, to get a sense of the cosmopolitan nature of the city (surprisingly, the majority of candidates who come for final rounds have never been in the twin cities), and take a short cab ride to our headquarters campus after breakfast downtown.

We usually have a maximum of three candidates per day, so as to afford the individualized attention we know is important.

Our assistant director of recruiting individually greets candidates and then walks them through their day. Once they are settled in, we start our creativity and business case assessments, followed by four interviews.

For lunch, they are individually hosted by another recent hire for a nonevaluative meal and a brief tour of the facilities.

Q: What mix of people from the company do you use to interview?

A: Our interview team usually consists of three middle and senior managers (most have a division president) and an HR director.

To participate in the callback process overall? The recent hires as stated above, middle and senior managers, HR, and the recruiting team captain.

Q: Would you give a sense of the kind of interviews you conduct?

A: Four interviews, primarily behaviorally based, and a few short cases during the interview. In addition, we have a formal business case, and a creativity assessment which, once the candidate has taken them, agree that we are assessing exactly the types of skills and abilities we will be calling on them to utilize during their positions.

Q: Does each interviewer probe on a different dimension?

A: Yes, with a little overlap.

Q: How do you let candidates know they have offers?

A: We call them immediately after a decision or even make an offer before they leave our offices. What makes recruiting especially fun is when our line managers are completely engaged and dedicated to the recruiting wars. CEO Steve Sanger, CFO Jim Lawrence, our vice chairmen, and executive officers are open to making calls or setting up meetings on short notice if it can make a difference with a candidate.

Q: Tell about your sell weekend or any follow up/wooing of the MBAs once you make offers.

A: We have ongoing programs at each school which manage systematic communications with all candidates with offers. We have three critical sell weekends, in addition to ongoing sell weekends throughout the year.

1. *An international weekend for all international students and candidates with global aspirations.* This is hosted by the president of our international division and most of our senior executives.

2. *Martin Luther King, Jr. weekend celebration, in January.* Starting with a black-tie gala attended by our chairman and senior management, and hosted by our Black champions network, this sell weekend for African-American candidates and their families continues through Monday morning when General Mills hosts a breakfast for 2,000 Twin Cities businesspeople.

3. *A weekend for our Hispanic candidates,* in January. This is held to better understand the growth of the Twin Cities Hispanic network, our senior management commitment, and availability of Latin culture (including salsa dancing) in the metropolitan area.

Q: What do you do that really sets you apart from others, that makes you world class?

A: Our line managers get very involved, they care, and it shows. People join us because they like what work we do, and they like to play—we try to show them both during their time here. Minneapolis is not first on anyone's list in terms of places to live, but once they feel the excitement of the job, and see the quality of life they can live here, it becomes an easy sell. The hard part is getting "piece of mind" in the beginning of the process, with so much other noise on campus.

Takeaways

- Act quickly to follow up on-campus interviews.
- Use a high-touch, personalized approach, engaging your line managers and executives.
- Overcommunicate plans; execute exceptionally; treat candidates well—even those you turn down.

DRILL-DOWN #9: MAKE OFFERS THAT GET ACCEPTED

Time Line: Within 2 Weeks of Your Second/ Final Rounds

Do Your Homework

Chapter 8 is an in-depth discussion of compensation fundamentals, considerations in developing offers, and talking points. Suffice it to say that doing your homework before making an offer is important. Depending on how many openings you have and what you predict will be your offer acceptance rate, you can decide on how many offers to make. Work with your compensation group to develop the offers, then start contacting the candidates. Most likely you'll call them unless you are in the area and can meet personally.

Note that as soon as you begin calling the candidates, other MBAs at those various schools will hear about it. News travels fast and cohorts share their job triumphs and woes, offer information, discuss their inclinations to accept or decline, and give their impressions, both positive and negative, about the companies that are pursuing them. The people in your organization making the offers need to be ready to move quickly. This goes for both giving offers and saying no.

Sequentially, in Waves, or Open

How you choose to make offers, sequentially, in waves, or open, can be a tricky issue. Each has pros and cons. It depends on the number and kinds of jobs you are making offers on, how good a handle you have on your offer acceptance rate, and the flexibility you have for overextending offers, thus potentially overhiring.

Sequential offers are best when you have a limited number of openings. For example, if you have seven openings total, say two openings in each of three groups and one opening in a separate group, you may call your first two choices for each of the two openings in each of the three groups and call only your first choice for the single opening. In other words, you call only the number of candidates you have openings for, giving them a time limit to respond, and waiting to hear whether they accept or decline. If they decline, you move sequentially down your rank-ordered list of candidate choices. This model takes much patience and time, because you're waiting to hear definitively before moving on to make other offers. You could also be losing out on qualified second- and third-choice candidates who must make decisions on offers they receive from other companies. Someone in your organization, the hiring manager alone or with HR, needs to stay on top of the offer process. You also need to be prepared to stick to your time limit and void an offer if a candidate keeps asking unreasonably for more time. Note that some schools have deadlines that require a company to hold an offer open up to a specified date.

Another model is to make offers in waves. This works best when you have only a few types of jobs but many openings for each type. Decide on your top tier of candidates as a single group and call them first. Based on prior experience with offer acceptances, you can forecast how many offers you need to make in order to end up with a certain number of yeses. Again, set a time limit to give you an answer. You can let other candidates, your second wave, know that you remain very interested in them but are not in a position to make an offer yet.

If you want to be bluntly honest, you can also tell these second-wave candidates that you are making offers in waves and ask them to sit tight. This could work to your advantage. The candidates who don't get offers right away from you will most likely find out anyway from their colleagues at school that you have made a first wave of offers. The downside is that these next-tier candidates may feel like runners up unless you make them feel like it's a really tough decision. They may accept offers from other companies, where they feel more wanted. On the upside, the candidates may view your jobs as more competitive and coveted and feel fortunate if you ultimately make them offers. The economy will most definitely impact the thinking and behavior of candidates. In a slowing economy, MBAs are more anxious and more risk averse about job offers. In a booming economy, they can exhibit overconfidence and hold out longer.

Success versus losing out on these second- and even third-wave candidates depends a lot on how you handle communicating with these MBAs during this tricky time. Warmth, being straight up, and caring about the candidates—*not* avoiding them until you have closure—will make a difference for you.

Open offering involves making offers to every one of your yeses. Some companies figure that given all the time and energy expended so far on MBA recruiting, *and* the openings they now have (TBHs) and expect in the future—by the time the students graduate in May or June and can start work, everything will work out. For this option, you would make clear that there were so many outstanding candidates that you've decided to make offers to all of them using your best estimate of acceptance rate, but that you'll be slotting people and confirming them in specific jobs and groups as they say yes. In other words, first come, first served. If a specific job role is not available by the time a candidate accepts, you can match him or her with other openings before graduation.

During most years, it is rare to have more candidates accept your offers than you have openings, but it can happen. If you find yourself in that enviable position and have some flexibility in staffing, you can actively work to find other openings within your company for the candidates. This would be an enormous testament to your commitment to people and show your agility as an organization.

Woo, Woo, and Woo

Once you've made your offers, turn up the volume—the real wooing begins. Many companies pull out all the stops and even invite those with offers back on site yet again. Investment banks are known for their effective sell weekends, but others, including high-tech companies, organize their own versions. Sell weekends are designed to make those students to whom you've made offers feel really special and to give them the opportunity to know you up-close. Examples of how companies have wooed their prized offerees include courtside tickets to sold-out sports events, sailing outings on America's Cup yachts, dinners at five-star restaurants, and expense-paid weekends at top-tier hotels in the cities where they'll work. These sell weekends involve concentrated time and interaction with senior managers and others within the company. Those who received offers have time to get any outstanding questions and concerns addressed and the opportunity to take a deeper, critical look at the firm to determine what it would really be like to work there.

Sell weekends are not deal breakers. Not all companies host them. Factors to weigh when considering a sell weekend include your resources, norms for recruiting, and the competitive picture and your standing in it. Just as effective as an elaborate sell weekend is having the hiring manager take the recruit to breakfast, lunch, or dinner and assigning someone as the point person to check in periodically with the recruit to answer questions or supply additional information. You can send the recruit a small gift or send an invitation to an upcoming companywide event, such as an all-hands meeting or a company picnic.

These high-touch efforts can work incredibly well. Some companies also let gatekeepers in the school (dean, faculty, other candidates who have said yes, career center director and staff) know which of their students have outstanding offers, so that they can put in a good word.

Make It Stick—No Buyer's Remorse

Make a point, without going over the top, to keep in contact with all those you've made offers to. Touch base to see whether they have questions and where they are in their decision making. Keep letting them know that you are excited about their joining you, and you hope that they will. Buyer's remorse is common for an MBA who has accepted an offer and hears of a friend who has accepted a job in another company or industry: *Did I make the right decision? Should I have held out for something else? Is the grass greener elsewhere?* Some of these thoughts are normal, but stay on top of your new recruits to keep them enthusiastic about having accepted your offers. Engage them through the time they start working with you.

DRILL-DOWN #10. GET FEEDBACK, GIVE THANKS, MAKE IMPROVEMENTS, START AGAIN

Time Line: May–August After You Finish the Offer Process

Initiate Unabashed Feedback

Be fervent about soliciting feedback so you can improve for next time. After you've made your offers and are starting to hear back on acceptances and declines, it's time to reflect on the year. You have probably gotten some feedback along the way from students, schools, and those involved from your company, but you'll want to be more systematic in initiating feedback and in evaluating your recruiting efforts:

- What are your numbers (cost-per-hire, or CPH, offer rates by schools, yields)? Refer to Appendix A.
- What worked and what didn't—internally, with the schools, the students, your recruitment materials, interview scheduling, job descriptions, pre-recruitment activities, on-campus interviews, second rounds, and offers?
- Should you keep recruiting at the same schools or edit your target list?
- Should you keep recruiting on campus or move to other less resource-intensive venues? (See Chapter 13 on recruiting on the fly.) Remember that most companies take 2 to 3 years before they start to achieve results

on the campuses. You may need to stick with it for a few years to see progress. Evaluate whether it's worth it.

- What are the ways you can improve for next time?

Seek out Student Impressions

Those that said yes and are joining your company are also a valuable source of feedback since they experienced recruiting first hand and now have a vested interest in the company doing well. You may wish to organize a lunch with the school recruiting team and the new hires to celebrate their joining you and ask for feedback. These new hires now can also act as an informal advisory board, provide extra help, or become members of your recruiting team next time around at their schools. Ideally, you'll also want to initiate feedback from the ones that got away, those to whom you extended offers but who didn't accept. For this group, a telephone or an e-mail survey, or a focus group, can be telling. They have nothing to lose by being direct, but they are time constrained, so you'll need a hook to get them to give you feedback. Use this time to let them know you'd like to keep in touch, and tell them that the door remains open for the future. Ask them to get you their contact information when they've settled into their new companies.

You'll want feedback on the effectiveness of each component of your recruiting efforts over the year: Your recruitment materials, Web site, job descriptions, company briefing, on-campus interviews, second-round interviews, and interviewers. You want to hear their impressions about your image and reputation and how to improve them, and who are considered your most formidable competitors and the best in recruiting. What do the competitors do better than you that makes them so effective?

Debrief the Schools

You'll also want to get feedback from the career center director or assistant director of recruiting. Spending 10 to 20 minutes with these folks should give you a big picture view of your efficacy at the school, best practices of and insights on competitors, as well as student job choices for the year. Key questions to ask are: How was the recruiting year overall? Are there any interesting themes and changes from previous years? How did we do? What worked and didn't? What specifically could we do better next time?

Thank them if they were helpful to you. Voice your commitment to your relationship. Give them feedback too on how they did, positive and constructive suggestions. Let them know specifically how they can help make your experience more enjoyable and productive next year.

Spread the Wealth

You don't want to sing from the rooftops, but you will want to spread the news about your MBA recruiting. Especially if you've started the program from the ground up, you'll want to celebrate getting through the first cycle and over the biggest start-up hurdles. Convey results in a summary or send a brief report describing the results. Give hearty, vociferous thanks and recognition, especially if you achieve some wins, like going from no hires the year before to three top MBAs, or making it onto a top employer list at a challenging school. Write a story for your company newsletter or Web site, or send a short broadcast e-mail to managers in your company, if that's how you communicate successes in your company. Spread the wealth, the glory or praise, with *all* in the company who were involved and helped. Let people know how they can participate in next year's recruiting.

Thank those who were involved on the recruiting teams or in pre-recruitment—the Web designer for the MBA recruiting Web site, the travel agent who made all the callback arrangements—profusely. Writing them a personal letter with a copy to their boss and giving them a thoughtful gift are my favorite ways of saying thank you. Examples of gifts include a sweatshirt with a team logo, special world desk clock, a cool something for their office so others see it (a small desktop water fountain or office accessories are the rage right now), gift certificates, movie passes, or a gift basket. Some companies give extra days off and make sure the person's contributions are duly noted in the performance review. You can also host a celebratory lunch. Team captains can give a brief summary of how they did, people can share war stories, and you can start to seed interest and enthusiasm for the next year. Lunch could be simple or a more elaborate spread in the partners' dining room or at a nice local restaurant. You don't have to give a formal speech, but do let them know, for closure, the overall results and what's in the works for next time, asking for feedback while it's on their minds on how to improve.

Refine Your Plans for Next Time
Time Line: June–August

In general, evaluate all the feedback you've received from students, the career center staff, and your recruiting teams. Brainstorm on improvements you need to make, prioritize them, and figure out their timing. You're refining your MBA recruiting efforts with the objective of continuously learning and getting better. The good news is that with a full recruiting cycle under your belt, you'll know what to anticipate and can be more realistic in your plans. Think about any edits to the list of schools (adding, deleting, or moving away from on-campus interviews to another venue), interview team changes, and all your processes and any improvements. If you recruited only for full-time jobs, think about adding summer internships; or if only for internships, consider full-time openings. Get ready to start all over again. Review the sample time line and to-dos in Figure 2-2. If you had to skip any of them, you can pick them up this time around. Congratulations! Getting this far is a huge accomplishment.

Chapter 8

Structuring Compensation Offers

YOU ARE IN THE HOME STRETCH when you are ready to make offers to your top candidates. If you haven't already, you'll need to start working with your compensation experts, in house or outside your company, to develop your best offer packages.

FOUNDATIONAL KNOWLEDGE: WHAT IS TOTAL COMPENSATION?

Offers form a subset of your overarching compensation strategy and philosophy, so for foundational knowledge, we'll first take a look at what total compensation is, defining each component and seeing how all the pieces of the pie fit together. Next, macrocompensation and microcompensation considerations will be addressed in the context of doing your homework before making your offers. We'll then bring it down to the nuts and bolts of what you need to know of the elements of negotiation, talking points for your offers, comparative compensation for popular MBA career fields, and sources of information on the going market rates. We'll circle back and cover in more detail why intangibles and perks really matter and cover what you need to know about options. At the end of this chapter are recommendations for compensation experts and resources—some of the best in the field—to call on for further help.

As a hiring manager, I appreciate the strategic and practical aspects of compensation, and particularly enjoy making offers to top candidates and closing the deals. Over the years, however, even in my role as an HR generalist, I have learned that the compensation arena is a highly complex, specialized, and technical field. We are fortunate to have experts who really know their stuff and can teach us or help us with putting together plans and practices.

For this chapter, I've called on compensation expert Linda E. Amuso, co-founder and principal of iQuantic, an 8-year-old national performance and rewards consulting firm, to provide some of her 15 years' experience.

Amuso notes that the components of compensation are base salary; short-term incentives, benefits and perquisites; and long-term incentives, according to these formulas:

Base salary + short-term incentives = total cash compensation

Total cash compensation + long-term incentives =
total direct compensation

Total direct compensation + benefits and perquisites =
total remuneration

A visual depiction of the components and their definitions is given in Figures 8-1, 8-2, and 8-3. Now that you have the fundamentals, what's the context for developing and making winning offers?

A MACRO VIEW: EXTERNAL CONSIDERATIONS

It is critical to establish a context for developing your compensation packages by looking outside your organization to your competitors—those companies both inside and outside your industry that are pursuing the same kinds of talent—and to the market overall.

What are the top companies recruiting at your schools? What are they offering? How are their offers structured: base salary, signing bonus, year-end bonus, options, and perquisites? What are the trends or new twists in placement and compensation at the school (co-investing, interest carry-forwards, tuition reimbursement)?

A lot of this information will not be in print; you'll need to ask for it or hunt for it. Most likely you'll come up with a band of compensation for all your MBA recruits, but you may make higher offers for certain schools or for certain candidates based on their experience and backgrounds. What-

Figure 8-1. Total Cash Compensation.

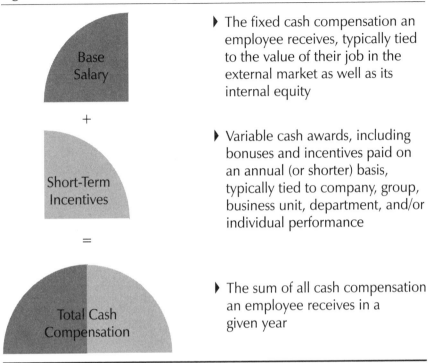

▸ The fixed cash compensation an employee receives, typically tied to the value of their job in the external market as well as its internal equity

▸ Variable cash awards, including bonuses and incentives paid on an annual (or shorter) basis, typically tied to company, group, business unit, department, and/or individual performance

▸ The sum of all cash compensation an employee receives in a given year

Source: iQuantic

ever offers you end up making, remember that the students will talk with each other and compare them. So if you offer three different candidates three different packages, you must have a logical explanation for doing so. I'd suggest you deal with this up front by communicating about how you developed the offer (e.g., based on the MBA market and your own internal compensation structure and philosophy) and why offers among candidates may differ (e.g., based on years of experience or that the different groups within your company pay differently). This is part of managing student expectations and being proactive.

A MICRO VIEW: INTERNAL CONSIDERATIONS

When developing offers for your MBA recruits or others, there are several important considerations to take into account that are unique to your organization and internal picture.

What are your pay ranges for the jobs? If you've hired MBAs off and

Figure 8-2. Total Direct Compensation.

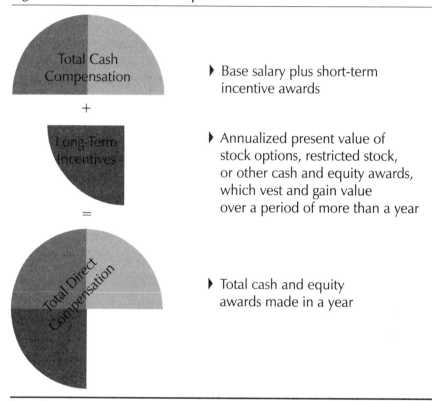

▶ Base salary plus short-term
incentive awards

▶ Annualized present value of
stock options, restricted stock,
or other cash and equity awards,
which vest and gain value
over a period of more than a year

▶ Total cash and equity
awards made in a year

Source: iQuantic

on over the years, where did you bring them in relative to others in your company, and do you wish to be more aggressive or conservative now? How can you rationalize an internal inequity if you bring in new hires at compensation levels way above others who have been in the company a long time with even more years of work experience? These are all questions you want to think through and feel comfortable with.

On a related note, you may have bigger issues to deal with, such as changing the competitors and industries against whom you benchmark, giving one-time adjustments for certain categories of jobs, deciding to live with the internal parity issues but use other compensation options like bonuses to close the gap over time. Right now you are trying to make offers that will be fair, competitive in the market, and exciting to the candidates you've just spent all the time recruiting. You'll want to juggle elements of the package

Figure 8-3. Total Remuneration.

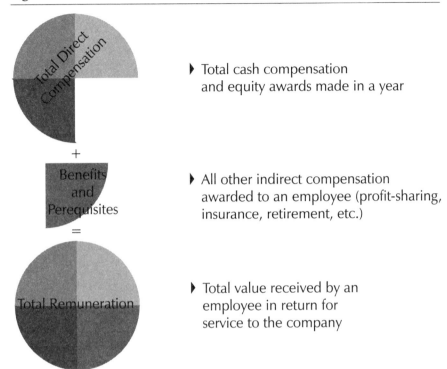

▶ Total cash compensation
and equity awards made in a year

▶ All other indirect compensation
awarded to an employee (profit-sharing,
insurance, retirement, etc.)

▶ Total value received by an
employee in return for
service to the company

Source: iQuantic

making sure that what you'll do fits within your existing compensation structure, philosophy, and policy. No small feat.

DOWN TO BUSINESS: ELEMENTS OF THE NEGOTIATION

I have three recommendations about negotiating in general:

1. Approach the negotiation as if you are already on the same side of the table with the candidate and on the same team. Try to create a win-win situation.
2. Ascertain the candidate's motivations, what he or she values most, and what components of the total package, tangible and intangible, are have-to-haves or giveaways. Get a sense of what would make the candidate say yes or walk away.

3. Know your own degrees of freedom—what you can or cannot negotiate or are willing to do or not to do. Know your walk-aways as well, since eight out of ten candidates will try to negotiate for more.

The sum total of the elements you are negotiating include:

- Base salary
- Sign-on bonus
- Stock option grant
- Title
- Start dates
- Relocation support

- Timing of first salary review
- Bonus target
- Relocation features
- Vesting schedules
- Benefits
- Vacation

TALKING POINTS FOR MAKING YOUR OFFERS

Ideally the hiring manager will make the offer, cover key elements of the package, and then ask HR or someone knowledgeable in compensation to follow up on the details, including benefits. The hiring manager would remain involved for any back-and-forth negotiation with the candidate and work with HR for recommendations and any exceptions.

In sum, you'll want to cover these sample points when making your offers, translating them into your voice and style:

- How excited and happy you are to be able to make an offer.
- The main components of the offer as listed above. For stock options, any pertinent information you can share (how many? current valuation of the company, and the vesting schedule). Any special circumstances of the job, such as three rotations of 8 to 12 months, each including one international assignment.
- For the compensation components that are more complex or detailed (relocation or medical benefits), let them know that someone in HR will be calling to follow up. If your company has a brochure, a Web site address, or a one-pager with this kind of information, you could give that to them for reading and they can ask questions later when the HR manager follows up.
- Time to consider the offer, and the deadline for responding. It helps here if the deadline is firm, and if you tell them why. An explanation

may be that many candidates are waiting in the wings, and if the candidate doesn't accept your offer, you need to go to other candidates before they have already accepted other jobs. Appeal here to the sense of fair play and responsibility to peers.

- Ask whether the candidate has questions or needs more information to make a decision, and indicate how you'll follow up.

Many times, those to whom you made offers will want to circle back to their hiring managers or others in the company with outstanding questions or concerns. Help them talk with the people they need to in order to get the best information they can to make a decision. In any follow-up interactions, convey your continued excitement about working with them. Keep in touch, checking in periodically without being overly aggressive, until you achieve closure.

HELP FOR DOING YOUR HOMEWORK: RESOURCES AND EXPERTS

For understanding the market and the going rates for MBA compensation, useful sources of data are the career center's Web sites, placement reports, and the summer interns you had work with you. For the broader view on what your industry and other industries are paying, experts in the field include:

- Brecker & Merryman at www.bandon.com. The firm has a specialty practice in campus and MBA recruiting. It produces annual surveys on the recruiting outlook including "Snapshot" and "MBA Compensation."
- The Fuqua Report—www.fuqua.duke.edu. This is a periodic national survey of MBA graduates of top-tier business schools. The survey objective is to determine the graduates' prevailing attitudes, career plans, and values. Produced by the Fuqua School of Business at Duke University, it also covers employment and compensation. The report is published every other year. The next report will be available in summer 2002. To view the report, you can either report the exact URL below, and click on the link entitled "The Fuqua Report" in the right-frame menu or

the main Fuqua address, www.fuqua.duke.edu, and locate career services under the corporate relations menu.

- Hay reports on executive talent compensation may be ordered by telephone, 781-239-1111. Hay reports are a comprehensive source for compensation and benefits practices. Reports provide benchmarks of pay and benefits across industries.

- Salary.com's salary wizard. This is not geared to MBAs or employers per se, but it can show you the going rates for numerous functions and industries in different locations.

COMPARATIVE COMPENSATION FOR POPULAR MBA CAREER FIELDS

So many words in a chapter on compensation and offers! Here are some numbers for those of you who like numbers. From the Fuqua Report, Table 8-1 provides a snapshot of market rates for top MBAs in popular career fields. These include common components such as base salary, signing bonuses, year-end bonuses, second-year tuition reimbursement, and stock options.

THE INTANGIBLES REALLY COUNT

In thinking about and making offers, it's important not to lose sight of the fact that for many MBAs intangibles are equally important as money. Ask your own employees, and much of the time they'll tell you that money is important but not *the* most important reason they accepted the job. Other dimensions of work are also valued. Most often, you'll hear about the importance of liking the people they work with and for, learning opportunities, stimulating work, and company culture and values. Intangibles really count.

According to a recent Wetfeet survey for MBAs in the graduating class of 2001, the top five factors swaying their job choices were people, professional development, company image/résumé power, value of the compensation, and job location.

For the past 10 years, Stanford MBAs have noted that most important in their career decisions are intangibles, such as the people they'd be working with and for, intellectual stimulation, responsibility as quickly as they can handle it, and opportunities for career broadening. Compensation has always been in the top five, but not always in the top three. Other intangibles mentioned are love for the work, belief in the company, and the quality of life.

David Stuart, VP of operations for Computer Motion, gives his advice. He uses intangibles strategically.

> *If you are a start-up company, certain characteristics may not exist that do exist in a more mature company. Things like IT systems, company processes, human resources to support you, nice buildings, comfortable furniture, and money. Although not having these can seem like a challenge to attracting good people and convincing them to work for many years in a skeletal environment, there are many intangibles that you can point to that may attract very talented employees. Things like freedom to create without bu-* reaucratic decision makers; lean and mean teams that make things happen; *being a part of creating a company from scratch; leaving your signature on the world rather than following the rules of other people; and a chance to think outside the box to create products no other people have created. And with the absence of capital to invest in the frills, a great substitute is to spend a little money on some perks that will return huge productivity dividends. Things like paying for all coffee, sodas, spring water; bringing in lunch once a week (or more); bringing in dinner for anyone who works late; and having lots of celebrations. Celebrate everything, but be genuine in offering thanks.*

PERQUISITES (PERKS)

Intangibles and perks often get discussed together. A simple distinction to keep in mind is that perks are the more concrete things and benefits that a company pays for and provides for its employees, individually or collectively. Intangibles are things you can't touch and that don't have a specific dollar value. For some real-life examples, look no further than Silicon Valley companies, which started the extensive use of perks and still use them for advantage in this tight labor market.

Paul Ning, Director of Platform Engineering of Netergy Networks, says,

> *For candidates we're making offers to, we've sent flowers to their homes, given away company apparel with offer letters, taken them out to follow-up*

Table 8-1. Comparative Compensation in Popular Career Fields

	All Respondents		Women		Men	
	Average*	Percent Receiving Bonuses	Average*	Percent Receiving Bonuses	Average*	Percent Receiving Bonuses
Consulting						
Base Salary (yearly)	$97,770		$94,815		$99,179	
Signing Bonus	$23,033	94	$19,859	88	$24,424	96
Guaranteed Annual Bonus	$18,949	40	$18,444	35	$19,147	42
2d Year Tuition Reimbursement	$28,591	25	$33,313	27	$26,049	24
Stock Options (average number of shares)	4,268	16	6,065	13	3,605	17
Investment Banking						
Base Salary (yearly)	$78,905		$76,692		$79,480	
Signing Bonus	$25,607	97	$24,423	100	$25,927	96
Guaranteed Annual Bonus	$33,431	92	$27,818	85	$34,745	94
2d Year Tuition Reimbursement	$31,700	8	$24,000	8	$33,625	8
Stock Options (average number of shares)	0	0	0	0	0	0

Marketing and Management

Base Salary (yearly)	$80,595		$77,987		$81,865	
Signing Bonus	$18,160	89	$19,587	87	$17,487	90
Guaranteed Annual Bonus	$15,975	36	$24,220	26	$13,398	41
2d Year Tuition Reimbursement	$17,415	9	$25,667	8	$13,879	9
Stock Options (average number of shares)	8,594	43	2,223	34	10,832	47

Internet/e-commerce

Base Salary (yearly)	$88,738		$85,167		$89,333	
Signing Bonus	$17,682	79	$11,250	67	$18,569	81
Guaranteed Annual Bonus	$16,917	29	$0	0	$16,917	33
2d Year Tuition Reimbursement	$27,000	12	$0	0	$27,000	14
Stock Options (average number of shares)	27,349	83	8,360	83	30,513	83

*Averages in U.S. dollars are taken over those responses that reported some nonzero level of that compensation type.
Source: Fuqua Report 2000. Reprinted with permission.

lunches and dinners with more employees, invited them back for more prod-
uct demos and tours, and generally tried to keep them engaged throughout
their decision process. For our employees, we've organized a range of activi-
ties that keep people connected to each other and the company: Friday after-
noon beer/wine/cheese parties; Monday night football parties; project
milestone bonuses; companywide outings to movies; monthly socials with
theme food and corporate communications; ski and sports activities.

A recent story by Michelle Crowe, in the *High Technology Careers* magazine, Fall 2000, entitled "Perks Plus—Best of Silicon Valley Company Benefits," touted a list of some of the best and most unusual benefits offered by
Bay Area companies at the height of the dot-com frenzy. These included
R&R, services to make life easier, lifestyle adjustments, mentoring and career
training, and celebrations and rewards. Notable examples include week-long
orientations in Hawaii; concierge services like having your wedding coordinated or dry cleaning picked up or the dog walked; shoeshines, oxygen bars,
flextime; ongoing online educational opportunities; and celebrating birthdays. Although the start-ups and old companies alike are watching their
budgets, most are preserving the good changes they have made to their cultures, both to attract and to hold on to their valuable talent.

WHAT YOU NEED TO KNOW ABOUT OPTIONS

Options have been around a long time. Old companies, like Microsoft,
have used them for years for their executives, but the dot-com frenzy brought
them to popular attention and gave them, at times, mythical proportions.
Options have been glorified, vilified, and now demystified. Simply put,
many companies use equity compensation, stock or options, as part of the
pay package for employees, consultants, and board of directors members.
The underlying advantage to equity compensation is that it provides the
recipient with a stake, a piece of the pie, in the success of a company.

Options are such an expansive topic; however, here are some key aspects
of designing an options program, according to Linda E. Amuso of iQuantic:

- Statement of the objectives of the program.
- Eligibility and participation. Who is included in the program and who
  actually receives an award.

- Timing to IPO if prepublic, including anticipated rounds of funding and capitalization structure.
- Competitors. Who in the public market do you compete with for talent and labor, and, secondarily, for products and services? This peer group is used to examine and benchmark aggregate equity compensation packages.
- Hiring plans. The number and types of positions to determine equity requirements.
- Types of grants and participation in each type for new hires, annual grants, promotional grants, special awards.
- Plan to communicate the program.

David Stuart tells how he has used options at Computer Motion in a strategic and planned approach. For a start-up, he advises to share equity:

Provide stock options to all employees. Be as consistent as possible. Let people constantly earn stock options by completing important projects. Issue stock options in smaller amounts more frequently, maybe every 6 months rather than annually. Communicate clearly the possible value of a stock option. Share in a macro sense the cap tables so people realize that their options can be worth a lot of money if the company can be successful. Carefully explain the dilution problems, if too many seed rounds are required prior to an IPO.

Stuart goes on to suggest:

. . . giving textbook examples of well-done private investment rounds through IPO, including companies entirely self-funded after only one small investment round. And show examples of companies that kept going back and giving away more and more of the company for added capital. Show how their options will dilute if goals and objectives are not achieved in accordance with the plan. Present these concepts quantitatively in ranges. Set reasonable dilution goals that you can surely beat, so you do not set expectations that will be disappointed even if reasonable results occur. Present this model frequently. Make sure everyone understands the model.

If you are a start-up, a helpful source of information is *Consider Your Options: Get the Most from Your Equity Compensation* (Kaye A. Thomas,

Fairmark Press, January 2000). Although more geared to the employee, it is useful for employers too. This book covers the basics, the nuances of non-qualified and incentive stock options, vesting, fair market values, 83b elections, exercising options, frequently asked questions; gains, losses, and taxes related to selling stock. Another resource, again more from the employee's viewpoint but which can give you information on options, is www.myStock Options.com, which blends educational information with advice. It offers an in-depth and ever-growing library, ranging from the basics to detailed reports on exercise strategies, legal issues, and psychological factors.

COMPENSATION RESOURCES AND EXPERTS

Consulting firms with compensation expertise include iQuantic; Hay Group; Advanced HR for pre-IPO companies; and Towers Perrin or Watson Wyatt Data Services, which typically focuses on Fortune 100 clients.

iQuantic (415-437-6200; www.iquantic.com), an 8-year-old national performance and rewards consulting firm, addresses the three critical components of new economy strategies and people processes: organization performance, compensation and rewards program design, and communication/implementation strategies. It also publishes a suite of compensation survey databases for the high-tech and life sciences industries.

The Hay Group (www.haygroup.com) is one of the world's largest human resources consulting firms and has been in operation for more than 50 years with 70 offices in 34 countries. Hay has the largest single database on people and pay worldwide. It also provides human resources products and services on the Internet through its <ebusiness.asp>.

Watson Wyatt Data Services (www.watsonwyatt.com; www.wwds surveys.com) is a leading provider of global compensation, benefits, employment practices information, and HR and consulting. It specializes in the design and development of both U.S. (focused nationally, by region, or by industry) and international (non-U.S.) compensation and benefit surveys, electronic HR, and employee communications. It has over 5,500 associates worldwide, with corporate offices in Reigate, England, and Washington, D.C.

Advanced HR (www.advanced-hr.com) is a compensation design and consulting firm to pre-IPO companies. It has an extensive database on executive pay and stock information.

Chapter 9

Best Practices and Worst Mistakes: A Multi-Industry Perspective

THIS CHAPTER SYNTHESIZES LESSONS LEARNED from working with and observing all kinds of companies that recruit MBAs. These seven best practices and seven worst mistakes represent the collective experience of hundreds of organizations across a variety of industries, including consumer products, manufacturing, high technology, venture capital, management consulting, investment banking, retail, entertainment, and non-profits—start-ups to large, global Fortune 500 companies.

BEST PRACTICES

1. Develop an Integrated Year-Round Plan

In Chapter 2, the sample time line and to-dos show what it takes to build an MBA recruiting program from the ground up. While carrying out a strong program of activities and efforts throughout the year, you must critically assess how to improve for next year's efforts, realizing that it takes at least 2 years to build a presence, cultivate relationships, and see results. Companies that are successful on-campus are those that have a plan, work the plan, and execute it in a thoughtful and coordinated manner. All their efforts and activities work together to make progress on their objectives.

You'll begin with your recruiting needs and program objectives. Develop your plan with action items and deliverables strategically timed throughout the year. Coordinating everyone involved is no small feat. Execute your plan with an eye to the big picture but with attention to the details. Make sure that your activities, recruiters' assignments, communications with the schools and internally, callbacks, and offers all work together and are not at odds with each another.

From the overarching plan, customize specific plans at the school level. Do your research on the schools, initiate relationships with people, and get to know your customers. Understand all your schools' respective cultures, their student demographics, and the nuances of recruiting there. Seek to know your most important customers, the students, beyond the surface; and understand with whom you're working in the career centers and how they operate. Review the fifteen dimensions in Chapter 3, Drill-Down #2, that give you a roadmap to researching the MBA programs. Take the time to do your homework on each school so you can better tailor plans for each. In the profiles of my top twenty school picks, in Chapter 10, the career center directors give you their thoughts on what works and what doesn't at their schools, along with other recruiting advice.

2. Don Your Marketing Hat

Companies that do a superb job of recruiting are excellent marketers. They know what they have to offer and clearly communicate it to students. They have effectively positioned themselves vis-à-vis their competition. They convey a compelling overall package pinpointing why it would be exciting to work with them. These companies are clearly aware of the marketing five Ps—product, price, place/distribution, promotion, positioning—and use them to their advantage. Applying this marketing framework to recruiting, you would think about how to position, price, promote, and so on, your company to your MBA school customers, the students.

Product. What do you do? What do you have to offer? What are your benefits and features? What do you have that would be of interest to your potential customers, who in the recruiting context are the students? What are your target markets and segments? Can you use a pull or push strategy: push your product through to the customer or build up demand and have the customer clamoring for you?

Price. Are you premium, high end, and elite? Do you need to offer a discount (extra incentives) for customers to be interested in you? What's the market perception of the value of your jobs and company environment compared with your competitors'?

Place/Distribution. How do you best deliver your product to your customers? By what avenues do you distribute your product to market? In this context, avenues are on-campus recruiting or one of the other options discussed in Chapter 13 on recruiting on the fly, such as participating in a school career fair or using the résumé book to target students directly.

Promotion. What's your communication strategy? How and when will you convey your key themes and messages—your strengths, what you have to offer, who you are? How will you vie for the attention of your targeted market? How can you interest potential customers to try you out? How do you promote your brand so that your customers keep coming back for more as your repeat customers? How can you build your visibility, reputation, and image to keep yourself on customers' minds? What can you do to be a product (i.e., an employer) of choice? Are you optimizing your PR on campus and elsewhere to serve your recruiting purposes? Do your activities, efforts, and people you choose to represent you promote what you are trying to accomplish among customers or deter them from it?

Positioning. What are your points of difference relative to competitors in your industry and to all the other companies that would be interested in the same kinds of students? What are your unique qualities, and how can you get those across to your potential customers? What are your strengths and weaknesses in contrast to your competition? Where does what you have to offer fit in the grand scheme of all the opportunities in your customers' choices? How can you carve out a place in the consumers' minds and stand out from the pack so they remember you—distinguish you?

Packaging. Sometimes, marketers also employ a sixth P, Packaging. In the context of MBA recruiting, packaging questions relate to how you appear to the students. How do you present yourself? For example, do you look disorganized and disjointed, or world-class and strategic? How does your total package look from the outside to the students, career centers staff, and others with whom you're interacting?

3. Build Multiple, Broad Relationships

Since recruiting is all about relationships, not transactions, companies that post strong recruiting results are those that realize they are dealing with people at the center of the flurry of activities, and at the heart of the company strategy. It's absolutely fundamental to initiate and to cultivate relationships among the students, career center staff, faculty, and other key people within the schools.

Beyond relationships with the students and career center staffs, it can be beneficial to build broader, multidimensional relationships within the school. If you have the opportunity, seeking out people in the office of alumni relations or corporate relations within each school can prove highly useful. Alumni relations can help connect you with alumni 2, 5, 10, and 15 years out of school. Corporate relations, in many schools, does more than fund raising. Depending on its charter, corporate relations may be able to open doors to faculty and in general advise a company how it can become more visible in the school, building a stronger presence, for example, with opportunities to sponsor high-profile student or school events. Corporate relations may also be able to make introductions to specific faculty for developing new case studies for use in their courses or broker opportunities for research initiatives or other joint projects.

Realistically, relationships require attention year in and year out. They call for consistent interaction, mutual trust, and open communication, which take time and build over the years.

4. Integrate into the Educational Process

Faculty are receptive to companies in varying degrees. Getting to know the faculty can prove to be of enormous advantage, even when it means a longer-term courtship. Faculty relationships offer you a window into the curricular and academic life of the school, which in turn lends genuine insight into the students' thinking and their educations. Knowing the faculty may also mean increased direct access to students, for example, by providing an invitation to speak to a class. A professor may be willing to make an announcement about your company's event. Many faculty and professors are company friendly and receptive. They already consult with companies, and seek out companies with which to develop case studies, or to share ideas and conduct research.

Developing case studies, providing an illuminating speaker for a relevant class, or participating in school or faculty research, programs, or initiatives are promising ways for companies to integrate into the educational process.

5. Communicate Strategically and Often

Companies with world-class recruiting are superb communicators. They communicate well internally with those involved in recruiting. They communicate well with the schools and students. They have a communication strategy, including key messages and themes that they reinforce consistently through words, actions, and attitudes. Refer to Chapter 3 for advice on communication strategy.

Companies that communicate well also address head on anything negative appearing in the press or which could cause concern to students. These issues have included a merger; lower than expected revenues; firing a CEO or the departure of key executives; a layoff or the closing of international offices; a defective product and criticism of taking it off the market too slowly; and new, formidable competitors. Respect is afforded to those companies that take the time to tell it like it is, and students realize that these sorts of challenges occur in dynamic businesses.

6. Try for Brilliant Execution

We all know brilliant execution when we see it, but it's difficult to describe. It's the mega-event that seemed effortless from start to finish, with everyone having a great time to boot. It's the overflowing interview schedule that went off with no hitches that couldn't have been better even if scripted! Companies that recruit effectively know that the best-hatched plans don't mean a whole lot if they are not translated to action—implementation—that is thoughtful, complete, and as quick as possible.

7. Offer Great Summer Internships

For many companies, offering a summer program can be the single most important recruiting tool they use for several reasons. Summer interns can generate some of the best word-of-mouth, viral marketing, and positive buzz on campus—since cohorts influence each other so much. Interns are also a viable source of full-time talent, if they decide to return to your company after graduating, that's road tested and acclimated to your environment. Anecdotally, we also know that companies on average make offers to about 50 to 75 percent of their interns to lure this proven talent to return full time. About 30 to 50 percent of those interns accept full-time jobs with their summer employers.

In brief, companies that offer great summer internships keep the following in mind:

- *Tease out real jobs for the interns.* It's a misconception that interns don't really do anything since they are with you only about 10 weeks. Meaningful work that they can sink their teeth into is key. This may mean a discrete project or responsibilities that one could be expected to handle during the time frame. The work could also be a part of a larger project. If you're not an investment bank or a consulting firm in which summer interns can work on deals or engagements as part of a team, examples of realistic short-term jobs can include the market research phase of a plan to launch a new product, the due diligence for a potential acquisition, the business plan for an e-business initiative, and the analysis and recommendations for cost cutting. Whatever the case, give the interns jobs that let them experience what it'd be like to work full time with you later on.
- *Give them a home.* Interns need to have a manager, a team of people to be part of, and deliverables they need to produce, even though they may work with several groups over the course of their short time with you. Clue them in to your activities and what's on the horizon. Treat them as insiders on the team by inviting them to participate in what you're doing for other employees, for example, an all-hands meeting, press briefings, or a company event. Engaging them in these ways helps them feel connected to the company, and, again, it lets them experience first hand what it will be like to work with you full time.
- *Expose the interns to senior management across a diversity of areas.* This will make them feel special and give them critical perspectives on your business. Several of the best types of activities and programs we've seen: a Friday weekly lunch series talking with a different senior manager

invited each week; a slate of online chats with different executives from around the world; and an ice cream social where senior managers serve ice cream and spend time socializing with the interns.

- *Connect interns throughout the company and with alumni from their schools.* Think about assigning a summer mentor, host, or buddy from their alma mater, if you have one. A sister school will work too. Organize one event early on in which all the interns, even if only a few, can meet each other. Then plan another event later on, culminating their summer program, as a thank you and send off back to school. The interns could organize activities themselves and you could allocate a small budget to cover their activities.

- *Seek out and give feedback.* Take the time to find out how your interns are enjoying their summers, and make any midcourse corrections if necessary. Make a point to find out about their long-term career interests after they graduate and discuss what opportunities you may have. If you'd like to have them back, let them know it, perhaps facilitating interviews before they return to school with the groups they are most interested in. Make sure managers give their interns performance coaching and feedback. Let them know how they are doing, how they are being perceived, and the developmental opportunities for them.

- *Don't leave them hanging.* Be frank about whether they'll get offers to return. If you don't think there's a fit, be sensitive but let them know. Help them save face by giving them useful and constructive feedback and, without being defensive, a brief reason for that rejection. In this way, they won't have to dream up a reason to tell their classmates why they didn't want you.

- *Involve the interns in recruiting at their schools.* Brainstorm about ideas for their campuses; hear their views on best practices and key competitors. Let them know what you plan and keep them informed and engaged throughout all phases of your recruiting efforts. When I was head of recruiting, I always created group e-mail distributions for interns at each school and copied them on any recruiting updates I was sending out internally. For example, one savvy investment bank, as a kickoff to each campus's recruiting, hosted a breakfast and asked all their former associates—summer interns and those who had worked with them prior to business school—to invite five other students to the breakfast. This was highly effective, yielding valuable employee referrals and early interest in the firm.

There's a catch to all of this. By far, it is better to have no summer program than one thrown together or that doesn't measure up. Company recruiting efforts can nosedive if just thrown together as the cool thing to do, or if there is not commitment from managers to provide real summer jobs. A summer program needs to be part of your overall strategy, and thought through and planned as such.

Companies that have conducted abysmal summer programs, treating their interns poorly, then wonder why the buzz on campus is negatively impacting interest in their events and their interview schedules. They then must suffer efforts to clean up the company's image and reputation. So keep in mind the very real downside to doing a bad job with summer interns, who can seriously damage your reputation if they had a bad experience, felt mistreated, or honestly came to believe your company is not a good place to work. Weigh the tradeoffs carefully.

COMMON MISTAKES

✗ 1. Recruiting MBAs Like Undergraduates

There are some commonalities between MBA and undergraduate recruiting. For both you must research and choose the best schools, build relationships with the career center staff and students, and host pre-recruitment activities. You also conduct on-campus and second-round interviews and make offers. The resemblances end there.

MBA recruitment is different in the level of the playing field: There are higher stakes and more money being spent on recruiting efforts and offers; more intense competition among companies; and with that, much higher expectations among these more experienced students. Quite often, MBAs are looking to change their industry focus from what they did before B-school. This means that your recruitment processes will need to be more sophisticated in looking beyond the students' previous industries and job titles to decipher the skills and experience that are transferable to your opportunities and needs.

Also, in contrast to undergraduate recruiting, working with the MBA career centers is more complex. There are more time frames (start and end of company briefing periods, due dates for closed invitation lists for schedules, interviewing dates); more policies (disclosure of grades and GMAT scores, offer consideration time, exploding offers, reneges); and more dimensions to consider in the job offer (compensation components, titles, any promises beyond the initial start year such as international assignments, bonuses, trailing partner issues).

Whereas one employer briefing may suffice for undergraduates, a company doing that alone at a top MBA school would not be noticed. You may be able to get by with less-seasoned interviewers on undergraduate campuses, but at an MBA program, a poor showing could be quite detrimental to your results. An undergraduate offer may involve a $35,000 base; MBA base compensation could easily come in higher than $85,000.

MBAs and undergraduates are two distinct markets. This is part of knowing your customer. Treat them differently. Tailor your strategy and plans. No one size fits all.

✗ 2. Decentralizing Too Much

Can you visualize these company missteps? Two separate employer briefing sessions from the same company at one of their top schools conveyed inconsistent messages about their corporate direction and strengths. Three different divisions from a company send interviewers to a school on the same day, unaware of each other, which the students perceived as a lack of coordination and questionable business sense. A company makes competing offers, at different salaries, to the same candidate as two separate divisions unintentionally compete against each other for the same person. These are real-life examples of mistakes caused by companies going too far in decentralizing their recruiting efforts, undercutting some level of central coordination.

While it's common and useful for companies to decentralize their efforts, giving the responsibility and autonomy to the people closest to the action who can best make the decisions, it is a mistake to bypass some level of coordination across all the MBA recruiting activities in the company. For example, at a minimum, some central source like the campus recruiting group in HR needs to have a handle on overall recruiting needs and plans for the company. If more than one group will recruit at a school, someone needs to flag this so those groups can coordinate with each other.

The following four coordinating activities will result in more efficient, cohesive, and productive efforts at the schools:

- Consolidate overall needs for MBA and other openings in the company. HR should keep track of what each group will do at which schools, when. HR then has a big picture view of what's being done by your company, and can apprise the managers who need to know. Information, such as school research, and resources, such as budget dollars or interviewers, can be shared or combined for greater impact. Groups can be guided to work together to leverage their initiatives at key schools.
- HR can serve as the point group for the schools so they bypass the headache of dealing with too many people within the company. Any specific inquiries or issues can be redirected from HR to the appropriate hiring group. By having a point group or person, you'll look like one firm. The schools won't be confused dealing with many different people. The HR group can also serve as the experts for your interviewers in scheduling details and subtleties, institutional knowledge on the school, its policies, key dates, and other recruiting aspects—avoiding the redundancy of multiple people figuring out these same things. The operating groups can still make decisions and the interviewing teams can handle activities such as building relationships at the schools. You're just using your resources wisely by centralizing some efforts, with sensible coordination and efficiency.
- HR can actually handle all the logistics of scheduling interviews, company briefings, and any other pre-recruitment or recruitment activities. HR can also supply job descriptions and recruitment literature as required by the schools and organize the callbacks. You'll benefit immensely from one group handling the day-to-day operations, without the redundancy of multiple groups covering the same ground.
- HR should also coordinate the offer process, developing the offers with input from the compensation department and line hiring managers. HR can also call out when different groups are pursuing the same MBAs within the same schools and help design a solution that is best for the company.

✗ 3. Playing Dirty

Schools have different recruitment policies. The underlying purpose of these policies is to create a level playing field for all the companies that recruit, given their diversity in location, industry, size, number of hiring needs, cultures, and timing of recruiting. The firms that don't respect a school's policies will lose out. For example, is there a school policy on how much time students should get to consider an offer without it going away? If a company disregards that policy and pressures students to decide early, the students could sense this is underhanded and the company reputation will suffer, resulting in a rash of no's to offers or a shunning next interview time. Another way companies play dirty is being derisive about a competitor. This is fodder for the student grapevine that can damage a company's image and affect recruiting results for years to come.

✗ 4. Overexpecting

Companies that believe in their first year they can hire as many students as they would like to implement a smoothly running, perfect plan; or set themselves up to attain other unrealistic objectives are most often sorely disappointed. Overexpecting is a common mistake that has negative repercussions. It can cause those involved in recruiting for your company to feel let down and demoralized because of a perceived failure. It can also influence a lack of future support for the program if senior management thinks the results are a disappointment. At worst, it can make you seem naïve or not knowledgeable about MBA recruiting. But although it is a common mistake to overexpect, it *is* a good practice to set stretch goals. It's just that there is a fine line between the two that you'll need to distinguish through your knowledge of the schools and of your company's being able to achieve these goals.

✗ 5. Turning Your Faucet On and Off

By this I mean a company that recruits like crazy one year, but barely has a presence the next. Or, a company is a top employer/recruiter a few years in a row but then decides not to recruit for the next 3 years, returning to the school afterward assuming it can pick up where it left off.

Companies that make this mistake do themselves a disservice by not building momentum at the schools. There may be bona fide reasons you modulate your recruiting efforts from year to year, but since relationships are living entities, you need to at least keep a consistent level of effort with those. It's sometimes difficult to keep the faucet on at your target schools because situations do change. Heads of recruiting or the school teams come and go, taking with them the institutional knowledge of your history with the school and your recruiting efforts. Sometimes the energy and drive for the MBA recruiting wanes. This is why it's critical to have some centralization of recruiting in HR so that some group can be the repository of learning as well as the keeper of reports, files, and recruitment literature.

We see companies recruit on and off because of changes in senior management support or in budget dollars, and because of the ebbs and flows of hiring managers' interest in MBA recruiting. There could be a hiring freeze, impending layoffs, or the uncertainty of a potential acquisition. These reasons are understandable; however, a strong program requires stick-to-itiveness through consistent efforts at a certain watermark level over the years on each campus.

It may be practical to pull back your interview schedules, cancel them completely and participate in a career fair only, or pare down pre-recruitment activities or number of offers, but you should always maintain relationships with the career center staff or faculty and identify ways to keep a presence with the students.

If you need to modify your recruiting mid-season, or from one year to the next, openly communicate your course change to the career center staff and students, who will appreciate that. Honesty is the best policy, letting everyone know the reasons behind the changes and when realistically you may pick the pace back up.

✗ 6. Failing to Market the Program Internally

Those leading recruiting often fail to build internal support for the program, which results in its diminution. On a wholesale level, a misunderstood or undervalued program could cause more friction between employees who feel like have-nots pitted against the haves, your MBA new hires. The importance of internal marketing, PR, and internal communication are discussed on page 37. Suffice it to say that the more believers and champions you have in your company, the better. An employee base that feels good and welcoming about the new recruits, not threatened or bitter, impacts on how well those new MBAs perform once in the company—the level of support, shared information, and resources they receive. This also influences how much the new recruits like the people they're working with, their satisfaction, and how long they stay.

✗ 7. Arrogance

This is a common complaint from companies about MBAs in general
and for some schools' students more than others, but career centers also hear
it from students about recruiters. Most would agree that one or a handful of
arrogant people within a school or a company does not mean that everyone
else in that school or company is also arrogant. When first impressions about
your company are being formed quickly by students and you are investing
so much of your time and resources to MBA recruiting, it would serve your
best interest to utilize enthusiastic, professional, and accomplished representatives. Call on those with whom you would most want to work.

Chapter 10

School Profiles of the Top Twenty Picks

THERE ARE MANY EXCELLENT MBA programs available. No one can be the definitive expert on which are the best, because that really depends on you, your business needs, preferences, and resources. My picks are not scientific; there's been no rigorous research and evaluation. Rather they are practical suggestions from a manager who has done a lot of MBA recruiting and who has been on the inside as a career management center director as well. These twenty programs are my top picks from a couple of vantage points: from many years as a recruiter in terms of quality of the students; ease of working with the career center; value for the money; and how the recruits performed once in the company. From my seven years at Stanford, I have also added to the mix what I know about the programs from working directly with colleagues from our sister schools.

Note: The dates and statistics in the profiles are the most current available at the time of going to press with this book. They are representative of the individual school, but for the most current information, contact the career center directly. Also, I asked each one of my career center director colleagues to give their insights and advice on a list of questions/topics that would be most beneficial to those considering recruiting their MBAs. There are some variances across schools' information, based on the directors' personalizations. Also note Table 10-1, Comparative Student and On-Campus

(text continues on page 134)

Table 10-1. Comparative Student and On-Campus Recruiting Information

School	Applicant Selectivity / # Applicants	Admission Rate	# on Campus and Total Companies	Recruiting Dates 2000/01 as Sample	Student Compensation/ Placement Highlights
Carnegie Mellon GSIA	Class of 1999: 1417 Class of 2000: 1265	30.6% 29.8%	on campus: 314 total: 374	Career: after first mini-semester, around October 20 Summer: January	Base median: $82,960 Base mean: $86,032 Total median: $104,300 Total average: $110,217
Columbia Business School	Class of 1999: 7200 Class of 2000: 6328	11.0% 12.0%	on campus: 300 total: 700	Career: October 13–December 7 Summer: January 25–March 2	Total compensation: $146,000
Dartmouth TUCK	Class of 1999: 3192 Class of 2000: 2916	14.0% 14.5%	on campus: 160 total: 500	Career: October 16–November 9 Summer: January 16–February 22	Base median: $90,000 Base average: $91,223 Total median: $130,750 Total average: $135,000
Duke FUQUA	Class of 1999: 3612 Class of 2000:	15.4%	on campus: 400	Career: October 26–December 3 Summer: December 3–January 7	Base median: $90,000 Base average: $86,500 Total median: $130,000 Total average: $136,000
Harvard Business School	Class of 1999: Class of 2000: 8124	13.0%	on campus: 803	Career: November–April Summer: January–April	Base average: $100,000 Total median: $130,000
HEC ISA	Class of 1999: Class of 2000: (Applicant Pool: 1 for every 4)		on campus: 49 total: 192	Career: June, September, October, November Summer: October–April	Base median: $58,333 Base average: $72,905 Total median: $74,200 Total average: $94,717

School	Class Size	Percentage	Jobs	Recruiting Schedule	Salary
IESE	Class of 1999: 1000 Class of 2000: 1092 (31%)	61.0% 72.0%	on campus: 325 total: 910	Career: October/November–April Summer: January–April	In Euros— Base median: $62,664 Base average: $60,495 Total median: $82,247 Total average: $80,495
Indiana KELLEY	Class of 1999: 1770 Class of 2000: 1819	35.0% 33.0%	on campus: 138 total: 305	Career: October 2 and December 8 Summer: January 22 and March 15	Base median: $78,000 Base average: $78,664 Total median: $93,000 Total average: $94,574
INSEAD	Class of 1999: Class of 2000: 650		on campus: 183 total: 500 +	Career: December grads for full-time jobs Summer: July grads for full-time and December grads for summer	Base median: $95,000 Base average: $91,000 Overall base median: $110,000
London Business School	Class of 1999: 1333 Class of 2000: 1094	20.0% 24.0%	on campus: 163 total: over 400	Career: October–January Summer: January–April	Base average salary (in English Pounds) Consulting: £61,000 Finance: £62,500 Industry: £64,000 E-Business: £71,000 Startups: £56,000
Massachusetts Institute of Technology SLOAN	Class of 1999: 2927 Class of 2000: 2756	14.5% 15.4%	on campus: 221	Career: October 30–November 17 Summer: January 22	Base median: $90,000 Base average: $92,343 Total median: $135,000 Total average: $137,726

(continues)

Table 10-1. (Continued)

School	Applicant Selectivity Applicants	Admission Rate	on Campus and Total Companies	Recruiting Dates 2000/01 as Sample	Student Compensation/ Placement Highlights	
New York University STERN	Class of 1999: Class of 2000:		on campus: 133	Career: October 16–December 6 Summer: January 29–March 2	Base median: Base average: Total median: Total average:	$80,000 $82,861 $135,000 $117,600
Northwestern KELLOGG	Class of 1999: 6107 Class of 2000: 6128	13.0%	on campus: 320 total: 605	Career: October 16–December 1 Summer: January 29–March 2	Base median: Base average:	$90,000 $92,000
Stanford GSB	Class of 1999: 6559 Class of 2000: 5431	16.0% 8.0%	on campus: 379 total: 1170	Career: Fall/Winter/Spring Summer: Winter/Spring	Base median: Base average: Total median: Total average:	$100,000 $98,108 $150,000 $139,994
University of Pennsylvania WHARTON	Class of 1999: Class of 2000: 7428	14.0%		Career: October 26–January 26 Summer: January 29–March 30	Base median:	$95,000
UCLA Anderson	Class of 1999: 4926 Class of 2000: 4564	14.0% 15.0%	on campus: 221 total: 831	Career: October 23–May 25 Summer: January 29–May 25	Base median: Base average: Total median: Total average:	$80,000 $84,636 $110,000 $112,172

University of Chicago GSB	Class of 1999: 4239	18.47%	on campus: 283	Career: October 17–November 30	Base median:	$85,000
	Class of 2000: 3271	25.4%	total: 545	Summer: January 28–February 28	Total median:	$140,000
University of Michigan	Class of 1999: 4000	20.0%	on campus: 221	Career: October 9–December 7	Base median:	$90,000
	Class of 2000: 4000	20.0%	total: 1000	Summer: January 16–February 16	Base average:	$92,343
					Total median:	$135,000
					Total average:	$137,726
University of Virginia DARDEN	Class of 1999: 2682	18.7%	on campus: 212	Career: October 24–December 7	Base median:	$80,000
	Class of 2000: 2510	19.0%	total: 434	Summer: January 22–February 28	Base average:	$85,116
					Total median:	$130,000
					Total average:	$128,243
Vanderbilt OWEN	Class of 1999: 1313	38.0%	on campus: 95	Career: September 26–April 26	Base median:	$75,000
	Class of 2000: 1112	47.0%	(2d yrs.)	Summer: January 16–April 26	Base average:	$77,904
					Total median:	$100,000
					Total average:	$103,873

Source: School Career Management Center Directors, Web sites and publications; *U.S. News and World Report,* April 2, 2001.

Table 10-2. Comparative Demographic and Placement Statistics

School	Student Demographics	Top Industries	Top Locations	Top 10 Employers
Carnegie Mellon GSIA	2000 full-time enrollment: 442 GMAT median: 660 Women: 29% Men: 71% International: 41% Minority students: 22% Mean age at entry: 22–44 Full-time work experience: 5.3 Countries represented: 34 Universities represented: 180	Consulting: 30.2% Financial services: 15.6% Hardware/software: 15.6% High tech: 9.4% E-commerce/Internet: 8.3%	West: 27.5% Northeast: 23.6% Mid-Atlantic: 18.1% Midwest: 12.1% Southwest: 8.2% Top Cities: San Francisco/ Silicon Valley Pittsburgh New York City Boston Chicago	Diamond Technology Partners, Intel, PRTM, Booz Allen & Hamilton, Corning, Deloitte, Ford Motor Co., Citigroup, FreeMarkets, Inc., Hewlett-Packard, McKinsey & Co., Price-waterhouseCoopers
Columbia Business School	2000 full-time enrollment: 1400 GMAT middle (80%): 640–750 Women: 37% Men: 63% Minority students: 23% International: 27% Average age at entry: 27 Age range: 22–37 Full-time work experience: 4 Countries represented: 50	Financial services: I/B & brokerage: 38% Other financial services: 17% Consulting: 22% Manufacturing: 12% Other services: 11%	Europe: 49% Asia Pacific: 33% Central/South America: 11% Middle East: 5% Canada: 2%	Goldman Sachs, MSDW, McKinsey, Lehman Bros., American Express, Citigroup, Booz Allen & Hamilton, JP Morgan, Merrill Lynch, DLJ

School	Statistics	Industries	Locations	Top Employers
Dartmouth TUCK	2000 full-time enrollment: 400 GMAT average: 693 Women: 32% Men: 68% Countries represented: 32 Students from undergraduate schools: 187 Full-time work experience: 100%	Consulting: 45% Financial services: 31% Technology: 14% Entrepreneur: 4% Consumer goods/services: 3% General management: 3%	Boston New York City Bay Area/San Francisco Other New England Chicago/Midwest (tie with New England)	Bain & Co., McKinsey & Co., Goldman Sachs, Mercer Mgmt., Andersen/Accenture and Bowstreet (tie)
Duke FUQUA	2000 full-time enrollment: 676 GMAT mean: 690 Women: 41% Minority students: 20% International: 30% Average age at entry: 28 Full-time work experience: 5 Average undergraduate GPA: 3.33 Countries represented: 40	Consulting: 31% Investment banking: 19% Computers/business machines: 11% Other non-manufacturing: 7% E-commerce: 6% Consumer goods: 6%	New York: 16% International: 13% California: 13% Georgia: 10% North Carolina: 8%	Goldman Sachs, Booz Allen, Pricewaterhouse Coopers, Deloitte Consulting, Johnson & Johnson, McKinsey & Co., Dell, Lehman Brothers, Cap Gemini Ernst & Young, General Motors

(continues)

Table 10-2. (Continued)

School	Student Demographics	Top Industries	Top Locations	Top 10 Employers
Harvard Business School	2000 full-time enrollment: 1770 GMAT mean: 700 Women: 32% International: 33% Mean age: 27 Age range: 23–36 Full-time work experience: 4 Countries represented: 69 *Undergraduate major—* Business: 24% Humanities/Social Science: 41% Engineering/Natural Science: 31% Other: 4%	Consulting: 24% Computers/software: 11% Investment banking: 9% Venture capital: 8% Private equity: 5% Investment management: 5%	New York City: 21% California: Bay Area: 18% Boston: 18% Texas: 4% International: 14%	TBI
HEC ISA	2000 full-time enrollment: 160 GMAT median: 624 Applicant pool: 1 for every 4 Women: 28% Men: 72% International: 70 (incl. U.S.) Average age at entry: 29 Age range: 23–41 Full-time work experience: 5 Countries represented: 33	Consulting: 32% Industry: 32% Services: 26% Finance: 9% Other: 2%	France U.S. Germany U.K. Switzerland	Gemini Consulting, L'Oréal, Merrill Lynch, Renault/Mercer Mgmt. Consulting, Lilly/Bain & Co., Booz Allen & Hamilton, Hilti, GE Medical

IESE

Average GMAT score: 655
Women: 24%
Average age at entry: 28
Full-time work experience: 3.8
Students from abroad: 65%
Countries represented: 55
Undergraduate major—
Economics: 29%
Management: 16%
Engineering: 38%
Law/Political Science: 5%
Science: 10%
Humanities: 2%

Consulting: 37%
Finance: 24%
Consumer goods: 6%
Telecommunications: 6%
Academic/not-for-profit: 5%

Europe: 81%
Latin America: 8%
Asia Pacific/Caribbean: 6%
North America: 3%

Andersen Consulting, Arthur D. Little, A. T. Kearney, Diamond Cluster, Eli Lilly & Co., Europraxis Group, La Caixa, MarchFIRST, McKinsey & Company, Media Planning, Netpraxis, Uno-e bank

Indiana KELLEY

2000 full-time enrollment: 306
GMAT: 648
Women: 20%
Men: 80%
Minority students: 8%
International: 38%
Average age at entry: 28
Full-time work experience: 5

Electronic computers: 14%
Consulting: 12%
Auto/transport equipment: 11%
Household products: 7.5%
Pharmaceutical: 7.5%

Midwest: 49%
Northeast: 17%
West: 16%
Southwest: 6%
South: 5%

Eli Lilly & Co., Bank of America, Ford Motor Company, General Mills, Procter & Gamble, Cummins, Hewlett-Packard, Bristol-Myers Squibb, Intel, IBM, BP Amoco, Toyota

(continues)

Table 10-2. (Continued)

School	Student Demographics	Top Industries	Top Locations	Top 10 Employers
INSEAD	GMAT: 683 Women: 24% Men: 76% Average age at entry: 29 Full-time work experience: 5	Consulting: 39% Industry: 31% Finance: 21% New Economy: 9%	Europe: 52% Asia/Asia Pacific: 18% Other: 11% North America: 8% Central/Eastern Europe: 6%	McKinsey, Bain & Co., BCG, Goldman Sachs, Salomon Smith Barney, Merrill Lynch, L'Oréal, Bertelsmann/Lycos, Novartis, Eli Lilly & Co.

London Business School	2000 full-time enrollment: 240
	GMAT: 690
	Women: 25%
	Average age at entry: 29
	Full-time work experience: 5
	Countries represented
	  Asia: 25%
	  Africa/Middle East: 2%
	  North America: 22%
	  U.K.: 17%
	  Western Europe (excl. U.K.): 13%
	  Australia/New Zealand: 7%
	  Central/South America: 7%
	  Central/Eastern Europe: 7%
	Undergraduate major
	  Accounting/Finance: 28%
	  Advertising/Media/PR: 4%
	  Consulting: 19%
	  Energy/Engineering/Industry: 20%
		Finance: 40%
		Consulting: 33%
		Industry: 12%
		Startups: 9%
		E-Commerce: 6%
			U.K.: 67%
			North America: 10%
			Europe: 8%
			Australasia: 8%
			Asia: 6%
			South America: 2%
			Africa & ME: 1%
				McKinsey, Goldman Sachs, Merrill Lynch, Deutsche Bank, Schroders SSB, Credit Suisse First Boston, Bain & Co., Booz Allen & Hamilton, Lehman Brothers, Morgan Stanley Dean Witter, Deloitte Consulting, UBS Warburg

FMCG: 4%
IT/Telecomm: 9%
Leisure/Retail: 3%
Not for Profit/Public: 7%
Other: 6%

Massachusetts Institute of Technology SLOAN

2000 full-time enrollment: 350
GMAT: 700
Women: 26%
Men: 74%
Minority Students: 8%
International: 38%
Average age at entry: 28
Full-time work experience: 5
Countries represented: 50

Consulting: 30%
Software/e-commerce: 17%
I-banking/brokerage: 16%
Computers/electronics: 8%
Telecommunications: 5%

Massachusetts
California
New York
Midwest
Southwest

McKinsey & Co., Goldman Sachs & Co., Bain & Company, Intel Corporation, Morgan Stanley Dean Witter, Boston Consulting Group, Diamond Technology Partners, Inc., Booz Allen & Hamilton, Inc., A. T. Kearney, Inc., Merrill Lynch

New York University STERN

2000 full-time enrollment: 837
GMAT median: 686
Women: 42%
Men: 58%
Minority Students: 19%
International: 31%
Average age at entry: 27
Full-time work experience: 4.4
Countries represented: 44
Undergraduate major
Business: 22%
Economics: 20%
Engineering/Sciences: 27%
Social Sciences/Humanities: 31%

Investment banking: 37%
Management consulting: 17%
Diversified financial services: 8%
Consumer products/ commercial banking/ new media: 6%

None Provided

Lehman Brothers, JP Morgan/Chase, Deutsche Bank, McKinsey & Co., Salomon Smith Barney, American Express, Bear Stearns, Goldman Sachs, Merrill Lynch, Booz Allen & Hamilton, Credit Suisse First Boston

(continues)

Table 10-2. (Continued)

School	Student Demographics	Top Industries	Top Locations	Top 10 Employers
Northwestern KELLOGG	GMAT: 690 Women: 31% Minority students: 19% Average age at entry: 28 Full-time work experience: 5 *Undergraduate major* Business: 22% Economics: 20% Engineering/Sciences: 33% Social Sciences/Humanities: 26%	Consulting: 33% Banking: 14% E-commerce: 8%	Chicago Bay Area New York	McKinsey & Co., BCG, Bain, Goldman Sachs, A. T. Kearney, Mercer, Booz Allen & Hamilton, Lehman Brothers, Siebel Systems, Hewlett-Packard
Stanford GSB	2000 full-time enrollment: 735 GMAT mean: 730 Women: 29% International: 31% Minority students: 26% Mean age: 28 Full-time work experience: 4.7 Countries represented: 35 *Undergraduate major* Applied/Natural Science: 5% Behavioral/Social Science: 25% Economics: 26% Engineering/Computer Science: 25% Humanities: 11% Mathematics: 3%	Management consulting: 18% E-commerce/Internet services: 14% Venture capital/private equity: 14% Entrepreneurs: 10% Investment banking/ brokerage: 9%	San Francisco/Bay Area New York Austin Los Angeles Miami	McKinsey & Co., Goldman, Sachs & Co., Bain & Company, Intuit Inc., Siebel Systems, Inc., BCG, Loudcloud Inc., Morgan Stanley Dean Witter, Cyclone Commerce, Yahoo! Inc.

UCLA Anderson	2000 full-time enrollment: 651 GMAT mean: 698 Women: 28% Minority students: 23% International: 24% Average age at entry: 28 Full-time work experience: 4.3 *Undergraduate major* 　Business: 16% 　Economics: 22% 　Engineering: 22% 　Humanities: 9% 　Math/Science: 12% 　Other Social Sciences: 13% 　Other: 6%	Investment banking: 22.7% Internet/computer services: 18.6% Consulting: 17.2% High tech: 10.5% Venture capital: 5.5%	Southern California: 50.7% Bay Area: 18.7% New York: 10.8% Asia: 6.1% Latin America: 3.6%	Intel, Goldman Sachs, Robertson Stephens, McKinsey & Co., Salomon Smith Barney, Diamond Cluster, Lehman Brothers, Morgan Stanley, Bank of America Securities LLC, Digital Coast Partners, Mattel
University of Chicago GSB	2000 full-time enrollment: 1100 GMAT mean: 684 Women: 26.1% International: 30.5% Minority students: 8.2% Advanced degree holders: 16% Mean age: 28.6 Full-time work experience: 4.7 Mean undergraduate GPA: 3.35 Countries represented: 34	Investment banking/brokerage: 34.5% Consulting: 32.1% Technology: 11.2% Investment management: 4.3% Venture capital: 3.2%	New York: 24.8% Chicago: 22.4% San Francisco: 6.3% London: 4.1% Boston: 3.3%	McKinsey & Co., Lehman Brothers, Booz Allen & Hamilton, Goldman Sachs & Co., Merrill Lynch, Andersen Consulting, Chase, BCG, Bain & Company, Morgan Stanley Dean Witter

(continues)

Table 10-2. (Continued)

School	Student Demographics	Top Industries	Top Locations	Top 10 Employers
University of Michigan	2000 full-time enrollment: 866 GMAT: 675 Women: 28% Minority students: 21% International: 33% Average age at entry: 28	Consulting: 31% Banking and financial services: 19% Consumer goods: 12% Automotive/transportation: 7% High tech/electronics: 16% Pharmaceutical/health care: 6%	NE/Mid-Atlantic: 22% South: 6% Midwest: 25% Southwest: 4% West: 9%	McKinsey & Co., A. T. Kearney, Dell Computer, American Express, Diamond Technology, Ford Motor Company, Chase Manhattan, BCG, Accenture, Salomon Smith Barney, Goldman Sachs
University of Pennsylvania WHARTON	2000 full-time enrollment: 1554 GMAT mean: 700 Women: 28% International: 39% Minority students: 15% Mean age: 29 Age range: 19–41 Full-time work experience: 6 *Undergraduate major* Liberal Arts & Science: 30% Business Administration: 19% Economics: 16% Engineering: 16% Other: 19%	Consulting: 31.8% Investment banking: 21.7% High tech: 17.2% Venture capital: 5.5% Investment management: 4.7%	Northeast: 36% West: 23.9% International: 16% Mid-Atlantic: 10.4% Midwest: 5%	McKinsey & Co., Goldman Sachs & Co., Bain & Co., Boston Consulting Group, Merrill Lynch, Morgan Stanley Dean Witter, Donaldson Lufkin & Jenrette, Andersen Consulting, Deloitte Consulting, Booz Allen & Hamilton

University of Virginia DARDEN	2000 full-time enrollment: 503 GMAT mean: 680 GPA mean: 3.3 Women: 30% Men: 70% Minority students: 18% Average age at entry: 27 Countries represented: 33 *Undergraduate major* Business Administration: 28% Economics: 15% Engineering/Science/Math: 31% Humanities/Social Science: 25% Other: 1% Universities represented: 113	Consulting: 33% Investment banking/ portfolio management: 30% High tech/ telecommunications: 15% Consumer products: 4% Diversified manufacturing: 4%	Northeast: 27.3% Mid Atlantic: 24.9% South: 11.5% West: 10.6%	A. T. Kearney, Booz Allen & Hamilton, Diamond Technology Partners, Donaldson Lufkin & Jenrette, Enron Corporation, Ernst & Young LLP, Goldman Sachs & Co., JP Morgan, Lehman Brothers, McKinsey & Co., Merrill Lynch, Morgan Stanley Dean Witter, Pricewaterhouse Coopers, BCG
Vanderbilt OWEN	2000 full-time enrollment: 432 GMAT mean: 631 GPA mean: 3.18 Women: 28% Minority students: 13% International: 33% Average age at entry: 28 Age range: 22–41 Full-time work experience: 4.8 Countries represented: 26	Financial service: 27% Management consulting: 17% Computer/tech: 11% Internet: 11% Consumer products: 6% Travel & transportation: 6%	Atlanta, GA Nashville, TN New York, NY Austin, TX Charlotte, NC	PricewaterhouseCoopers LLC, First Union, Dell, Goldman Sachs, Deloitte Consulting, KPMG, Mastrapasqua & Associates, Morgan Stanley Dean Witter, Johnson & Johnson, Arthur Andersen

Source: School Career Management Center Directors, Web sites and publications; *U.S. News and World Report*, April 2, 2001

Recruiting Information, and Table 10-2, Comparative Demographic and Placement Statistics.

CARNEGIE MELLON: GRADUATE SCHOOL OF INDUSTRIAL ADMINISTRATION (GSIA)

Dean: Dr. Douglas Dunn

MBA Program Overview/Mission

GSIA sets the world standard for educating leaders who can harness technology as well as use analytical tools to identify and solve complex business problems. A fundamental approach to teaching management makes their graduates effective managers, creative problem solvers, and strong business leaders. The objective is to develop in students the business savvy to jump in and address problems never seen before. Through a wide collection of electives, students are given the flexibility to concentrate in areas of special interest as part of their broad interdisciplinary education. This generalist approach develops the conceptual building blocks needed for students to comfortably lead organizations to achieve excellence.

Degree Programs

Full-time MBA: 2-year program with twelve concentrations: accounting, e-commerce, economics, finance, information technology, international management, organizational behavior, production and operations management, quantitative analysis, strategy, marketing, and entrepreneurship.

Flextime MBA: 3-year program for people working. This curriculum is the same as the full-time MBA program.

Masters in e-Commerce; Masters in Computational Finance; PhD Program.

Unique Features

Twenty-seven new electives introduced in the past three years. In the Management Game course students work with boards of directors from private industry and compete with teams around the world. The minisemester structure allows students to take more than thirty different courses. Known for graduates solidly grounded in business analysis and technology. Low student-to-faculty ratio.

On-Campus Recruiting Offerings and Advice

Offerings: Interview schedules of 30 minutes, 45 minutes, or whatever preference the employer has. All schedules are preselected by the employer. Most of what the employer needs to do concerning the schedules can be done online. There is also a Recruiting Guide outlining process, programs, and so on. Students have access to employer information twenty-four hours a day.

Pre-recruitment: At Carnegie Mellon the student clubs are very active, and many companies offer presentations and case competitions through the various clubs. Also, many companies work closely with the student groups by bringing in people to speak on significant topics. Informal preinterview dinners to get to know the candidates work well too.

Employer/Company Briefings: Students appreciate when the company knows something about the school and presents less general information about itself and more information that is specific to the work it will be doing. Company finances are often considered boring. A range of presenters from senior executives to recent MBA hires is recommended.

Interviews: Consult your interns from last summer to help identify talented and interested students. There is a strong preference for interested and interesting alumni and/or line managers. If not using alumni to interview, at least have them on hand on interview days to greet. Choose interviewers who understand the school's program.

Callbacks/Second Rounds: Timing and turnaround for letting students know the next steps and conducting follow-up interviews is important.

Student Communication: Recruiters should follow up with answers to student questions within a reasonable time. Within 24 to 48 hours is great. Maximum to follow-up is 3 to 5 days.

Top Three Dos and Don'ts

1. Do be accurate.

2. Do be timely.
3. Do have the recruiter be accessible to students.

1. Don't be tardy.
2. Don't be unfair.
3. Don't promise what you can't deliver.

Other Recruiting Options

GSIA Career Fair; treks to New York, Boston, Austin, Seattle, and Silicon Valley; case competitions sponsored by student business clubs; résumé reviews.

How to Find Out About Recruiting Options, Dates, Events, and Student Clubs

There is information for companies on GSIA's Web site under "Information for Recruiters." You can also glean information from the Recruiting Guide, or even by calling the recruiting coordinator. Club presidents' e-mail addresses are listed in the student newspaper and the career center's Web-based "Guide to Recruiting."

Key Contacts/Go-to People

Jo Bodnar, Recruiting Coordinator—Ph: (412) 268-1311; e-mail: jbodnar@andrew.cmu.edu

Kenneth Keeley, Ph.D., Director—Ph: (412) 268-3092; e-mail: kk4p@andrew.cmu.edu

Jean Eisel, Ph.D., Associate Dean, Admissions, Career Opportunities & Alumni—Ph: (412) 268-2277; e-mail: jeane@cmu.edu

School Web site: www.gsia.cmu.edu

Office Web site: www.gsia.cmu.edu/coc

Source: Jean Eisel

UNIVERSITY OF CHICAGO GRADUATE SCHOOL OF BUSINESS

Dean: Edward A. Snyder

MBA Program Overview/Mission

Founded in 1898, the University of Chicago Graduate School of Business prepares students to engineer their own success. The goal is to teach

MBAs to think and prepare for success in any business, anywhere. The approach to business education is, therefore, not trend based. Students study the fundamental disciplines of economics, statistics, and the behavioral sciences and gain analytical tools to solve business challenges that are yet unknown.

Degree Programs

Chicago GSB offers nine degree programs in North America, Europe, and Asia, seven leading to a masters of business administration degree (MBA), one program granting a doctor of philosophy degree (PhD), and joint degree programs.

> *Full-Time MBA:* 2-year MBA program at Hyde Park campus. Thirteen options for concentration include accounting, econometrics and statistics, economics, entrepreneurship and ventures, finance, analytic finance, general management, human resource management, international business, managerial and organizational behavior, marketing management, operations management, and strategic management.
>
> *Other Programs:* Evening MBA, Weekend MBA, International MBA, Executive MBA North America, Executive MBA Europe, Executive MBA Asia, PhD, joint degree programs.

Unique Features

Recognizing the maturity and intellectual curiosity of its students, the GSB allows considerable flexibility in designing an individual course of study. The curriculum enables students to build on their previous education and experience. More than half of the course credits required for graduation are electives. The GSB promotes research through numerous centers and institutes, including the Center for Research in Security Prices, James M. Kilts Center for Marketing, and the Entrepreneurship program. Chicago GSB has produced many firsts in the field of business education. It was the first business school to have a Nobel laureate on its faculty. It is the first and only business school to have had five Nobel Prize–winning faculty members. And it was first to offer an executive MBA program—in 1943—as well as the first to establish a minority relations program.

On-Campus Recruiting Offerings and Advice

Offerings: The career services staff is committed to assisting recruiters in connecting with students. All companies recruiting at the GSB are assigned an account manager. Each of the account managers is knowledgeable about a given industry, the current recruiting environment, and the campus. The account manager is the recruiter's main contact on campus and can assist with scheduling interviews and presentations.

Career services will facilitate all aspects of on-campus interviewing, including providing student résumés, advertising recruiters' visits, providing job descriptions online to students, notifying students invited to interview on recruiters' closed schedules, and scheduling the students' interview times. There are several scheduling options to choose from. On-campus interviews take place in a modern thirty-five-room interview facility at the Hyde Park campus.

Pre-Recruitment: Personalize as much as possible. Follow up with leading prospects. Use a combination of large-group and small-group events.

Employer/Company Briefings: Bring some senior alumni. Bring enough company representatives for a 5:1 recruiter-to-student ratio. Be prepared to answer questions about next steps and hiring needs. Keep presentations to a 25-minute maximum. Use only skilled presenters. Train all company representatives on answers to FAQ

Interviews: Use alumni as much as possible. Train your interviewers. Keep on schedule. Get back to students quickly.

Callbacks/Second Rounds: Offer flexible scheduling. Consider a "night before" event so that students walk into the place already knowing some people. Make sure students don't get "lost," that is, that handoffs from one interviewer to another are smooth. Assign the student a "buddy." Include senior staff on the interview team.

Student Communication: Use multiple media. Keep it short. Use breakthrough creativity. Follow up on critical communications.

Top Three Dos and Don'ts

1. Do commit to getting involved in many campus activities.
2. Do plan your strategy ahead of time.

3. Do make sure summer interns have good experiences, that is, deliver on your promise to them.

1. Don't send company representatives who cannot speak knowledgeably and enthusiastically about all of the opportunities at your company.
2. Don't try to fly in the same day for an 8:30 a.m. interview.
3. Don't leave students hanging on the outcome of interviews.

Other Recruiting Options

Throughout the year, there are numerous opportunities to showcase your company on campus through career fairs, conferences, and other student group activities. In addition, throughout the year, GSB students travel to San Francisco, Los Angeles, Houston, Denver, New York, and selected European cities for recruiting and networking activities. These trips represent additional opportunities for a company to host a student group or participate in a career fair. Career Services will work with recruiters to determine the best opportunities to meet their needs.

How to Find Out About Recruiting Options, Dates, Events, and Student Clubs

Visit the Web site or contact Career Services.

Key Contacts/Go-to People

Glenn Sykes, Director—Ph: (773) 702-7405; e-mail: glenn.sykes@ gsb.uchicago.edu

Julie Morton, Senior Associate Director—Ph: (773) 834-3591; e-mail: julie.morton@gsb.uchicago.edu

Kevin Baltz, Associate Director—Ph: (773) 702-9188; e-mail: kevin. baltz@gsb.uchicago.edu

School Web site: gsb.uchicago.edu

Source: Glenn Sykes

COLUMBIA BUSINESS SCHOOL

Dean: Meyer Feldberg, MBA 1965

MBA Program Overview/Mission

Columbia Business School, founded in 1916, builds on its unique strengths—a premier faculty, a global curriculum, and world-class resources—to prepare students to assume leadership and entrepreneurial roles in the marketplace. The broad-based, general business management curriculum, heterogeneous student body, New York City location, and active alumni network enable Columbia Business School to provide a unique learning environment. Whether through the full-time MBA, part-time Executive MBA, or the nondegree Executive Education programs, Columbia Business School educates men and women to become leaders, builders, and managers of enterprises that create value for all their stakeholders and constituencies.

Degree Programs

MBA: General business management curriculum with twelve areas of concentration: accounting; entrepreneurship; finance and economics; human resources management; international business; management; management science; media, entertainment, and communications; operations management; marketing; public and nonprofit management; and real estate. Other programs: Executive MBA program, Executive Education, PhD program.

Unique Features

Columbia Business School is known for finance and international business. The new Eugene M. Lang Center for Entrepreneurship opened in 2000. Columbia also has the Center for Japanese Economy & Business, the Chazen Institute for International Business Education, and the Center for Global Brand Leadership. The university offers the Distinguished Leader Lecture Series and Millennium Lecture Series, and features formal faculty partnerships called research alliances with financial services and high-tech companies. Noted Professor Bruce Greenwald's value investing class is one example of a course in which such alumni as Warren Buffett and Mario Gabelli participate each year.

On-Campus Recruiting Offerings and Advice

Offerings: 30- and 45-minute interviews are available, and can be flexible to address most needs.

Pre-Recruitment: Successful events for recruiters can include case studies, mock interviews, drop-in information sessions, or résumé writing slanted toward a specific sector. A company can take sign-ups for 20-minute "coffee chats" at coffee shops or do information sessions in restaurants near campus. Special dinners or programs can be offered for certain groups—women, minority clubs, international students (by region), and so on—at a variety of restaurants or in private spaces at company facilities. Avoid offering too many events. Students might feel pressured to attend all programs and feel guilty or penalized if they do not show up.

Employer/Company Briefings: Companies should target presentations specifically toward the group of students they hope to hire. Do not invite first years if there is no internship program for MBAs.

Interviews: Select individuals to interview who care about recruitment and understand the process and timetable for MBA recruitment.

Student Communication: Companies should communicate with students honestly and in a timely fashion. They should be sure calls are made or letters sent by the date and time announced or contact students to indicate the reason for any delay in following up. Feedback is appreciated, especially if an individual specifically phones to ask for suggestions to improve.

Top Three Dos and Don'ts

1. Do start on time, and avoid sign-in delays by distributing a card or sheet of paper to be returned after remarks.
2. Do come well prepared and be interesting.
3. Do target the audience invited in presenting all MBA opportunities within the company.

1. Don't send the same speaker or show the same video 2 years in a row.
2. Don't make corporate presentations if you're not hiring.
3. Don't send so many representatives of different business units and seniority levels that it's overkill.

Other Recruiting Options

There are various study tours, both domestic and international. The most popular include Silicon Valley in January and a European study tour to London in November. The Media Management Society and Internet Technology Business Group hold a career fair. "Silicon Valley Uptown" is a day-long event of panel discussions and networking. The Black Business Student Association holds a weekend conference, as does CWIB (Columbia Women in Business). These student groups generally reach out to companies for sponsorship, funding, and participation.

How to Find Out About Recruiting Options, Dates, Events, and Student Clubs

CBS Recruiters' Guide, which is published in hard copy and mailed to recruiters, is an excellent resource. It is also available on the CBS Web site. Recruiters are welcome to call staff members for information. For student clubs, listing is available via the B-School Web site, and is also distributed to recruiters by staff members whenever there are meetings to discuss recruiting strategy.

Key Contacts/Go-to People

Regina Resnick, Assistant Dean and Director, MBA Career Services—
    Ph: (212) 854-5471
School Web Site: www.columbia.edu/cu/business
Office Web Site: www.columbia.edu/cu/business/career

Source: Regina Resnick

DARTMOUTH: TUCK SCHOOL OF BUSINESS

Dean: Paul Danos

MBA Program Overview/Mission

The Tuck School of Business was founded in 1900. Tuck's mission is to provide the world's best full-time MBA program created by a faculty committed to teaching, scholarship, and thought leadership. Tuck strives to develop a sense of community; respect each individual in that community; promote diversity, inclusiveness, and integrity; create opportunities for intellectual and overall personal growth; and achieve comprehensive excellence in all its undertakings.

Degree Programs

MBA, General Management

Unique Features

A new core curriculum has been launched for the class of 2002, which focuses on developing the fundamentals of business (accounting, finance, marketing, strategy, decision analysis, etc.) and applying them to all industries in the current and future economies. There are new classes in entrepreneurship and technology and new self-designed student team projects. Also new is the Tuck General Management Forum, a year-long series of speakers and workshops that brings in real-world practitioners to apply academic learning to live examples. Recent guests include Meg Whitman, Orit Gadiesh, and John Pepper. Tuck has recently launched five new research centers: The Center for Private Equity (with offices in Hanover and Silicon Valley), The Center for Global Leadership, The Center for Digital Strategies, The Center for Asia and the Emerging Economies, and The Center for Corporate Governance.

On-Campus Recruiting Offerings and Advice

Offerings: Interview schedules of 30, 45, and 60 minutes; 100 percent open and 50 percent/50 percent open/closed schedules.

Pre-Recruitment: Be inclusive—from the very start. It's difficult to know the stars yet, so be a great host and mentor to all interested students. Club trips, by industry, to Boston, New York City, and Silicon Valley work well in preparing students. In addition to the standard company briefings, Tuck holds numerous "landing a job in _____ industry" panels.

Employer/Company Briefings: Interviewers who are early in the cycle of briefings should spend 3 minutes on the basics of the industry (especially more technical areas like sales and trading), and then focus on why and how their firm is different and best. It is also good to give some tips on interviewing well for the company.

Interviews: Maintain a "whole-company" perspective. Someone who may not be right for one group could be a strong fit in another, so make the introduction personally to the other group. The best recruiters are those who can assess candidate strength in general and then help them navigate their way into the correct position. Bring alumni to help in the interview process. Students love talking to interviewers who have experienced what they are currently going through.

Callbacks/Second Rounds: Do them as soon as possible, and do dings (rejections) at the same time as callbacks. Information travels at the speed of light at Tuck. Be flexible in scheduling second-round office visits; offering a few dates as options will minimize scheduling conflicts and maximize the opportunity of seeing lots of good candidates.

Student Communication: Be consistent, and be timely.

Top Three Dos and Don'ts

1. Do employ the personal sell with an individual mentor/champion who is well matched to a candidate's background.
2. Do give real feedback when you ding candidates.
3. Do treat this as a long-term relationship.

1. Don't be rigid about callback dates.
2. Don't interview fifty people if you are only planning to make one offer.
3. Don't forget to utilize alumni from the school, when possible.

Other Recruiting Options

The Tuck General Management Forum is a great way to get in front of students in an academic setting—through workshops, mentoring student projects, and the like. The student office and clubs (such as consulting, finance, investment, and technology) sponsor trips to Boston, New York, Silicon Valley, and elsewhere. Clubs often look for sponsorship of key events, such as Winter Carnival, the Work-Life Symposium, Soccer Tournament, and Hockey Tournament, all of which are great opportunities to support favorite events that include Tuckies and many other top schools.

How to Find Out About Recruiting Options, Dates, Events, and Student Clubs

Visit the school Web site, www.tuck.dartmouth.edu, or Tuck's specific career services site, www.tuckjobs.com. Calling the career services office or club chairs is also good. Tuck's *Recruiter Guide,* published annually and available from the Career Services office, is a good source.

Key Contacts/Go-to People

Office of Career Services: www.tuckjobs.com

Source: Erin Cochrane

DUKE: FUQUA SCHOOL OF BUSINESS

Dean: Dr. Doug Breeden

MBA Program Overview/Mission

Duke University's Fuqua School of Business prides itself on its unique approach to the business of management education and research. The school has actively embraced innovation in its programs, from the design of the world's first Global Executive MBA to the adoption of new methods and technologies for creating a richer and more rewarding educational experience. The curricula of Fuqua's programs are designed by faculty who rank among the world's leading experts in their fields, but who also have embraced an integrative approach to learning. These programs offer a well-rounded education in management, blending practical know-how, critical thinking, communication skills, and a strategic, global perspective. Fuqua has created an overall academic program and school culture designed to help people operate as part of an international network of individuals managing change on a daily basis.

Degree Programs

Full-time MBA program with general management emphasis. The only formal concentration is Health Sector Management.

Additional programs include the Global Executive MBA program,

Weekend Executive MBA program, Cross Continent MBA program, PhD program, and Short-Term Executive Education programs.

Unique Features

The school is known for its "Team Fuqua," a culture strongly driven by teamwork, collaboration, and student initiative. Recent innovations in technology and distance learning and two executive MBA programs that rely heavily on Internet-mediated learning. Has recently spun off the Duke Corporate Education program as a standalone, full-service provider of customized, enterprisewide management education. The Center for Customer Relationship Management (CRM), with sponsorship from NCR, is another recent addition.

On-Campus Recruiting Offerings and Advice

Offerings: Interview schedules of 30, 45, or 60 minutes; also offered are rotating or back-to-back interviews. Both 100 percent open interviews or 50 percent closed/50 percent open interviews.

Pre-Recruitment: Activities during first-year orientation provide great early and informal exposure. Activities during student campout weekend for Duke basketball tickets are informal and personalized, a very "Duke" opportunity, with high visibility.

Presentations of business cases (either in classroom or as standalone activities) allow students to learn more about a company's business and new initiatives.

Employer/Company Briefings: Bring people from a variety of levels and business units within the company. Have at least one senior representative to present charismatic vision of the company's future and how MBAs fit into that future. Keep presentations brief; focus more on Q&A and interaction. Bring a Fuqua alumni to discuss cultural fit between the two organizations and what Fuqua teaches that allows a student to be successful in the company's environment. When doing other pre-recruitment activities, the most important things are to make sure (1) that the activities chosen are in alignment with the type of message the company wants to send out about its culture, opportunities, and people; and (2) that the people who represent the company at these activities reflect how the company wants to be viewed.

Interviews: Make sure *all* interviewers have a clear picture of what questions they should be asking and what they should be looking for, and have received some basic instruction in what's legal and appropriate in the interviewing process. Some companies have had huge discrepancies in interviewer behavior, even among those screening candidates for the same position. As a result, students began to view the interviewer as a factor in whether or not they were advanced through the process. Talk to graduates and interns. They can be a very valuable source of information in helping to select an appropriate recruiting team. Make sure there's a general sense of buy-in from any selected recruiter that MBA recruiting in general, and recruiting at Fuqua specifically, is of value. If the recruiter has a negative attitude about MBAs or a specific school, that will likely come out during interactions with students.

Callbacks/Second Rounds: Have a clear agenda and share it prior to the callback so that students know what will be expected of them. Provide opportunities for students to meet people within a variety of business units and levels of seniority so that they receive a broad understanding of the company and its culture. Follow up very promptly. Provide opportunities to get to know the city and surrounding geographic area, especially for full-time hires. Location is a critical factor in the decision-making process.

Student Communication: Keep it short and to the point. Students are always on information overload. Mailbox stuffing does not work at Fuqua. E-mail or electronic b-board is usually best. Try to personalize communications when appropriate.

Top Three Dos and Don'ts

1. Do be clear and consistent.
2. Do personalize and build relationships.
3. Do build presence and show commitment.

1. Don't forget to follow up.
2. Don't send uninterested, uninformed recruiters.

3. Don't be rigid or inflexible.

Other Recruiting Options

Corporate Partner Career Fair, September 21, 2001
Career Fair, October 3, 2001
High Tech and Growth Company Recruiting, March 2002

On a less formal level, there are many more events, club-sponsored and otherwise. Each club does a half-day symposium addressing relevant, career-related topics in the early fall. Fuqua Fridays are informal "happy hours" after the conclusion of classes on Friday. Some have structured activities, others are come and go, but corporations can sponsor a Friday event. The MBA Games are held annually in April. This event is a major fundraiser for NC Special Olympics. Teams composed of MBA students from across the country "compete" in team and individual events. Week-in-cities trips are held over both fall break and holiday break and generally include trips to New York, Boston, Washington, D.C., Atlanta, San Francisco, Los Angeles, Seattle, and Denver.

How to Find Out About Recruiting Options, Dates, Events, and Student Clubs List

Dates and details about options and events are included in the *Recruiters' Guide,* which is distributed in late June with the placement report, and available on the Web site, or may be discussed in meetings or phone conferences between company representatives and CSO staff. Attend Recruiters' Day. Meet with their account manager or other Career Services Office (CSO) staff. Student club contacts for each year are also identified in the *Recruiters' Guide.*

Key Contacts/Go-to People

Sheryle Dirks, Director—Ph: (919) 660-7813: e-mail: sheryle.dirks @duke.edu
Career Services Information Desk—Ph: (919) 660-7810; e-mail: csoinfo @fuqua.duke.edu

School Web site: www.fuqua.duke.edu

Source: Sheryle Dirks

HARVARD BUSINESS SCHOOL

Dean: Kim B. Clark

MBA Program Overview/Mission

Harvard Business School's mission is to develop outstanding business leaders who will contribute to the well-being of society. The general management education offered at HBS is a transforming, developmental experience that stimulates intellectual and personal growth by building deep, practical knowledge and fostering sound judgment. Located on a thirty-acre campus in Boston, it is a residential MBA program. The hallmark of the learning model is the case method, pioneered at HBS. Students learn how to exercise judgment, make decisions, and take responsibility. It's committed to being the leader in the use of information technology (IT) in business education and works to create an unparalleled environment for learning and growth. Much of the research and course development at HBS is also used by academic institutions and organizations worldwide. Faculty research is close to practice and field-based, and the school has research centers in Latin America, the Asia-Pacific region, and one to be opened in Europe in 2001.

Degree Programs

Full-time MBA program
MBA/JD Program, DBA, PhD program, Executive Education

Other Recruiting Options

Manufacturing and Technology Management Club
High Tech and New Media Club
Marketing Club Career Fair
The Finance Club Career Fair
The Management Consulting Club Career Fair
Entrepreneurship Conference

Europe Business Conference
Women's Student Association Conference
Venture Capital and Principal Investment Club Conference
Asia Business Conference
Cyberposium 2001
Africa Business Club Conference
Latin American Business Conference

TREKS

WesTrek, Bay Area, CA
EuroTrek, several European locations
Hollywood Trek, Los Angeles, CA
Denver Trek, Denver, CO
Boston Trek, Boston, MA
Austin Trek, Austin, TX
D.C. Trek, Washington, D.C.
Seattle Trek, Seattle, WA
Asia Trek, several Asian cities
Maine Trek, Portland, ME
New York Trek, New York, NY

Key Contacts/Go-to People

MBA Career Services—Ph: (617) 495-6232; fax: (617) 495-8947;
e-mail: mbacs@hbs.edu; Web site: www.hbs.edu/career_services/; mailing address: MBA Career Services
Harvard Business School
Soldiers Field
Boston, MA 02163
School Web site: www.hbs.edu

HAUTES ÉTUDES COMMERCIALES (HEC): INSTITUT SUPÉRIEUR DES AFFAIRES (ISA)

Dean: Bernard Ramanantsoa
Associate Dean, MBA Program, Jean-Paul Mournier

MBA Program Overview/Mission

The mission of the HEC MBA (ISA) Program is to prepare highly ambitious individuals for careers as future leaders competing in the international arena. The MBA program provides management education to students who have leadership potential, a strong educational background, and a maturity of experience that will enable them to become successful leaders. A successful manager in a global company should have a number of crucial qualities: an integrative management style, good communication skills, exposure to cross-cultural experiences, the ability to make decisions, and the capability to adapt to different situations. HEC's admissions process and teaching methods are built around these qualities.

Degree Programs

Full-time MBA program of 16 months' duration, two classes per year
Executive MBA TRIUM has just been launched with the London School of Economics and Stern University in New York.

Unique Features

The MBA embodies HEC School of Management's mission statement: *Local roots, global reach.* The program curriculum is entirely bilingual. The teaching offers a truly international perspective. Students come from more than thirty countries. Participants can personalize their curricula since the program duration is 16 months. Graduation rate of 160 graduates per year, split into two classes, is considered optimal, and it fosters a true class spirit and community ethic. Graduates become part of one of the most influential alumni networks in the world—21,000 people in forty-two different countries.

ON-CAMPUS RECRUITING OFFERINGS AND ADVICE

Offerings: HEC offers a customized service to companies with a range of interview schedules. The most popular interview slot is 45 minutes. Companies generally preselect candidates for interview using the profile book (résumés), but they are strongly encouraged to leave a number of open slots for candidates who are keen to interview with them.

Pre-Recruitment: The careers office should be the recruiter's first point of contact. Recruiters will be advised on how and when to make their impression. Since campus visibility is highly important, sponsoring sports events, purchasing publicity space in publications, and inviting students to events (dinner, competition, film, industrial site, brainstorm weekend) are good options to consider.

Employer/Company Benefits: Companies are encouraged to come on campus to make recruitment presentations. Remarks in the presentations should be no longer than 30 minutes and should be lively, dynamic, and as original as possible. It is essential that the speakers be from top-level management and masters of the subject they address. The presence of recent and less recent alumni is also crucial. The remaining 30 minutes can be used for Q & A. Some companies choose the latest evening slot so that they can host a cocktail afterward to encourage informal exchange.

Interviews: There should be a minimum of 2 weeks between the company briefing and interviews. This enables students to prepare fully. Companies are encouraged to be up front about their expectations and the format the interview will take. The names and functions of the interviewers should be communicated to the careers office in good time.

Callbacks/Second Rounds: Give a time frame within which you will follow up with candidates and stick to it. Verbal offers should be followed quickly by written confirmation. Be prepared to give feedback to rejected candidates.

Student Communication: Always go through the careers office—ask for advice on your marketing message. Develop a coherent approach for all campus communications.

Top Three Dos and Don'ts

1. Do offer well-paid summer internships.
2. Do be bluntly honest with students.
3. Do give specific information about job opportunities.

1. Don't be vague about career opportunities.
2. Don't bring speakers who are ill prepared for their presentations.
3. Don't give contradictory information on the selection process.

Other Recruiting Options

Among the major events coming up are:

Consulting Forum: October 25, 2001 (Twenty-five companies represented)

International Finance Forum: November 8, 2001 (Twenty-five leading investment banks)

International Career Fair: January 29 and 30, 2002 (140 companies representing all sectors)

In addition, recruiters can participate in information sessions on specific functions, career orientation afternoons with alumni, conferences on recruitment issues, mock interviews, and student-led events (marketing awards, luxury goods, etc.). There are also opportunities to provide support to student interest groups (e.g., third-generation Telecom, consulting club, legal and fiscal associations), use the e-mail forwarding service, buy publicity space in the profile book, and sponsor specific projects (e.g., Web site creation, the career information center).

Companies that make substantial financial donations on a regular basis are sometimes offered the opportunity of intervening in the classroom in connection with an academic course.

How to Find Out About Recruiting Options, Dates, Events, and Student Clubs

Make contact with the careers office. Ask that the profile book and recruitment calendar be sent to you. The careers office will give you the appropriate contact details for the presidents of student clubs.

Key Contacts/Go-to People

CAREERS DEVELOPMENT OFFICE

Helen Farrow, Director—e-mail: farrow@hec.fr
Clare Gaffney, International Development—e-mail: gaffney@hec.fr

Claudine Guimaraes, Corporate Relations—e-mail: guimaraes@hec.fr
Valerie Leroy, Careers Information Center—e-mail: leroyv@hec.fr
School Web site: www.hec.fr
Office Web site: www.HEC.FR/hec/eng/groupe/orientation/index.html

Source: Helen Farrow

INDIANA: KELLEY

Dean: Dan Dalton

MBA Program Overview/Mission

Employers praise Kelley MBAs as self-determined, hard-working business leaders. And Kelley is particularly well known for its focus on teamwork.
Ranked third in teaching by *Business Week,* Kelley is characterized by a high
degree of student access to faculty. The school has a number of academies
to support career interests: Telecom Academy, Sports & Entertainment
Academy, Investment Banking Academy, Investment Management Acad-
emy, Retail & Consumer Marketing Academy, Healthcare Academy, Entrepreneurship Academy, Consulting Academy, Global Experience Academy.
The programs in marketing, finance, and general management are nationally
ranked.

Kelley has also recently initiated the "problem based," integrated core
curriculum for first-year students. The school offers many distinct student
leadership opportunities. There is a favorable academic fee structure, even
for out-of-state students. A new MBA home, the Corporate & Graduate
Center, is scheduled to open in Fall 2002.

Degree Programs

MBA Full-Time Program. This is the residential program at Blooming-
ton. It is a 2-year, full-time, fifty-four-credit-hour program with
concentrations in finance, marketing, management, production/
operations, international business, entrepreneurship, information systems, business economics and public policy, strategic management

consulting, strategic human resources management, and design-a-major.

Other Programs: MBA Evening, MBA in Accounting, Master of Professional Accountancy (MPA), Master of Science in Information Systems (MSIS), PhD/DBA, Executive, Kelley Direct.

On-Campus Recruiting Offerings and Advice

Offerings: 30, 45, and 60 minutes. No requirement to have 50 percent open/50 percent closed.

Pre-Recruitment: Get involved with faculty and clubs to improve yield from the program.

Employer/Company Briefings: Corporate presentations are September 11–December 8 and January 9–31.

Guidelines: No presentations scheduled before 5:30 p.m.

Keep presentations to 1½ hours in length.

Formal presentation of 15 to 20 minutes.

Allow a minimum of 20 minutes for Q & A.

Allow 30 or more minutes for networking.

Consider alternative venues besides presentation (dinners, receptions, etc.).

Consider students' time commitment when scheduling events.

Interviews: Use the preference schedule to preselect students who are a good fit for your organization. Select representatives who will represent the organization with a passion. They do not have to be alumni.

Communication with Students: The best way to communicate with students is by e-mail.

Top Three Dos and Don'ts

1. Do establish a presence on campus with faculty, clubs, career services, and academies. Designated school recruiting teams work well.
2. Do communicate with students promptly after on-campus interviews.
3. Do be considerate of the MBA's time and keep presentations within a 1½ hour time frame.

1. Don't mix undergraduate events with graduate events.

2. Don't hold excessively long, formal presentations.
3. Don't offer noncompetitive compensation programs.

Other Recruiting Options

MBA Roundtables: Ninety-plus recruiting companies welcome students to campus and provide a networking opportunity before classes start.

Business Seminar: This is a student-driven event sponsored by the Marketing Network Club and the Finance Guild. Companies participate in a 1-day program for first-year MBAs.

Kelley Forums in major metro markets.

TREKS

The Consulting Academy makes annual trips to Chicago and Cleveland to visit consulting firms. Approximately fifty to seventy-five students participate.

The Retail & Consumer Marketing Academy makes an annual trip to metropolitan areas to visit retail and consumer marketing firms in the Chicago area.

The Investment Management and Investment Banking academies make trips to New York and Chicago annually to visit I-banking and I-management firms.

The Telecommunications Academy and e-Business Club are two new organizations. They plan trips to Dallas and the Bay Area.

Job postings, résumé books, video conferencing, invitations to students to home office visits, and participation in career development workshops are some other opportunities for recruiters.

Key Contacts/Go-to People

Director, Dick McCracken—e-mail: dmccrack@indiana.edu

Associate Director, Susie Clarke, Career Development—e-mail: eclarke @indiana.edu

Associate Director, Allyn Curry, Corporate Relations—e-mail: curry @indiana.edu

Source: Dick McCracken

INSTITUTO DES ESTUDIOS SUPERIORES DE LA EMPRESA (IESE)

Dean: Carlos Cavallé

MBA Program Overview/Mission

IESE Business School, the graduate school of management of the University of Navarra, is located in Barcelona and Madrid. It offers the MBA, Global Executive MBA, Executive MBA, and PhD in Management degrees, as well as a wide range of executive education programs for global senior executives and continuing education programs for alumni. Some 20,000 graduates of IESE programs work for major corporations and new business ventures in more than seventy countries.

Providing action-oriented learning opportunities tailored to the personal needs of all program participants and designed to bring them to new levels of professional achievement.

Developing new ideas for the global business community based on a solid platform of research.

Placing people and the development of society at the heart of managerial decision-making.

Degree Programs

Master of Business Administration (MBA)
Executive MBA
Global Executive MBA
Ph.D. in Management

Unique Features

A general management program, the IESE MBA develops sound business judgment, leadership qualities, and the ability to work effectively in character and content. It offers dynamic, student-centered learning opportunities keyed to the latest developments on the global business scene. The program places strong emphasis on e-business, entrepreneurship, and communication skills. Other unique features include the option of doing the

MBA program in English or Spanish; a personalized education in which the student is the focal point of the MBA program; and a student/teacher ratio that gives students frequent access to professors, a key factor in making the IESE MBA such a rich learning experience.

The IESE faculty consists of seventy-three full-time, thirty-eight part-time, and eleven visiting professors.

During the first semester of their second year, students also have the option of participating in the International Exchange Program at leading business schools in the United States, Europe, and Asia. Admission to the program is on a competitive basis.

On-Campus Recruiting Offerings and Advice

Offerings: IESE's annual MBA Career Forum and European E-Business Forum are two key sources of job offers for students.

MBA Career Forum: IESE was the first European business school to hold an MBA fair that combined company presentations with interviews in a two-day format. It was held early in the recruiting season in October. The fifty participating companies carried out 1300 interviews in two days. They responded very well to a format that offered them one-stop shopping. Instead of making two trips to Barcelona—one to present, the other to interview—they were able to accomplish both things in one trip. Moreover, combining interviews and presentations made the scheduling of companies recruiting later, outside of the Career Forum, a lot easier and reduced the pressures occasioned by limited space. The reformed process was a big hit with both recruiters and students.

E-Business Forum: IESE's annual E-Business Forum involves a conference conducted by a number of movers and shakers *from* the world of e-business and venture capital representing the "hot centers" of new business development. Representatives of the same kinds of companies are in the audience along with students. The company representatives stay on an extra day to meet MBAs and discuss job opportunities with them. Many companies have ended up making offers to students through this event.

Pre-Recruitment: Posters and flyers provide more of the feel of an "event." Summer cocktail receptions are effective, as well as off-campus dinners and receptions.

Employer/Company Briefings: Briefings on substantive business and economic issues relating to a company's work have more impact than briefings focusing on career path and opportunities. Substantive briefings give companies the chance to show that they are involved with cutting-edge issues of relevance to the real world and thus attract interest on the part of MBAs.

Interviews: IESE is flexible and offers all types of interview schedules, depending on company requirements. There is no bidding system. Interviewers should hold to the schedule. When interviews run over on time, there is a domino effect which disrupts the schedules of students waiting to be interviewed. This creates the impression of disorganization. Interviewers should always come from the department or division of the company that is doing the hiring. In interviewing at international business schools for hires from a number of countries, it helps if the interview team is made up of diverse nationalities.

Student Communication: e-mail works best.

Top Three Dos and Don'ts

1. Do provide company briefing as early as possible in the season, while interest is still high.
2. Communicate quickly with the students.
3. Give the exact dates on which results will be known.

1. Don't do a big presentation and then let the recruitment process drag on.
2. Don't hesitate to say no or send a rejection letter.
3. Don't appear disorganized when it comes to following up on applications.

Other Recruiting Options

MBA Career Forum; E-Business Forum; with the E-Business club; various conferences set up through direct contact with student clubs.

How to Find Out About Recruiting Options, Dates, Events, and Student Clubs

MBA Career Forum information can be found under the company information on the IESE Web site or through MBA Career Services. Or review the Web site, recruiters' guide, or e-mail, call, or fax Career Services. Also, student club information and contacts can be found on the IESE Web site.

Key Contacts/Go-to People

Mireia Rius, Director of MBA Career Services—e-mail: rius@iese.edu
School Web site—www.iese.edu
Office Web site—www.iese.edu/companies/index.html

Source: Anthony Salvia

INSEAD

Dean: Gabriel Hawawini

MBA Program Overview/Mission

The first business school to pioneer a one-year MBA program, and the first to open a campus in Asia, INSEAD has prepared outstanding individuals for leadership of the top-ranked schools for more than 40 years. The principal objective of the INSEAD MBA is to provide a solid foundation for a future career in general management in a constantly changing global business environment. With campuses on two continents and the possibility to spend some time studying on both, INSEAD is widely recognized as the world's most international business school. Its participants represent more than fifty different nationalities, and faculty originates from almost thirty countries. At INSEAD equal emphasis is placed on both teaching and research, ensuring that through their research efforts and their close links to business, faculty provide the most relevant and up-to-date information in the classroom.

Degree Programs

Full-time MBA program (General Management): 1-year program for high-potential young professionals aiming at an international business career.
PhD program

Unique Features

INSEAD's uniqueness lies in the diversity of its faculty and students: Africa/Middle East (9.5 percent); Asia/Asia Pacific (17 percent); Benelux (7 percent); Central/Eastern Europe (8 percent); France (9.5 percent); Germany (5 percent); Latin America (6 percent); Nordic countries (5 percent); North America (8 percent); southern Europe (14 percent); rest of Europe (2 percent); United Kingdom (9 percent).

On-Campus Recruiting Offerings and Advice

In 2000, 183 companies recruited at INSEAD, many of them participating in both the Spring and Autumn recruitment campaigns. More than 800 company executives conducted over 8500 interviews on campus. Companies ordered the profile books for on-campus recruitment as well as for direct contact.

The Career Management Service (CMS) at INSEAD provides advice and assistance to companies wishing to recruit INSEAD's MBA participants. CMS organizes its recruitment campaigns as follows:

Autumn: December graduates for full-time positions.

Spring: July graduates for full-time positions; December graduates for summer internships. The On-Campus Recruitment (OCR) is an integral part of CMS activities. Regular on-campus recruiters receive advance notification of the next recruitment calendar in a special mailing. A typical recruitment visit involves a one-hour presentation, followed by a series of individual interviews arranged with a Web-based scheduling system. The use of amphitheaters and equipment is free of charge. All recruitment events are published via Intranet and posters on campus. Often the companies choose to offer a cocktail reception after their presentation, which can be organized by an on- or off-campus caterer.

Apart from OCR, recruiters can purchase the profile book of each promotion, which contains the CV of each participant available for employment (also available on the Internet, with a specific research system for candidates). There is also a Web-based posting system for job descriptions that the students consult regularly.

Pre-Recruitment Activities: Establish and maintain a broad relationship with school.

Employer/Company Briefings: Mix of high-level speakers, alumni, and HR.

Other Recruiting Options

With the increasing number of companies competing for limited presentation slots, CMS offers Career Days in each recruitment campaign. Companies can also participate in special events, such as the Career Context Conferences that are organized by students and supported by the Career Management Service.

Key Contacts/Go-to People

Diane Yelland, Manager, On-Campus Recruitment—Ph: +33.1.60. 72.45.06/42.40
Career Management Service—Ph: +33.1.60.72.42.24 (general)
School Web site: www.insead.edu

Source: Mary Boss

LONDON BUSINESS SCHOOL

Dean: John Quelch

MBA Program Overview/Mission

London Business School is as international as the individuals and businesses it serves. Its faculty and staff, who come from all six continents, reflect the internationalism of program participants and corporate clients. The school is located next to beautiful Regent's Park and combines excellent communications, access to the City of London and London's international airports, and an infrastructure that offers the latest technology. The school is working with Los Angeles–based Quisic to create six online courses, and with Sun Microsystems to create a virtual learning network. The school has access to over thirty data sources on company and financial information. LBS has also developed an intranet. An advanced computing facility is being built to support the school's activities in e-business, e-commerce, and Internet teaching. An extensive, enterprisewide network and server infrastructure has also been commissioned. Taunton Place, a £12 million building housing the school's information and IT facilities and a fully equipped sports complex, completes the well-balanced learning and recreational environment LBS offers its students.

The MBA comprises a highly international class—80 percent from outside the United Kingdom, from more than fifty countries—and offers a lively and cooperative atmosphere with considerable emphasis on teamwork. The 21-month program includes fifteen core courses in the first year and more than eighty electives, allowing breadth and depth of study.* Emphasis is placed on projects and out-of-classroom learning, including the shadowing project and a major paid second-year project. Students are given the opportunity to learn a language. A key to the MBA is continuous innovation in curriculum and support services, examples of which are the Leadership Days (such as Becoming a Socially Responsible Leader) and the new Career Management Center, which features a resource center, recruiters' center, and dedicated interview rooms.

Programs/Degrees Offered

Full-Time MBA: A top international MBA of 21 months offering a full range of general management courses with opportunities for personal specialization in key areas and including a language program. Attracts outstanding young professionals (aged between twenty-four and thirty-five) from over fifty countries.

MS Management (Sloan Program), Masters in Finance, Executive MBA (EMBA), EMBAGlobal, PhD program, Executive Education.

Unique Features:

The MBA program has a number of special features, including:

Extensive language program: French, German, Spanish, Japanese, and Mandarin Chinese are taught as part of the elective portfolio, and all students graduate with at least two languages.

*www.lbs.ac.uk/mba/about_the_mba/course_structure_mba/electives/electives.html

The first-year "shadowing" project, in which students shadow, or observe, a manager for a week.

An extensive range of electives in e-business produced by faculty who have researched the area for several years. An established program of support for entrepreneurship, including a range of electives, a venture capital fund which invests in student and alumni ideas, and support through serviced office accommodation close to London Business School—all supported by a group of strategic partners from banking, consulting, and industry. A world-renowned range of finance electives, including field trips to New York and London.

International exchange with thirty-two top schools.

The MBA Program Office at London Business School boasts a rigorous admissions process. This includes all entering MBA students having benefited from a face-to-face interview with a member of the MBA alumni community. The conversion rate of offers to accepts has improved year-to-year, and is typically around 70 percent.

On-Campus Recruiting Offerings and Advice

LBS runs a full on-campus recruiting facility for all companies that recruit at the school, with a dedicated staff to manage the whole process. A dedicated recruiter's lounge and fourteen interview rooms are available in a dedicated suite. There are no "open/closed" interview schedules or bidding systems at LBS.

A recruiter's briefing event's held in July of each year to update top recruiters on the year and let them know trends and concerns and give them feedback. Briefings and updates on a recruiting issue can also be done by bringing in "experts." For example, there have been sessions on employment law, cultural awareness issues, and interview techniques.

Employer/Company Briefing: LBS provides advice to each company on the best way to market itself to students. Companies should contact the school for help and guidance.

Pre-Recruitment Activities: Engage early with the CMC, which can assist in pre-recruitment. Inviting students to company premises for a familiarization visit is a successful technique. Invitations to discuss opportunities and issues over dinner is another.

Interviews: Make contact with the CMC as early as possible for advice and scheduled slots. When selecting interviewers, using school alumni is really important.

Communication with Students: If at all possible, always channel communication through the CMC.

Top Three Dos and Don'ts

1. Do deal with students professionally throughout the recruitment process.
2. Do honor commitments made at presentations.
3. Do provide feedback as and when required.

1. Don't pressure students to make early decisions on offers.
2. Don't raise expectations and then fail to deliver.
3. Don't ignore student communications.

Other Recruiting Options

LBS has a very active group of student clubs that help CMC in hosting companies and giving them opportunities to network with students. The school offers two treks each year, one to Silicon Valley (the Eclub and the Industry Club hold a trek to the United States in the autumn). In addition, there is an annual careers fair each November, and the student clubs hold their own networking evenings. All these are coordinated through the CMC.

How to Find Out About Recruiting Options, Dates, Events, and Student Clubs

Make contact with the CMC and speak with June O'Connor (JO' Connor@london.edu). The best way to contact a student club is also through the CMC.

Key Contacts/Go-to People

June O'Connor—Ph: +44 (0) 20 7706 6764; e-mail: JO'Connor@ london.edu

School Web site: www.london.edu

Source: Chris Bristow

UNIVERSITY OF MICHIGAN

Dean: B. Joseph White

MBA Program Overview/Mission

The University of Michigan Business School has become known for its unendingly innovative attitude and for producing a unique breed of creative, results-producing MBAs who are truly able to lead. Essentially, Michigan has set a new benchmark by blending the full-range intellectual prowess of a top research university with a richly diverse program and the remarkably human-scale but intensive hands-on development of the skills and abilities that make things happen. The school has also earned consistently high marks for its global orientation, development in specialty areas, commitment to corporate citizenship, and emphasis on leadership opportunities for minorities and women.

Degree Programs

Masters Program: A 2-year, full-time program which can boast nearly twenty dual degree programs with other schools at the University of Michigan, including engineering, law, and the School of Natural Resources.

Other Programs: Variable length part-time MBAs, PhD program, Executive MBA, "Global" MBA.

Unique Features

Multidisciplinary Action Plan (MAP): More than 10 years after its introduction, MAP remains the most in-depth and effective method of teaching MBA students how to deliver results in a real-world, real-time business project executed for corporate partners under faculty guidance. Ongoing innovation in the program keeps it ahead of the pack.

MAP is part of the required core curriculum for MBAs. The MAP model is also used globally, offering students elective opportunities for in-country and highly demanding project work throughout the world. In addition, UMBS is home to a number of world-leading institutes:

The William Davidson Institute, headquartered at UMBS, is a center for emerging market expertise. The institute reflects Michigan's signature blend of rigorous research and hands-on, in-company learning and development. It is also the hub of an international network of scholars. It evolves and makes an impact through ongoing assistance to companies and institutions in emerging markets.

The ZellLurie Institute for Entrepreneurial Studies is a leading center of expertise on entrepreneurship. Its programs, too, reflect the Michigan signature style of blending the academic and the practical, intensifying the developmental impact on MBAs. The institute, for instance, operates a school-run venture capital fund, a business incubator, and funds entrepreneurial internships for students.

The Tauber Manufacturing Institute was established to meet industry's need for business leaders who can blend engineering and business knowledge and ability. This institute is a joint venture between the business school and the University of Michigan College of Engineering, blending the expertise of both areas. Like the others, Tauber Institute reflects Michigan's signature approach to development by including intensive in-company team and leadership development project work in its degree programs.

On-Campus Recruiting Offerings and Advice

Recruitment guidance and Web advice is available at www.bus.umich.edu/companies/ocd/index.html. Baseline involvement includes a corporate presentation or career fair, club sponsorship, faculty support, internship interviews, MAP proposal submission, and personal knowledge of targeted students.

Other Recruiting Options

West Coast Recruitment Forum
Wall Street Recruitment Forum

International project sponsorship
Off-campus postings

Key Contacts/Go-to People

Allan Cotrone, Director, Office of Career Development—e-mail:
Acotrone@umich.edu
Ph: (734) 647-4920

Source: Allan Cotrone

MIT—SLOAN

Dean: Richard L. Schmalensee

MBA Program Overview/Mission

Sloan's mission is to be the leading academic source of innovation in
management theory and practice. Its top-ranked academic programs draw
some of the finest students from around the world, people who see technology not just as the basis for new products, services, processes, and industries,
but as a major component in operational and strategic decisions. Sloan is
committed to educating professionals who have the will to lead and to risk
and to deal with complex systems, because today, nearly every business is a
high-tech business.

Degree Programs

Master's Program: A 2-year program whose curriculum integrates the
latest developments in management theory and practice.
Other Programs: Leaders for Manufacturing Program, Management of
Technology Program, Alfred P. Sloan Fellows Program, PhD program, System Design and Management Program.

Unique Features

Sloan pioneered the concept of "management tracks." Beginning in the
second semester and continuing through graduation, students affiliate with
one of eight management tracks. These tracks give students a blend of aca-

demic disciplines and business functions related to a specific career. Students complete course work, participate in professional development activities, and complete a ProSeminar. The ProSeminar, a cornerstone for each track, is a forum that brings students, faculty, and business leaders together to discuss and work on current industry issues. The eight tracks include eBusiness, Financial Engineering, Financial Management, Information Technology and Business Transformation, Manufacturing and Operations, New Product and Venture Development, Strategic Managment and Consulting, and the self-managed track.

On-Campus Recruiting Offerings and Advice

Offerings: A recruiting schedule typically offers twelve 30-minute or nine 45-minute interviews per job position. Interviews normally begin at 9:00 a.m. and end at 4:30 p.m. Sloan CDO can offer up to three interview schedules per job position. CDO offers both open and closed interview schedules. If a company reserves more than one closed schedule per position, then at least one schedule has to be an open schedule. Each company can have a total of six interview schedules on campus per recruiting cycle (fall second year, winter first year, and winter second year). This can be broken down in a variety of ways.

Pre-Recruitment: Company involvement in preinterview preparation and career-related activities, such as case interviews and a Career Options Day. Have a dedicated alumnus as the liaison for the school.

Employer/Company Briefings: Be concise and well prepared. Set clear time lines for résumés and recruiting.

Interviews: Have an alumnus help students prepare for the interview. The interviewer should reflect the culture of the company.

Callbacks/Second Rounds: Clearly communicate the process to the student.

Student Communication: Be concise with all communications. Have fewer contacts for students to create less confusion.

Top Three Dos and Don'ts

1. Do provide good customer service.
2. Do be flexible.
3. Do cultivate a nonelitist attitude.

1. Don't be inflexible.
2. Don't view recruiting as mostly operations.
3. Don't be unwilling to go the extra mile for the students.

Other Recruiting Options

Student-run treks, company visits, and charitable events.

How to Find Out About Recruiting Options, Dates, Events, and Student Clubs List

CDO, student clubs, Web site, Recruiter's Guide. The Recruiter's Guide has all the e-mail addresses for the student clubs.

Key Contacts/Go-to People

Jacqueline Wilbur, Director of MBA Career Development Office
Susan Kline, Associate Director, Recruiting Services
Tricia Martin, Recruiting Coordinator, Career Development Office
School Web site: mitsloan.mit.edu
Office Web site: mitsloan.mit.edu/cdo

Source: Jacqueline Wilbur

NYU—LEONARD N. STERN SCHOOL OF BUSINESS

Dean: George Daly

MBA Program Overview/Mission

The Stern School of Business seeks to play a leading role in the development of ideas that shape the worlds of business and management, and to deliver the highest quality education on the forefront of management thought and practice to a large and diverse group of students as well as to practicing executives. It is also committed to maintaining an enduring, mutually enriching, and intellectually stimulating relationship with its distinguished alumni and with the community of leading management practitioners around the world.

Degree Programs

Master's Program: 2-year full-time MBA with eight specializations: accounting, economics, finance, information systems, management and organizational behavior, marketing, operations management, and statistics and operations research.

Other Programs: PhD program, part-time MBA program (The Langone Program), Executive MBA, Trium MBA, Executive Education.

Unique Features

Although known for its strong finance program, which includes one of the largest and most distinguished faculties in the world, the Stern academic program offers a rich menu of opportunities to broaden and deepen your business knowledge. More than 160 courses are offered within the Stern curriculum. Business related courses are also offered at other schools, such as the Robert F. Wagner Graduate School of Public Service, the School of Law, the School of Education, and the Real Estate Institute. There are program initiatives in Digital Economy, Entertainment, Media, and Technology, Law and Business, Quantitative Finance, Real Estate Finance.

On-Campus Recruiting Offerings and Advice

Offerings: Interview schedules of 30 and 45 minutes; 75 percent closed/invite and 25 percent open schedules.

Pre-Recruitment: Go through the Office of Career Development; work with student clubs. On-site (a day in the life) visits and social events in New York City have proven effective for companies.

Employer/Company Briefings: Schedule a conference meeting with the Office of Career Development staff for specific and customized advice.

Interviews: Use recruiting team and alumni.

Callbacks/Second Rounds: Work with the Office of Career Development.

Student Communication: E-mail, phone, Office of Career Development.

Top Three Dos and Don'ts

1. Do cultivate student interaction (multiple visits on campus).

2. Do work with student clubs.
3. Do use alumni.

1. Don't use pressured (exploding) offers.
2. Don't limit schedules.
3. Don't forget to work with the Office of Career Development.

Other Recruiting Options

Among the student groups and events recruiters should know about are Technology and New Media Group (TANG) West Coast Tour and European Tour, Media and Entertainment Association (MEA) West Coast Tour; student conferences, Latin American Business Association, Association of Hispanic and Black Business Students (AHBSS), Graduate Finance Association (GFA), Stern Women in Business (SWIB), Asian Business Society (ABS), Entrepreneur's Exchange (EE), and Emerging Markets Association.

How to Find Out About Recruiting Options, Dates, Events, and Student Clubs

Contact the Office of Career Development.

Key Contacts/Go-to People

Gary Fraser, Assistant Dean—Ph: (212) 998-0623
School Web site: www.stern.nyu.edu
Office Web site: www.stern.nyu.edu/ocd

Source: Gary Fraser

NORTHWESTERN—THE KELLOGG SCHOOL OF MANAGEMENT

Dean: DiPak Jain

Degree Programs

Master's Program: Full-time 2-year MBA program with majors in accounting, technology and e-commerce, entrepreneurship and innovation, finance, health industry management, human resources management, international business, management and organizations, management and strategy, economics, marketing, operations management, media management, public/nonprofit management, real estate, and transportation.

Full-time 1-year MBA program, with majors in the same areas as above.

Full-time 2-year joint MBA degrees with engineering (Master of Management in Manufacturing) and law (JD/MBA).

Other Programs: PhD program, Manager's Program, Executive Master's.

Unique Features

Kellogg's primary strength is the ability to quickly make changes to curricula. They are continually reviewing current classes and adding new ones based on student demand. New majors in e-commerce and technology, biotechnology, and media management were student initiatives with support from a number of faculty. Kellogg averages about fifteen new courses a year. In order to expand its global reach, Kellogg has formed partnerships with prominent MBA programs in Germany, Israel, and China. The school partnered with Wharton in building a new business school in India.

On-Campus Recruiting Offerings and Advice

Offerings: Companies may have interview schedules comprised of 30-minute, 45-minute, or 1-hour interviews. They may have either all-open schedules or a fifty-fifty split of open and closed schedules. Details are available at www.kellogg.nwu.edu.career/employer/emprac.htm.

Students may start summer or full-time positions when it is most convenient for them and the company. Most students begin their full-time position in August or September. Summer internships generally begin the middle of June and terminate the end of August.

Pre-Recruitment: Be sensitive to the various time demands students are juggling. Try not to host too many events where they would need to be at a four-hour dinner before they've interviewed and received an offer. Examples of what has been effective include smaller dinners/cocktail parties for particular offices of multinational companies and casual meetings in the Atrium (a popular place for hosting gatherings) with company representatives (usually recent alumni).

Employer/Company Briefings: Keep them brief. Students want lots of time for mingling and gathering information about you that they can't get from the Web or company literature.

Interviews: Be honest with students on decision time frames. Return phone calls when asking for feedback. Make sure people are trained in the dos and don'ts of interviewing.

Callbacks/Second Rounds: Be sensitive to the school calendar, and to the fact that each school is on a different schedule.

Top Three Dos and Don'ts

1. Do give quick turnaround on decisions.
2. Do keep presentations within the time allotted by the school (usually one hour).
3. Do consult with the Career Management Center on logistics for interviews and presentations.

1. Don't be unresponsive to student phone calls, even if it means that you have someone else return the calls to get more information or to let the students know you may be delayed in getting back to them.
2. Don't ever mislead students as to the disposition of their interview.
3. Don't send group e-mail dings.

Other Recruiting Options

Kellogg hosts a High Tech Career Fair, an Entrepreneur's Career Fair, and speaker series through the various clubs (Consulting, Investment Banking, Sales, Trading & Research, Marketing, High Tech, Entertainment, Women's Business Association, or WBA, etc.). The WBA hosts a Wines of the World career night. Other events in which companies may participate are student conferences (Real Estate, Marketing, Digital Frontiers, Venture Capital/Private Equity, Business of Healthcare, Global Business, Biotech, Manufacturing, Philanthropy, Black Management Association, and India Business). Many first-year students participate in the Global Initiatives in Management course, which brings in outside speakers from various businesses and then culminates in a 2-week visit to businesses located in a particular country or region of the world. There is also a TechVenture class, which includes a 1-week trip to the West Coast, with over eighty companies hosting Kellogg students.

Companies are contacted directly to participate in these and other events and also find out about them through the school's Web site. Alumni networks are also used to publicize the various trips.

How to Find Out About Recruiting Options, Dates, Events, Student Clubs

This information is available either by mail, phoning in for information, or the school Web site. Student club contacts are available at www. news.kellogg.nwu.edu/scripts/clubdir/clubdir.asp

Key Contacts/Go-to People

Roxanne Hori, Director of Career Management—Ph: (847) 491-3168; e-mail: cmc@kellogg.nwu.edu

School Web site: www.kellogg.nwu.edu/index.htm

Office Web site: www.kellogg.nwu.edu/career/employer/index.htm (for employers); www.kellogg.nwu.edu/career/prospective/index.htm (for prospective students)

Source: Roxanne Hori

STANFORD GRADUATE SCHOOL OF BUSINESS

Dean: Robert L. Joss

MBA Program Overview/Mission

Stanford aims to be the world's leading academic school of general management, combining academic rigor with entrepreneurial enthusiasm to create an educational experience with lifelong value. Understanding that leadership is more than being the best, the school aspires to be an organization that others look to for guidance and inspiration. The research and teaching at Stanford are aimed ultimately at the challenges faced by the integrative general manager, the person who must put it all together and then see to the effective implementation of whatever decisions are taken, achieving this largely through the efforts of others.

Degree Programs

Masters Program: The MBA is a 2-year, full-time residential program designed to prepare students to be outstanding global senior-level managers. Each fall, approximately 360 students begin an academic program consisting in its first year of core courses in key functional disciplines, such as finance, economics, operations, human resources, and marketing, for developing a strong foundation. During the second year, students choose from more than 100 electives, ranging from entrepreneurship to corporate finance, from supply chain management to HR.

Other Programs: Sloan Program (1-year), the doctoral program, and various joint degree programs, the MSE/MBA (engineering) and JD/MBA (law), among others.

Unique Features

Stanford Graduate School of Business represents a community of people who make an impact on the world around them, who believe in the power of ideas, and who lead the waves of innovation that new ideas generate. The tremendous changes in technology that Stanford has witnessed and been a part of have enabled the school to reach beyond the traditional classroom and campus in novel and powerful ways. In November 2000, the school announced a collaboration with Harvard Business School to explore a project to develop and deliver online executive management education. The Silicon Valley location also offers an unparalleled resource in research and in providing educational opportunities for students and alumni.

Successful in one of the most selective admissions processes among top business schools, Stanford students represent a diversity of perspectives, backgrounds, and managerial potential. The school enjoys a sense of community centered around such core values as entrepreneurship, intellectual risk taking, and teamwork. Leadership in technology, along with entrepreneurship, global management, and public management, is reinforced with centers for Electronic Business and Commerce, Entrepreneurial Studies, and Social Innovation. Also in 2000, the school joined with McKinsey and Company to establish the Global Organization of Business Enterprise to study organizational structures and practices used by large companies to meet the challenges of a globalizing economy.

On-Campus Recruiting Offerings and Advice

Offerings: Stanford offers 30-, 45-, and 60-minute interviews for full-time career opportunities and summer internships. Interviewers can request schedules and discuss options and what works best either online or by calling the CMC director or recruiting assistant director. Another helpful resource is the *Recruiter Guide,* available in hard copy or online on the school Web site. This guide includes a time line, recruiting best practices, and other information for effective recruiting.

Pre-Recruitment: Be strategic with regard to timing. Do your homework on what else is going on. Target students via the résumé book, student clubs, and in other ways to generate early interest and visibility. Especially effective are activities that are more personalized, unique, creative, small, and focused, such as a day on the job, small group dinners with alumni or senior managers, sponsorship of student events and conferences that reinforce your message and priorities.

Employer/Company Briefing: Call on a dynamic, engaging speaker. Utilize a mix of levels and functions, including a recent MBA hire. Timing is key; they must be early enough to influence interview sign-ups. Allow ample time for Q & A.

Interviews: Make sure all interviewers are briefed and know about big picture plans, follow-up timing, and history with the school, and that they have interviewing experience. Use alumni when possible or hiring managers who are knowledgeable about the position the student is interviewing for. A team approach works well.

Callbacks/Second Rounds: Follow up with students as quickly as possible. It's as important how you say no to someone as how you say yes. Involve the CEO and a broad mix of managers in the callback process, and use it to give the candidates an authentic picture of your company and what it would be like to work there. After making offers, stay connected with the students, even after they say yes or no. Get feedback on your whole recruiting process for improving next time.

Student Communication: Keep it concise, but know what resonates (language, tone, and medium) with the students and what will be compelling to them. Know your communication strategy for all your schools and the key messages and themes you want all those involved from your company to reinforce. Remember, job descriptions are a key communication tool.

Top Three Dos and Don'ts

1. Do develop an integrated, tailored strategy, plan for your recruiting efforts, and shoot for excellent execution.
2. Do build broad relationships within the school, among students, faculty, career management staff, and other key departments. Also, strive to integrate yourself into the educational process.
3. Offer a great summer internship program; this is powerful viral marketing for next year's recruiting.

1. Don't focus on the titles of the people you send for pre-recruitment and interviewing. Choose a diverse mix of people, with different backgrounds, levels, and functions, who have in common enthusiasm about your company and recruiting for it.
2. Don't forget to communicate 360 degrees—with students, the CMC office, other partners in the school, your recruiters and senior managers, and your MBA recruiting champions—about what and how you are doing.
3. Don't "overexpect" results. Recruiting takes time. Often, terrific companies take 2 or more years to start achieving the results they want. Do your homework on recruiting trends, student preferences, and competition for the talent, and let the school assist you on a productive and enjoyable effort.

Other Recruiting Options

Career Fairs: International, Growth Company, High Tech, and Cool Products/Manufacturing. Worldwide Recruiting Receptions in locations such as Los Angeles, New York, Chicago, São Paulo, London or Paris, and Hong Kong. Treks are planned for various cities in 2001–2002.

Mock interviews for second years in the fall quarter.

Share expertise in one of the thirty student career development workshops or panels. Participate in student-led conferences or events, such as healthcare, entrepreneurship, or manufacturing.

Use the recruiter e-mail distribution service. You can send an e-mail to an entire class at a time. Stanford also offers job listings, résumé books from which you can target candidates, and alumni career services.

How to Find Out About Recruiting Options, Dates, Events, and Student Clubs

Call or e-mail the CMC director or recruiting assistant director. Check the Web site and go to the special recruiter section. Ask to be included in mailings. Read the *Recruiter Guide* or the *On-Campus Recruiting Guide.* Contact student clubs directly via e-mail: www.wesley.stanford.edu/cmc/clubs.html.

Key Contacts/Go-to People

Sherrie Taguchi, Assistant Dean and Director—Ph: (650) 723-3651
Uta Kremer, Associate Director—Ph: (650) 725-3237
Matt Rees, Assistant Director, Recruiting—Ph: (650) 723-2857 or 723-2152
General numbers—Reception: (650) 723-2151; fax: (650) 725-5528
School Web site: www.gsb.stanford.edu
Career Management Center Web site: www.gsb.stanford.edu/cmc
Office Web site: www.gsb.stanford.edu/cmc

Source: Sherrie Taguchi

UNIVERSITY OF PENNSYLVANIA—WHARTON

Dean: Patrick T. Harker

MBA Program Overview/Mission

Wharton's top priority is essentially, and has always been, attracting and retaining the best faculty. Wharton operates from the philosophy that schools are nothing but people, and that buildings and technology really aren't important without the intellectual capital to deliver new and exciting content and ideas. Wharton attributes its success in the past year, a transition year, largely to the strength of its faculty. It is Tom Gerrity's greatest legacy to Wharton, along with former deans Russ Palmer and Don Carroll, that they developed a faculty that is hungry and that wants to be the best management faculty in the world.

How does a school continue to draw such people? The most important thing is to have an exciting intellectual environment. And that means great colleagues and great students. In other words, Wharton's approach to staying on top involves creating opportunities for its faculty to express ideas and creativity through innovative research and educational programs. The rest is really tactics.

Degree Programs

Master's Program: Wharton's full-time MBA program offers a unique combination of preterm courses, core courses, and areas of major concentration. With seventeen majors, more than twenty-five concentration areas, and over 200 elective courses, the Wharton MBA degree is designed to be as varied as the individuals who seek it.

Other Programs: Dual degree programs include Communication (MBA/ MA); Engineering (MBA/MSE); Law (MBA/JD); Medical Sciences (MBA/MD, MBA/DMD—Dental, and MBA/VMD—Veterinary, MBA/PhD, and MBA/MS); Animal Health; Economics Postgraduate Training Program; Nursing (MBA/MSN, MBA/PhD); and Social Work (MBA/MSW).

On-Campus Recruiting Offerings and Advice

Offerings: Wharton offers 30- and 45-minute interviews. Recruiters can visit the school's interactive Web site, Recruiting@ Wharton, to post a job, request dates for recruiting visits, monitor recruiting activities, view real-time student sign-ups on schedules, plan travel to Philadelphia, and much more. Recruiters can also subscribe to the *Recruiting@Wharton* quarterly newsletter for up-to-the-minute information. On-campus interviews run from the end of October through the last week in March for second-year students, and from the beginning of February through the last week in March for first-year students.

Pre-Recruitment: A successful strategy starts with understanding that recruiting is a long-term process. Plan appropriate events and components of a program accordingly. Recruiters should understand the school's culture—what works and what doesn't—and customize your recruiting efforts.

Employer/Company Briefings: Keep the formal part of the presentation short; the more time for questions and one-on-one discussion, the better. Bring a mix of staff to the event, senior level as well as entry level. Wharton alumni are a big plus. Be creative. Students attend many employer information sessions, so attempts to differentiate yourself with exciting venues or a novel delivery can pay off.

Student Communication: It is important to have clear and consistent communication. Advertising, presentation materials, speeches, even how your company representatives behave should be consistent with your overall image. During the course of a year, students are subjected to literally thousands of recruiting messages. Only the strongest messages will have the desired impact.

Other Recruiting Options

Treks to San Francisco/Silicon Valley, London, Seattle, Los Angeles.

Key Contacts/Go-to People

Office of Career Services—Ph: (215) 898-4383; fax: (215) 898-4449
Bob Bonner, Director of Career Services—e-mail: cdpweb@wharton.upenn.edu
Ursula Maul, Senior Associate Director—Ph: (215) 898-2894
School Web site: www.wharton.upenn.edu
Office Web site: MBACareers.wharton.upenn.edu

Source: Becky Scott

UCLA—ANDERSON SCHOOL OF MANAGEMENT

Dean: Bruce G. Willison

MBA Program Overview/Mission

The mission of The Anderson School is to create the intellectual capital that managers need for the global information age and to develop the entrepreneurial leaders who will create tomorrow's successful organizations. The MBA program offers a solid grounding in business fundamentals as well as the opportunity for students to choose an emphasis in one of fourteen areas or create an individual emphasis from several fields to support their interests and career goals. The Anderson School has built a reputation as a leader in globally focused management education, the uses and implications of advanced technologies in business and management, and entrepreneurship. At Anderson, each student takes active responsibility for integrating his or her own learning and has many opportunities to develop and apply the skills required to both organize and function in a productive team.

Degree Programs

Master's Program: The full-time 2-year MBA program has fourteen concentrations: accounting; decision, operations, and technology management; entrepreneurial studies; high-technology management; information systems; management; policy; business economics; entertainment management; finance; human resources and organizational behavior; international business and comparative management; marketing; and real estate.
The fully employed MBA program is a 3-year program designed for emerging managers with strong records of achievement who wish to pursue an MBA degree without leaving full-time employment. Classes take place during evenings and weekends.
Other Programs: Executive MBA; PhD in Management

Unique Features

The Anderson School has a long history of innovation in its curriculum. The management field study program, which serves as the capstone project for MBA students, was first created by The Anderson School in 1965 as a living laboratory where students could apply their MBA skills and knowledge to problems faced by real-world businesses. This innovative program is now incorporated into MBA curricula at many top business schools throughout the country. The school's Price Center for Entrepreneurial Studies was among the first such centers created to prepare MBAs to manage in a fast-paced entrepreneurial environment, and today it is considered one of the best in the country. Anderson was also the first school to create a virtual community by connecting every seat in every classroom, breakout area, and library reading room to the Internet as well as the school's intranet. Each student has been required to own a laptop since 1995.

On-Campus Recruiting Offerings and Advice

Offerings: Interview schedules of 30, 45, or 60 minutes, including rotational schedules and back-to-back interviews. The school offers open, closed, and split (open/closed) options.

Pre-Recruitment: A couple of well-timed, interesting activities usually suffice. Look for ways to really get to know the students. Among the approaches that have worked best are educational programs on a topic related to the firm or industry (e.g., Salomon Smith Barney presenting on the AOL/Time Warner merger; Goldman discussing its IPO; P&G covering unique product launches, advertising seminars). Social gatherings are also popular. One bank rented out a pool hall for the night, a very well-attended mixer. Another bank conducted true "informational interviews" for first years (using recent alumni) in the Career Center.

Employer/Company Briefings: No need to be fancy; just focus on the basics, like "A Day in the Life." Senior personnel are fine to bring along, but have them talk about topics of relevance to MBAs, and make sure more recent graduates are available as well to mingle and answer questions.

Interviews: Stay on schedule. Prepare in advance (students get the same advice). Have a roster of questions that will truly enable students to demonstrate their strengths and weaknesses and interviewers to make educated decisions. When selecting interviewers, use alumni whenever possible, or at least people with experience interviewing and judging the candidacy of MBAs. It's nice to have consistency of company representation; ideally, the same couple of folks who come out for the presentation and events should do the interviewing.

Callbacks/Second Rounds: Do them when you say you will. Avoid stringing along "B" candidates while "A" candidates are making their decision (or at least try not to be blatant about who's on the A and B lists). Be flexible regarding callback schedules. Students can get into real binds of multiple commitments and unforgiving professors, who can create academic nightmares.

Student Communication: Keep it clear, simple, and use students to get to students, i.e., alumni or summer interns.

Top Three Dos and Don'ts

1. Do show recruits and interviewees that you actually care about them and are committed to their growth and development.
2. Do be available for them.
3. Do find ways to connect with the students, to help them beyond what's necessary for the process.

1. Don't arrive late or run late.
2. Don't change the rules midstream, for example, give notice the day before interviews that international students can't interview; decide to have only closed schedules after students have begun bidding; notify the school last minute that the interviewer is only able to stay part of the day, after a final schedule has been set up for the full day.
3. Don't leave students hanging once the first round is complete.

Other Recruiting Options

Career nights; day-on-the-job visits; High Tech Career Fair; a multitude of on- or near-campus events and programs, with more of an "educational" and less of a "recruiting" approach; conferences.

How to Find Out About Recruiting Options, Dates, Events, and Student Clubs

Recruiter packets are mailed out in March. All information is also available on the Web site. Phone calls are welcome any time! Information on student clubs is provided in the recruiter's guide and on the Web site. To contact a student club, use e-mail or call the Employer Relations office.

Key Contacts/Go-to People

Donna Robinson, Employer Relations Coordinator—Ph: (310) 206-8890; e-mail: donna.robinson@anderson.ucla.edu
School Web site: www.anderson.ucla.edu
Office Web site: www.anderson.ucla.edu/cmc

Source: Alysa Polkes

VANDERBILT—OWEN

Dean: William G. Christie

MBA Program Overview/Mission

Owen @ Vanderbilt stays in front of the information curve by knowing what drives success in the global marketplace. Combining theory, practice, and professionalism, Owen @ Vanderbilt partners students, business leaders, and corporations to help shape the new economy. The school is known globally for its high academic standards; first-rate, research-driven curriculum; and real-world instruction.

Degree Programs

Master's Program: The full-time 2-year MBA program has seven specializations: accounting, finance, operations management, marketing, organizational management, human resources, and electronic commerce and information technology
There are six joint degree programs: MBA/JD (Law); MBA/MD (Medicine); MBA/MSN (Nursing); MBA/MLAS (Latin American Studies); MBA/ME (Engineering); MBA/BA (Arts & Sciences)
Other Programs: PhD program; Executive MBA

Unique Features

Innovative ideas help set Owen @ Vanderbilt apart from other business schools. Faculty bring their research, consulting, and previous professional experience into the classroom. A ground-breaking curriculum focuses on such current business issues as electronic commerce and financial markets. Noteworthy for its vision, Owen @ Vanderbilt was the first business school to offer electronic commerce to its students.

On-Campus Recruiting Offerings and Advice

Offerings: On-campus interviews can range from 20 minutes to 1 hour, depending on the recruiter's preference. Interviews are closed schedules. The Career Management Center caters to specific company needs in developing the best strategy for recruiting Owen students.

Pre-Recruitment: Through information sessions, private dinners, club-sponsored events, and classroom guest lecturing, recruiters have a unique opportunity to interact with the Owen student community.

Employer/Company Briefings: All recruiting companies are invited on campus to host an information session. The sessions take place Monday through Thursday at 5:30 p.m. and 7:00 p.m. A company may also opt to host a "brown bag" lunch information session, which begins at 12:50 p.m., Monday through Thursday. The Career Management Center advertises all company presentations in the weekly newsletter and on its Intranet central recruiting calendar. It is highly recommended that companies contact student clubs to get them involved in the planning and advertising of their events.

Interviews: All interview schedules at Owen are closed. Closed interview schedules allow recruiters the opportunity to select the students they wish to interview. Candidate selection may be done in three ways: the Career Management Center administering a résumé collection, choosing from the résumé book, or selecting from students whom you or a representative have met at events.

Callbacks/Second Rounds: Be accommodating of a student's schedule and course load when scheduling callbacks.

Student Communication: Maintain regular communication with students and clubs to keep them up to date on developments within your organization.

Top Three Dos and Don'ts

1. Do develop a strategy as to how your company will establish its presence on campus.

2. Do involve alumni.
3. Do communicate clearly.

1. Don't miss deadlines.
2. Don't delay on student follow-up.
3. Don't forget to work with the Career Management Center.

How to Find Out About Recruiting Options, Dates, Events, and Student Clubs

Contact the Owen Career Management Center at cmc@owen.vander bilt.edu or (615) 322-4069. Contacts for function-specific clubs can be found at the Web site.

Key Contacts/Go-to People

Steve Johansson, Assistant Dean, Career Services and Corporate Relations—Ph: (615) 322-4075
Amy Herr, Associate Director—Ph: (615) 322-4068
Suzanne Scott, Associate Director—Ph: (615) 322-3797
Christie St. John, Director of International Relations—Ph: (615) 322-2293
Leslie Albert, Assistant Director of Recruiting and Operations—Ph: (615) 343-1122
Mercy Eyadiel, Assistant Director of Recruiting and Operations—Ph: (615) 322-4975

Other Recruiting Options

Career Day (a Fall event); Owen Golf Tournament (a fall event); Atlanta and New York MBA Consortium; EC Club Silicon Valley trip; Finance Club New York and Charlotte trips; Consulting Club Atlanta trip.

Source: Leslie Albert

UNIVERSITY OF VIRGINIA—DARDEN

Dean: TBD

MBA Program Overview/Mission

The Darden School seeks to develop professionals who create, lead, and transform great organizations. It does so by combining extraordinary students, an unmatched level of faculty commitment, an academic model that delivers an integrated curriculum, and a vigorous career exploration program, all combined with a highly involved and successful alumni base. Darden is also defined by a greater sense of community, which is made up of more than just students. A diverse assemblage of faculty and staff, visiting executives, and loyal alumni, each group plays an important part in the school's growth.

Degree Programs

Master's Programs: Full-time 2-year MBA program in general management.

Four 3-year joint degree programs: MBA/MA in East Asian Studies; MBA/ME with the Engineering School; MBA/MA in Government or Foreign Affairs; MBA/MSN with the Nursing School.

MBA/JD 4-year program with the UVA Law School; PhD program.

Unique Features

In 2000, Darden founded the Batten Institute, a program center that focuses on how entrepreneurs and entrepreneurial organizations create, lead, and transform global enterprises. It has become a vehicle for implementing Darden's research and programs on major business issues and operates the Progressive Incubator, which provides opportunities for students to develop their business plans and concepts into viable ventures.

Also in 2000, Darden opened an office in Reston, VA, the heart of northern Virginia's high-technology corridor. From that office, Darden plans to develop outreach activities with local organizations, partner with local corporations through case studies and business projects for Darden students, develop specialized executive education programs, and assist and house participants in the Progressive Incubator.

On-Campus Recruiting Offerings and Advice

Offerings: On-grounds recruiting options for first- and second-year recruiting are 30-, 45-, and 60-minute interview schedules, with up to 75 percent of those schedules closed. Also offered are 30- and 45-minute rotating schedules.

Pre-Recruitment: Build an on-grounds recruiting strategy that effectively targets your company's interests. Always try to have alumni present at these events. Sponsoring a Career Discovery Program for incoming first-year students; sponsoring First Coffee, a break between classes every day; holding office hours in Career Development; and providing case and interview workshops are activities that have worked well for recruiters.

Employer/Company Briefings: Bring alumni. Have a short presentation and allow plenty of time for networking. Be clear about what a Darden student would do as an intern or in a full-time position.

Interviews: Be as up front and clear about the interview process as possible, and make sure that students understand what type of interview to expect and the timing of the decision process. Bring alumni if possible, but if not, make sure that the interviewers have had line experience and have successfully completed the associate or training program.

Callbacks/Second Rounds: Be clear about the callback process, and make sure that your responses are timely for both invites and declines.

Student Communication: E-mail is fine for casual exchanges, but personal contact is essential for interview and job offer communication.

Top Three Dos and Don'ts

1. Do be quick with feedback to students.
2. Do get back to each student individually, whether the status is positive or negative; personal attention is vitally important.
3. Do participate in all key events (briefings, panels, CDP, interviews, etc.) and send the appropriate person or mix of representatives (senior, junior, and alumni) to each event.

1. Don't fail to be consistent in communication content and style with all students, regardless of hiring location.
2. Don't let turnover in HR/recruiting roles affect your knowledge of Darden and disrupt any recruiting progress made.
3. Don't allow inconsistency in your company message (e.g., citizenship hiring policies, international assignment potential, salary expectations, hiring needs).

Other Recruiting Options

The Batten Institute; Darden Business Projects; Issue-Based Initiatives; Case Development; Distinguished Speaker Series; Corporate Advisory Board.

How to Find Out About Recruiting Options, Dates, Events, and Student Clubs

For a calendar of events, contact the Darden Corporate Relations Office. Ellen M. Briones, Associate Director of Corporate and Foundation Relations—Ph: (804) 924-4575; e-mail: BrionesE@darden.virginia.edu. Or call our office: (804) 924-7283, look in our Recruiter's Guide, visit our Web site: www.darden.virginia.edu/career/career_recruiter.htm.

To contact a student club, go either through the Corporate Relations Office or through the club Web sites and e-mail addresses: www.darden.virginia.edu/students/ss_affairs_orgs.htm.

Key Contacts/Go-to People

Anne Harris, Assistant Dean for Career Development—Ph: (804) 924-7685; e-mail: harrisa@virginia.edu

Megan McManus, Assistant Director, Recruiting Operations—Ph: (804) 924-3981; e-mail: mcmanusm@virginia.edu

School Web site: www.darden.virginia.edu

Source: Anne Harris

For Established Companies: Here Today, Here Tomorrow

THE DOT-COM FRENZY MAY HAVE been brief, but it did change the scenery substantially, particularly for companies vying for MBAs and the best and the brightest talent in this generation of recruits. Years from now, it'll be interesting to note what historians say about 1999 and 2000 when start-ups and the new economy were the stuff of sexy headlines. For now, many are still deciphering what it's all meant. The smart ones are figuring out what they've learned and how it applies for the future.

PROUD TO BE A NOT-COM

At the height of the dot-com popularity, some established companies, caught unprepared, got the wake-up call to retrench their strategy, rethink their plans, and reposition to address the reasons MBAs at top business schools were often reluctant to join them. By rediscovering their strengths and going back to basics, many established companies rebuilt or, in some cases, refined their recruiting strategies and plans and became more agile and fit to compete with their start-up brethren. Although they never garnered the same kinds of media hype surrounding the dot-coms, these companies showed staying power, many achieving strong recruiting results despite the intensified competition from the start-ups and other companies in pursuit of the still-limited supply of MBA talent.

Established companies that prevailed learned to become better at strategy and marketing; faster and smoother in execution; and more confident and compelling about what they can offer. They were proud to be a not-com. What did these established companies learn through the experience of competing with the dot-coms? Foremost, we watched them take away some valuable lessons.

- **Don't take success for granted.** It's something constantly worked at as hiring needs ebb and flow. Recruiting and keeping great talent takes hard work, imagination, and continuous effort.
- **Leverage marketing prowess.** Marketing prowess is a key to winning, and should be leveraged to the hilt as a competitive advantage. The marketplace is continuously changing, and thus a company's position within it is dynamic. It takes constant drive to know your customers and competitors and strategically position your company within that ever-changing context. It requires continually doing your market research on your customers: What do they now want and need? What now appeals to them in what you can now offer? It also takes knowing your competition, their strengths and weaknesses, which are your opportunities. It's about understanding your strengths and capitalizing on them.
- **Use your best marketers to tell success stories.** In your company briefing, your recruitment literature, your Web site, in your interviews, your callbacks—use the managers/executives who are your success stories, your role models. Trot out unabashedly those who have MBAs themselves, who have had opportunities to join "sexier" companies or start-ups over the years but have not and can explain why they have remained with your company. Call on those who are exemplary in interesting, diverse career paths. It doesn't matter that not everyone in your company is a success story. You are putting your best foot forward to intrigue the MBAs and open their minds to the possibilities of working with you while they are in exploration mode for considering new industries and companies. Success stories can be your hook to get them intrigued. Once you have their attention, you can show them a more balanced view of your company, both strengths and weaknesses.
- **Employees want a piece of the action.** Company ownership in the form of stock options can be a powerful incentive, not just for top manage-

ment but for everyone in the company. A person who is going to work long and hard for the company wants to benefit from the upside of a company. If you cannot offer stock options, offer career options. Talk about how you invest in people—their learning and development, their careers. What initiatives and programs do you have in place for career development? Highlight your internal processes that ensure employees get to voice their career interests and preferences. Discuss how you promote and move people into career broadening opportunities. Give concrete examples of recent MBAs who have come in and the types of career options afforded them. Do your succession planning; identify your high potentials. See Chapter 16, the section on continuous learning and career development as retention strategies.

- **Speed is needed.** When a candidate can interview with a CEO, the hiring manager, HR, and key colleagues in the course of an afternoon and have an offer by the time he or she walks out the door, you've broken warp speed for recruiting. Even with a cooling economy, the talent most in demand is still being hotly pursued. Companies have learned that if they want the best candidates, they need to move fast. Act like a nimble, small company in your recruiting execution.

- **Culture *is* important.** Having fun in a terrific environment and enjoying co-workers energizes employees to sustain working intensely and productively. Although you must always be cognizant of budgets and value adds, fun activities and gestures such as celebrating birthdays, casual dress days, and company outings are not frivolous. We've seen that having fun can energize your talent to become more productive, more intense about work, and more satisfied, thus staying longer in the company.

- **Stability is not a bad thing.** The S-word is, in fact, a good thing that we see many seeking out these days. After the whiplash of the dot-com frenzy and the enormous amount of uncertainty that many have survived in start-ups, candidates welcome stability in an employer.

Why MBAs Have Been Skittish in the Past

Although there seems to be a renewed interest in established companies at present, it's interesting to note why many MBAs have turned away from established companies over the years. They tell us their unabashed perceptions—many of them myths—of old, large companies, such as the following:

- They are hierarchical; we MBAs will get lost in the morass of people.
- They are not agile or quick; these companies are slow to change and to make decisions and act.
- We MBAs are scared of being bored or fear we won't continue to learn.
- The talent in the company may not be stimulating, smart, or ambitious.
- They offer inferior compensation to start with and limited future upside.
- They lack role models for us.
- While there is structured career development, they may not have the flexibility or fluidity to allow someone to take on as much responsibility as quickly as he or she can handle it.
- It will take much longer to wear lots of different hats and gain exposure to a variety of work in an established company than in a start-up.
- Loyalty doesn't guarantee you a job, as evidenced by the downsizings and rightsizings of the 1980s.
- You can't make an impact as fast as in a smaller, younger company.

Putting Net Start-Ups in Perspective

On the flip side, MBAs were attracted to start-ups and many still are as these young companies enter the second act of their evolution:

- The potential to be part of something huge; to make an impact; and help build a great company
- The gold rush and the monetary upside when and if options still pan out
- Thrill of the challenge
- Variety and the ability to work across groups and gain diverse experiences
- The media idealization of start-ups with everyone becoming a millionaire overnight

STRENGTH IN BUSINESS FUNDAMENTALS

In making sense of these pieces of the puzzle—why MBAs traditionally shied away from mature companies and were so drawn to dot-coms—you can begin to formulate the "aha" here.

If you know the misperceptions about you as a mature company, you can turn them around with examples to the contrary. Among the most pronounced strengths of established companies are what I call business fundamentals, which start-ups most often lack. Examples include global or extensive resources; experienced people, the gray hairs who can mentor from fonts of knowledge; proactive career development initiatives; and time flexibility such as job shares, telecommuting, and sabbaticals. For example, in a mature company, when someone leaves for 12 weeks on maternity leave, there is someone who can take her place.

Established companies can also offer very attractive compensation packages. These may not be the options of mythological proportions, but even in established companies there are millionaires. You just don't often hear about them as you did the dot-com legends. Another strength of a mature company lies in the ability to offer broad-based experience across functions and locations, including international assignments as a global manager. This broad foundation and wide collection of experiences can be an advantage for future career moves. For example, there are many testaments from converts, MBAs who started in mature companies and then parlayed their experience to leapfrog to a senior role at a start-up later on. These converts frequently extol the learning, breadth of experience, foundation, and confidence that working in an established company for 3 to 5 or more years gave them. The experience afforded them roots *and* wings.

How You Can Compete Effectively

Here are some real life stories and theories, some advice and ideas from remarkable managers who have been there and done it. The question posed to them was, How can established companies compete effectively with Net start-ups?

Today Alice Chow is vice president of business development for QED Global, a hot start-up technology ventures and management company based in Hong Kong. She gives a great deal of credit for her current success to the 4 years she spent with McKinsey and Co., where she had first-hand experiences that gave her a broad repertoire of skills and the confidence to handle a wide range of challenges. During her time at McKinsey, she benefited from the advice of experienced mentors and friends, and worked with many mature companies.

Chow has the following advice for established companies to keep top talent and to compete especially with Net start-ups in Act II: Reward your people well. One key reason why many people rush to start-ups is the potential upside they might receive if the venture is successful. Not only is the pay comparable to old economy jobs, the stock options represent a very powerful incentive. Established companies should consider tying more of the pay structure to performance, in the form of either options or bonuses, and letting the employees share in the upside of the company.

Be innovative in business approaches. The Internet offers opportunities to significantly change the way things are done. For young talent, this can be very exciting. Old companies can show they are also risk takers open to new ideas by allowing managers to test new approaches, creating greater chances for breakthroughs.

Allow people opportunities to learn and develop. Top talent is sometimes motivated by an environment where they can learn and feel challenged, with little time left to think about job hunting! This can come in the form of more responsibility and independence, challenging employees and pushing their limits, assigning them critical projects, and offering training opportunities.

Care about your people. Set high but reasonable standards and help your employees build their careers. If you give them responsibility and then support them when they hit rough spots, you will have a loyal staff. Employee satisfaction depends a great deal on the match with the overall company culture, but individual managers also have profound influences on the retention of key staff.

Jay Eum, also formerly with McKinsey and Co., now director of business development with Dialpad Communications, one of the largest and fastest-growing players in Internet telephony, cites the firm's innovative approaches to keeping its top talent: the opportunity to become partner in less than the typical 5 years; new compensation models in which associates share in equity; and the expansion into new areas of interest for the consultants, for example, BTO (Business Technology Office) and @McKinsey Initiative, an e-business incubator for McKinsey clients, among other strategies.

Paul DiNardo, managing director, High Technology Group at Goldman Sachs and the Stanford recruiting alumni team captain, has led his firm to record breaking for Stanford MBA hires over the past 3 years running, despite the tenuous interest from students in investment banking overall and even during the pinnacle of the start-up craze. DiNardo highlights his winning strategy, "To compete effectively against anyone, a firm needs to understand and articulate its value proposition. In the case of recruiting, it is critical to be able to make clear the opportunities that are available for bright, motivated people within your organization. It is also important to recognize that not every potential recruit will be attracted to those opportunities. The biggest danger is in moving away from the core value proposition in an effort to attract people."

Elizabeth Murphy, vice president, human resources and director of information management and recruiting, Goldman Sachs, goes on to underscore the importance of executive management commitment to recruitment as a critical part of being successful with MBA recruiting. "Goldman Sachs's commitment to recruit the best and brightest MBAs is supported at the very highest levels of the firm. Our chief executive officer and co-COOs have been involved in a number of campus and diversity recruiting activities. Our leaders realize the tremendous importance of campus recruiting in our overall growth strategy, and they can be credited for much of our success.

"Our alumni teams are led by managing directors or vice presidents who work with alumni line professionals and recruiters in differing hiring divisions. These teams bring a great deal of enthusiasm and firsthand knowledge of the school to our efforts.

"We also understand the importance of providing both student recruits and career services professionals with the most comprehensive information possible on the financial services industry and career opportunities at Goldman Sachs in particular. Many students enter business school to change careers, and we realize these educational exchanges help to demystify our industry and the associate hiring process."

The Punch Line

So what have we learned from all of this? As an established company, what can you do to tweak your recruiting strategy or reinvent it? The startups are not the threat they once were, but they've taught us well about getting a head start on readiness for the next big thing. I think we'd all agree that there's always competition for the most in-demand talent, from startups, your own industry, those outside, those coming in, and those TBD. Think about and imagine what you can do to use the following principles and practices to your advantage in recruiting:

- Shower your MBAs with attention and enthusiasm about how important they are to you. Treat them as you would potential customers. They will be your next generation of leaders after all.

- Have fun. Provide exciting, stimulating work and an enjoyable environment.

- Provide career development opportunities. These could include international assignments and working across functions.

- Keep the caliber of co-workers high. Attract and keep the best talent you can.

- Expose the MBA hires to mentors and role models. Leverage your managers' wisdom and experience in building the pipeline for your company's future leaders.

- Make sure they have a great boss. If the MBAs don't like or respect their managers, and they believe they have tried to do everything in their power to fix the situation, they will leave when a better opportunity comes along.

- Play up the S-word, *stability*. Let your talent know that although there are of course no guarantees, you will be as committed to them as you can. Then prove this in your actions.

Compensation Considerations

Using options as part of compensation and giving employees ownership in the company have been around for a while. Microsoft has been doing this forever. Now it seems like everyone is aware of options, and many expect them, given everything written about them during the start-up craze. MBAs know there are risks associated with options and that they may amount to nothing, but the concept of options for all employees has probably gone mainstream more than at any time we've seen. Giving options or not and to whom are now important considerations for established, mature companies. What else do they need to think about as they still compete with Net start-ups? Linda E. Amuso of iQuantic outlines the strategic kinds of considerations your compensation group or an outside consulting firm would ponder:

- Spin off business segments to create and release value.
- Allow for different pay philosophies and pay strategies in different businesses.
- Try new approaches in every aspect of your business. Typically, old-line companies like a one-size-fits-all approach because it is easier to administer and manage.
- Use a fourth currency, creating a venture fund in which the company in-

vests in other companies.* Employees can have the opportunity to own shares in the fund, based on the fund's performance.
*   New economy companies are in a fast-growth, innovative mode, as opposed to the maintenance mode of their old economy counterparts, and leadership attitudes and philosophies reflect this difference.

More specifically, fourth currency entails:

Upstream options for existing employees in the company being spun out.
Carried interest: An employee can make an investment, as in a VC, in the unit being spun out.
Phantom stock: Phantom stock in the company being spun off.
Internal mutual fund: A basket of equity equivalents in various business ventures with the intent of spinning them off. The idea is to be able to use equity or equitylike vehicles when you are planning on building and spinning out businesses to give people a piece of the value being created.

Amuso goes on to note:

High-growth companies create opportunities for meaningful job responsibilities, opportunities to change positions rapidly, and excitement around new products and services that will drive company success, which in turn lead to upside opportunities for compensation. These opportunities produce rewards based on merit, favor high levels of employee engagement and are not age- or level-limited, which is often the case in more traditional organizations. Compensation opportunities at traditional organizations have been largely reserved for leadership and management, in keeping with the established, command-and-control approach; therefore equity is typically held at the top of the company and not issued broadly.

In the new economy, there is a belief that the value of a contribution is not determined necessarily by the organizational level from which it springs. As such, reward (equity) opportunities are spread throughout the organization. New economy companies recognize that the value created by their employees is inseparable from the value created by the company. And they recognize that their employees have far greater choice about where they live, where they work, the types of work they wish to pursue, and the length of time they wish to be engaged with an employer.

*First currency = base salary
Second currency = bonus/variable compensation
Third currency = stock options
Fourth currency = equity/ownership access to a company being spun out, carried interest, phantom equity, internal mutual funds

For Start-Ups Only: Cracking the Code on the People Issues

LET'S BE HONEST, IN MANY start-ups HR is not as respected as other functions—engineering, product development, or marketing. In fact, HR may be the most disrespected group in the company, viewed as a necessary evil, understood as mostly an administrative function or as an obstacle of some sort. You know the Catbert character in Dilbert, the evil personnel director. This view is alive and well. A recent article in a respected publication advised start-ups to get rid of the HR department altogether, and to just let the employees each bring in one recruit and be done with it. As if that is all HR can do.

STRATEGIC HR—NOT FLUFF

HR, done well, is so much more. The visionary, successful companies leverage HR as an integral part of their business, not as fluff or "those people in personnel." HR in these companies is not looked down on as a cost center or support staff group (yes, HR is both). It is seen as *strategic* HR. Strategic HR, at its best, can be leveraged to build channels to recruiting sources, instigate meaningful discussion within the company on values and culture, and shepherd their evolution as the company grows by quantum leaps. Strategic HR can create fluid infrastructure and processes that will help the company manage its growth and not implode. It can play a key role in enhancing teamwork, employee productivity, a fun environment, communication flow, career development, and employee learning and overall satisfaction. Strategic HR can make sure that compensation is at market and competitive and that there's diversity in employee backgrounds and perspectives. Strategic HR can be a good, safe coach for the CEO and executive team on getting along, leading the troops, and getting through rough spots with resilience. From a pragmatic standpoint, in these times of employee lawsuits, layoffs, and entire companies closing their doors, an experienced HR manager or group can make *the* significant difference in continuing to exist or being sued or sullied by such negative PR that it's difficult to recover.

By all means, HR is not a panacea, but given support and respect, which albeit should be earned, HR can prove to be invaluable to a start-up's thriving or failing. The following stories and examples from some remarkable start-up executives, who happen to be HR savvy and understand its value to the business, illuminate what the HR function and staff in start-ups can do.

The Yahoo! HR Success Story

Yahoo! really doesn't need an introduction: It revolutionized entire industries, pioneered the portal category, and is the thirty-third most recognizable brand in the world. In an interview, Kirk Froggatt, VP of HR at Yahoo!, gives his insights on leveraging strategic HR for Yahoo!, particularly with respect to the staffing pipeline:

> *There is no single practice, in isolation, which makes the difference. For me, the power is in the integration strategy, the way in which the elements of the total recruiting pipeline play together to meet the unique needs and circumstances of a specific organization. For example, take a look at the "Staffing Pipeline" framework [Figure 12-1]. It depicts the key elements of our overall recruiting and staffing strategy here at Yahoo! While many of the elements are generic, the way we implement some of them is unique to Yahoo!*

Froggatt goes on to describe the unique challenges and needs at Yahoo!

- *Many of the high-volume jobs we need to fill don't exist elsewhere, or at least not in many places, since we are already one of the largest,*

Figure 12-1. The Staffing Pipeline.

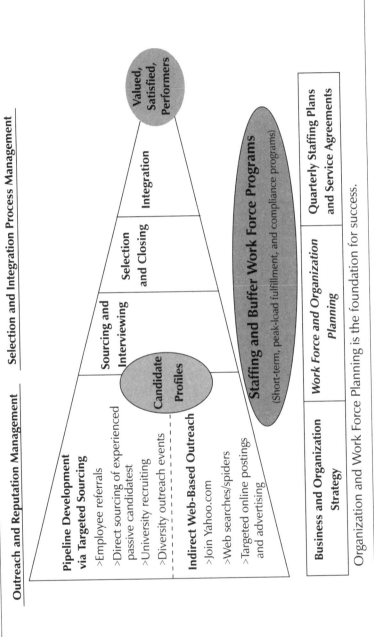

Source: *Kirk Froggatt, Vice President, Human Resources, Yahoo!.*

global Internet companies, so there aren't many places we can find people with bigger or better experience. Therefore we have to identify and hire foundation skills and attributes and train people on the specifics of surfing (editorial and directory services) and production (analogous to movie or media production, not manufacturing).

- *Because of our broad-based brand recognition, and our informal culture with job titles that sound fun and cool, we get a lot of unsolicited résumés, most of which are not a fit for our real needs.*

- *Some of the jobs we need to fill do exist in other industries (e.g., engineering and business development), and therefore are more competitive to attract. We need to identify and select people who want to be part of this industry, and Yahoo! specifically, for the right reasons and who are comfortable in a very organic environment. E.g., we don't have traditional product life cycles and the associated processes, but rather ongoing, organic adaptation on a daily basis with higher risk/higher reward potential.*

- *Because we have more than ninety Yahoo! properties (e.g., Yahoo! Sports, Finance, News, Weather, Mail, and Chat), we need to hire very different people who reflect and have passion and domain expertise in the user communities they serve. For example, we may hire kindergarten teachers who have never worked in our industry to work in Yahooligans, our children's education property; folks from bookstores and libraries to work in surfing; and television and movie broadcasters or producers to produce and MC our Finance Vision. This diversity of backgrounds requires that we organize our recruiters by our key functions or communities of practice that cut across many different properties and business units. Given these challenges, we have organized all recruiting efforts around several design principles.*

- *We have designated senior recruiters who are aligned with communities of practice and serve as the "one stop shop" for their hiring managers' varied needs. These lead recruiters are responsible for developing the appropriate recruiting strategy for each position they are working on, including direct sourcing and filtering the incoming, unsolicited résumés for fit.*

- *We have designated direct and indirect channels for developing the talent pipeline. The three primary direct channels are employee referrals, targeted sourcing for experienced candidates, and university rela-*

tions (UR) for entry-level talent. The primary indirect channel is our own Web site at www.join.yahoo.com.

- *We use a direct sourcing team and a UR team backing up the lead recruiters with targeted sourcing efforts. Think of these as channel development managers. We then implement each of the direct and indirect channels in ways that work best in our culture. For example, for employee referrals we offer a very average cash bonus, but we do several things to keep the program alive in our employees' minds: We send out new postings every week to all employees encouraging referrals; we have a monthly or quarterly prize drawing that anyone who makes a referral who is hired is entered in (to encourage thoughtful referrals vs. warm bodies); and we follow up with references provided by new hires as potential sources of additional referrals. In each of our channels, the channel manager is responsible for ensuring an effective and culture-specific differentiation strategy that yields the results we need. And, the foundation for all the recruiting efforts is the quarterly "workforce & organization plan" which translates any new or changing business priorities into the resulting HR implications for staffing and deployment needs, training and development needs, and change management needs. Without this, in our dynamic world, we could become very diffused and distracted by a large number of open reqs that are not aligned with the current business priorities.*

According to Froggatt, no single element makes the difference, but the effective combination of strategies, with differentiated implementation approaches given their unique needs and challenges, adds up to successful recruiting and retention for Yahoo! Wow! A short course on strategic HR with a focus on staffing from a VP of HR who has obviously been successful by integrating HR into his company as a business partner, a change architect, and a world-class developer and implementer of people practices, processes, and principles. Let's now turn to the hiring line manager's perspective and what they expect of HR.

Reality Bytes from Line Managers

Dr. Paul Ning, director of platform engineering for Netergy Networks, was one of the youngest in his PhD class at Stanford and one of the hottest recruits that year, with a host of high-tech companies pursuing him. In his current senior engineering role, he is actively involved in recruiting and managing talented people, including other PhD's. Ning says that attracting top people "begins with the key players or founding team. Top talent wants to work with other top talent, and you have to build a credible base of winners. Show them that a strong core team is committed to the venture, that their own contributions are critical, and that they will be able to continue learning. If the market space and technical projects are aligned with their professional interests, then you've got a good shot at attracting top talent."

Compensation has to be competitive and attractive, of course, notes Ning, "but the single most important factor is having a growth plan. You must identify what keeps someone interested, excited, and learning, and do whatever you can to accommodate. For some, that means moving into management roles. For others, a technical ladder needs to be in place to recognize superior individual contributors. For all, make sure that great work is publicly recognized. And look for opportunities to refresh and inspire with new projects in new areas."

At Netergy Networks, they've effectively leveraged a range of strategies and initiatives to recruit, including tapping into their employees' valuable contacts and letting candidates get to know them and feel special in the interviewing process. Says Ning, "We have standard referral bonuses for all reqs, and elevated bonuses (e.g., $10k) for certain critical openings."

Netergy pays attention to its current employees too, using a repertoire of tools, from activities and events that build strong bonds to project milestone bonuses.

"To motivate and retain your people, offer mentoring to employees who want to progress quickly and seek advice to do so. Send flowers or a handwritten card to a significant other when extraordinary requests at work are answered with dedication and sacrifice of personal time off being spent at work. Have every senior manager take people to lunch once a week in small groups with the objective of communicating about company goals. Rotate these small groups such that all employees get to do this at least once a quarter. Create fun spaces for different purposes: a game room, a quiet room, and a place to eat. This will keep things very balanced with a place to play, a place to concentrate, etc."

Jay Eum, director of business development at Dialpad Communications, a leading company delivering IP-based communications to consumers and businesses, was at McKinsey before moving to his current role. He's a good example of a great talent who gained an incredibly strong foundation in a world-class established company, then skipped over levels to a key senior role in a start-up. To Eum, recruiting and keeping talented people, the culture, and rewarding employees for their hard work make a significant difference in building a successful company.

Eum offers,

> *To find and keep talented people, Dialpad Communications has an employee referral program that has been very successful. Employees are awarded up to $3,000 for referring others. We have also tapped heavily into the telecom pool of talent with some of our senior executives who have so many contacts in the industry. We strongly promote a family atmosphere internally. We have regular lunch gatherings where the CEO hosts all-hands meetings and introduces newcomers. Even with the downturn in the market, we provided all employees with bonuses.*

Executives and senior managers play a critical role in people issues, but in order to stay focused on their core operating responsibilities, they must be able to rely on a strategic, value-adding HR group. Doug Chan, director of operations and manufacturing at Maple Optical Systems, says that he and other senior managers get very involved in hiring for the company, but there's an expectation that HR will do the lion's share so that their time can be focused most wisely. Chan embodies the quintessential qualities of a maverick and an entrepreneur. Starting his first business at eighteen—luxury foreign car auto parts, then windsurfing boards—he's done gigs as a senior manager in three successful start-ups. He is also said to be a fantastic manager who really knows how to keep people inspired and high performing. Chan told me his views on what he expects an HR group should do for the company:

> *In many start-ups HR has smart, capable but inexperienced people, uses a lot of contract recruiters or those without broader HR knowledge, and does everything on the fly with little process or infrastructure—making it tough for scalability when there are so many TBHs (to be hired). I want an HR department that understands our business, and can take a strategic lead on people issues. This means, for example, attracting and keeping talented em-*

ployees, figuring out how you keep the best of the culture while evolving it to support the company's growth, pulling together an offer to a hot candidate fast, and knowing the ins and outs when you need to fire someone or coach them to do better.

I've had the good fortune to work with some HR groups that added significant value to the companies. When you have a group like that, you're lucky—especially in the first few years in a start-up when the people-talent factor makes THE difference in tanking or thriving.

HR'S VALUE ADD

For HR to be a player in a start-up—besides the biggest hurdle of hiring an experienced and dynamic leader who knows the business, is great with people, can build teams, and is strategic and visionary—here's advice on the four core areas for which HR can add value, achieving early wins and setting the foundation for respect by contributing uniquely and significantly to the company.

Structure and Infrastructure

Ideally your head of HR should report to the CEO because it sends a signal about the importance of people in the company. HR can be the most valuable from this vantage point and positioning, because it can then be privy to the kinds of information and thinking about business strategy and priorities as well as what's on the horizon. If HR is to help drive the business by providing leadership on people issues, it needs support from the top. Many times HR reports to the CFO, which is OK too, but it's important not to make HR, at least in the early stages, get caught up in too many metrics and numbers. Metrics are integral to capturing the effectiveness of practices and activities, and there certainly needs to be discipline in measuring outcomes and results. But, numbers don't tell the whole story, for HR especially. HR needs a champion who realizes that it's one of those functions that can't quantify everything. Visionary HR organizations also have responsibility for internal communication, the environment (culture, of course, but also the physical space), and community relations (for philanthropic reasons and for building company visibility which will impact recruiting efforts).

One of the first mission-critical challenges for the head of HR is to recruit a supertalented, agile, and committed team. The HR function in start-ups has been a magnet for smart, capable people, but they often have little actual HR experience. The chief HR officer needs to bring in some gray hairs, those thirty plus with watermark experience, for key spots on the team such as a comp and benefits expert, a recruiting guru, a systems and a technology whiz. Then younger, less experienced folks can fill out the HR group, but the tools and guidance are needed early on.

Besides informal mentoring, there are numerous resources for giving HR staff access to the core tools and knowledge. The Society of Human Resource Management is a tremendous source and can connect you with regional associations in your area. The Northern California Human Resources Association, NCHRA, www.nchra.org/, for example, offers an HR certification program providing core classes in all the HR areas, e.g., recruiting, compensation, and employee relations. Business schools such as Stanford teach strategic HR executive education courses. There are also a plethora of HR books (try www.amanet.org, www.amazon.com, www.workforce.com, or www.saratogainstitute.com); community college classes; e-learning offerings; or conferences to attend. An excellent book is *Strategic Human Resources: Fundamentals for General Managers,* by Professors James N. Baron and David Kreps of the Stanford Graduate School of Business (John Wiley & Sons, 1999).

After you design your structure, you'll want to build some infrastructure. The dictionary defines infrastructure as the foundation or underlying system. In a literal sense, infrastructure means a system of public works in a city, country, or region, for example, the bridges, highways, and water supply. Infrastructure allows people to move freely. It supports their day-to-day activities. HR can also build infrastructure to ensure that its activities flow freely and are supported. It's a challenge to establish infrastructure when so many things are being done by the seat of the pants, but here are some brief examples of where it can be most beneficial in the long term.

For recruiting, make or buy a candidate and résumé tracking system. Have form acknowledgment letters (or e-mail or postcards) ready to go upon receipt of a résumé, which keeps someone from having to field numerous calls about the status of individual résumés. Develop one great application form in hard copy or for online. Create a professional job description template so they all look consistent, are easy for your compensation person to grade, and can readily be used (without creating a separate document) by potential candidates. Design a fluid interviewing and selection protocol:

Who has responsibility for scheduling? Who will interview at what points? How do you collect and evaluate feedback? What needs to happen to get an offer developed and made fast? Start to build inroads to business schools, executive search consultants, and other sources for talent.

For performance management, offer a process for managers and employees to set goals and objectives and to give and receive feedback. Facilitate ways by which employees can keep learning and developing. Establish norms for performance to be celebrated and recognized through awards, mentions at staff meetings, and bonuses.

For employee relations and development—create a system for employees to be able to voice concerns and to bring up problems like sexual harassment, a personal issue getting in the way of work, or a bad manager. Formulate HR policies that not only make clear to employees what's in bounds or what's not, but also serve as backup if you have to fire or lay off an employee. Make it a point that people have great bosses. Have mechanisms, formal or informal, in place to flag when a manager needs coaching or, in turn, when a manager needs to take steps with a problem performer. Put into place processes that support managers and the executive team, so they get care and feeding too. HR can play a role in keeping them connected and focused, providing coaching and the "What this would mean in terms of people" filter, and designing and facilitating quarterly off sites or retreats.

Harness Your Hiring Power

Figure out where the people you need are and build inroads to them. Foster heavy networking—with your employees, colleagues, competitors, at pink slip parties (for laid off dot-comers) or First Tuesday events. (See Chapter 14 for information on these and thirty best employment Web sites for locating top talent.) Host an open house. Use your whole arsenal to recruit: your Web site; select ads; undergraduate and MBA recruiting and alumni networks; some of the 2,500 employment Web sites for job listings and résumé databases; consulting or investment banking firms that help their employees who want to go into industry make a job change; and headhunters for the hard-to-fill or critical searches. Build your visibility and reputation as a great place to work in the community. Create an employee referral program (see Chapter 13) and challenge each employee as a group goal to refer one great candidate for a job, keep a fun tally, then celebrate and reward. (See Chapter 13 on recruiting on the fly.)

Delineate Roles with the Executive Team

In order for everyone's time to be used most strategically and efficiently, it is best to divide and conquer when it comes to involving the executive team or senior managers in people issues like recruiting. A recommended sketch of roles would make HR responsible for working with the hiring managers and incorporating into their portfolios what's on the horizon for the company's growth or contraction. HR would handle the sourcing of the candidates—knowing where the great people are and building the networks to them. HR would review the résumés, do the preliminary screenings, and orchestrate the interviewing through to making offers and hiring.

The executive team provides a vision of and input on the overarching qualities that *all* recruits should have in common no matter what function. Your executives should be used for high-profile events and activities to build company visibility and presence, and to cultivate strategic relationships, for example, with business school deans or community leaders. The executive team would be called on to interview the finalists for select positions, perhaps for director and above, or manager and above. They can be cheerleaders, getting other managers involved in recruiting, letting employees know the importance of doing their share to bring in other talent. They can also be utilized strategically at key points along the employee's life cycle in the company, for example, with a hot candidate for a critical role who has multiple offers; for new employee orientations; and for an all-hands meeting to keep employees informed about the company, about results, challenges, vision, growth or contraction plans, tackling ecosystem changes. The executive team would also work with HR to architect the people philosophy: setting direction on how you want to treat employees, what kind of company you aspire to be, and so on.

On Track with Compensation

I asked Linda E. Amuso, co-founder and principal, iQuantic, a respected performance and rewards consulting firm, to share her insights on specific compensation challenges and advice for Net start-ups. This is what she had to say:

The two most critical aspects in launching an organization are recruiting strategy and compensation strategy (both cash and stock). Many start-up organizations lack a compensation strategy and instead rely on their venture capital/law firms, search firms, or past experience for direction on equity compensation. Often their approach is, Let's make a deal.

    This approach, wherein compensation decisions are made outside a strategically defined compensation program based on relevant and current data, limits the effectiveness of cash and equity as tools for gaining buy-in and commitment to the organization. In addition, as the company grows, the Let's make a deal approach leads to internal equity issues, given that cash and stock were issued outside of a competitive framework. A strategically unfocused approach also presents issues, as the company grows increasingly reliant on relationships with investors, who have an interest in guarding against dilution of their ownership.

    It is crucial that the HR/Leadership Team understand the strategic nature of compensation as an organization design tool (shaping who is hired and how they are motivated). This understanding is gained through a deep and thorough understanding of competitive practices. Designing a formal compensation program requires access to benchmarking data and the expertise to analyze it. We recommend that companies outsource all design work and analysis until they reach approximately 300 people. At this point they should pursue a stock option administrator, benefits administrator, and compensation manager/analyst.

Amuso lists these factors to consider when designing a compensation program:

* Access to data
* Credibility of data
* Analysis capabilities
* Expertise in program design
* Timing
* Credibility with the leadership team and the board to ensure programs can be approved
* Expected shelf life of the program and other internal priorities

Amuso recommends that companies expecting to redesign monthly or quarterly because they have no clear strategy should hire a full-time compensation employee, because consulting support would be cost prohibitive. External resources are more cost effective for programs designed to last at least twelve months; external resources also tend to have greater content expertise, as well as better access to accurate and timely data.

FROM THE FRONT LINES

Jana Rich, Korn/Ferry International's managing director of software and emerging technology practice, has had a great deal of experience making offers to executive candidates or guiding her client hiring managers on the process to successful closure. Rich notes that:

> . . . *compensation discussions are primarily concerned with base salary, bonus, and sometimes signing bonuses. Industry norms and company guidelines are considered at this time.*

Rich goes on to articulate that there is much more to the negotiation process than these tangibles:

> *The negotiation process includes a lot of other less tangible aspects. For example, if the candidate needs to relocate, this is the time to include the spouse for a dinner with some of the key executives in the company. Offer to have them meet with a real estate agent to discuss and view various neighborhoods. You also want to find out other aspects that are very important to the candidate in a negotiation. Do they want to work from home one day a week? Do they have a spouse who might need to find a new job in a new location? By paying attention to the more human elements of a major life decision like this, the hiring company can increase the likelihood that they will sign the person and have them with the company for a long tenure.*

David Stuart, VP of operations with Computer Motion, has used compensation effectively in his various senior roles in high tech. His advice for start-ups:

• Use special bonuses discreetly. Offered in extraordinary situations they can go a long way. Be careful not to do this too often, and frame for the recipient how important it is to be discreet about receiving such a bonus. And do not set an expectation that this is a precedent for regular bonuses.

- MBO (management by objectives) bonus plans can be very exciting and motivating, and these can be factored into the budget when decisions about starting salaries are made, such that no substantial added costs are incurred. These are best managed as period bonuses, maybe once per quarter. Budgeted amounts should be exactly the same percentage of quarterly salary each quarter for every employee. Somewhere between 5 and 10 percent is meaningful.
- Performance bonuses should range from 0 to 100 percent, and a pay-for-performance structure should be maintained. Avoid an entitlement perspective, and do not unexpectedly remove the bonus system, or penalize an employee in some way that will surprise the employee. Set the rules ahead of time. Make the rules simple, and do not use the bonus to manage away bad results, but to reward good results. Otherwise, this MBO bonus can become a demotivator rather than a motivator. For example, one great way to manage such a system would be to offer 7 percent for very good performance (establishing 7 percent as the MBO bonus), but offer higher amounts to extraordinary performers, making the average payout for the entire company 10 percent.

A PEEK AT EQUITY PRACTICES FOR HIGH-TECH INDUSTRIES

Figures 12-2 and 12-3, from iQuantic, Inc., represent an overview of types of bonus and incentive programs as part of the strategic arsenal of compensation, and highlight how incentive opportunities are typically tied to competitive practice and level in the organization.

FAQs ON MBA RECRUITING

From working with hundreds of start-ups during the past few years, this is a collection of the top ten FAQs that we hear and advise on. The answers are applicable to most of the top business schools.

Q1: What can I do right now—real time—to recruit your students?
A1: Find out from the Web site or by calling the career center what the

Figure 12-2. Bonus/incentive programs.

▶ Discretionary Bonus

- Year-end "after-the-fact" recognition
- Management evaluation of employee's performance
- Performance criteria may or may not be established or communicated

▶ MBO Incentive Plan (Slice-of-Pie)

- Objectives set at beginning of each performance period (e.g., annual, semi-annual, quarterly)
- May include company (financial and/or milestones), group, team, and/or individual objectives
- Awards based on achievement against objectives
- May include a company performance threshold

▶ Pool-Based Incentive Plan (Zero-Sum Game)

- Incentive pool created based on company financial performance (typically revenue and/or earnings)
- Individual award allocations may be based on achievement against objectives
- No awards are paid until minimal corporate threshold performance is achieved

*. . . Incentive programs vary based on company
maturity and ability to measure and pay*

Reprinted with Permission from iQuantic, Inc.

Figure 12-3. Incentive opportunities are typically tied to competitive practice and level in the organization.

Award Opportunity	Target-Incentive Opportunities		
	Position	**50th Percentile**	**75th Percentile**
	VP	30–40	40–50
	Director/Sr. Director Sr. - Individual Contributors	20	25–30
	Sr. - Individual Manager	15–20	20
	Manager - Individual Contributors	10–15	15
	Staff - Individual Contributors	10	12.5–15
	Entry - Individual Contributors	5–7	6–8
	Nonexempt	3	5

Reprinted with Permission from iQuantic, Inc.

school is offering that is coming up. In any year, it will host career fairs, student-run conferences, and other recruiting events in which companies can participate. These give you instant access to students and you don't have to do the work. You can purchase a résumé book and target students directly, list a job with the center, call the director or assistant director of recruiting and ask for referrals, place an ad in the student newspaper, or send an e-mail with your job specs and how to apply. See Chapter 13.

Q2: How can we create immediate visibility?

A2: This is tough because unless you've been in the media overall or have a brand name product, founder, company name, or the like, that MBAs know, visibility is something that takes time to build. You can fast forward to establish a presence and generate some attention with students. Contact a student club about a mutually beneficial speaking opportunity, or sponsor a school event and host a lunch or reception after it. Do something spectacular in your community—beyond the philanthropic rationale, that kind of PR generates buzz. Create a summer internship program (see Chapter 9) but do it well since the word-of-mouth from it can impact positively or negatively the next year.

Q3: How and where do I find the candidates I need?

A3: Ideally, a company would start thinking about its MBA recruiting during the summer and be ready to execute starting in October. For start-ups, it's more realistic to start thinking about needs and plans in January/February and recruit March through May/June. This is the just-in-time approach, and most students would expect start-ups to recruit later in general than others. The calculated risk is that some students will have already accepted jobs and be off the market. Those joining investment banks and consulting firms will have already accepted offers, since those industries recruit early. If you cannot pull off on-campus recruiting, which is a significant undertaking to be done well, use Web sites that focus on MBAs. See Chapter 14 for thirty of the best sites. Also, refer to Chapter 13, which covers nine options for fast-tracking your recruiting when you have no time and need hires yesterday.

Q4: How can I most easily contact the schools—I can't call and visit each one—there's no time.

A4: Visit the Web sites for the thirty top business schools in Table 2-1, or review my top twenty picks and their school profiles in Chapter 10. To shortcut your research on schools and connect with key people fast: view their Web sites, call the career center director even for a ten-minute chat; ask for a recruiter guide or placement report if they are not on their Web site.

Q5: What is market (compensation) for your students?

A5: MBA base compensation is usually mid-to-high $80s across top schools and total compensation (base, signing bonus, and guaranteed year-end bonus) hovers around $100,000. There are wide variances among industries. School placement reports (on their Web sites) will show you the details. Also see Table 8-1 for comparative compensation for popular MBA industries across top-tier business schools. Take a look at the twenty school profiles in Chapter 10 and their placement highlights.

Q6: How can we work better with the school next time around?

A6: Realize that it's about relationships and not transactions. You'll want to cultivate relationships with key people in the school (faculty, students, career center staff). Integrating into the educational process is also key. It's one of the best ways that a company can build visibility and create a presence. Speaking in a class, working with faculty to develop a case study on your company, and participating in faculty research initiatives are not commonplace, but with focused attempts, they are doable for working with a school.

Q7: What have you seen as the best practices in MBA recruiting and the most common pitfalls?

A7: Best practices: develop an integrated year-round plan; don your marketing hat; build multiple relationships within the school; get integrated into the educational process; communicate strategically and often; try for brilliant execution; offer great summer internships. Pitfalls: approaching your MBA recruiting like undergraduate or other recruiting; decentralizing efforts too much; playing dirty; overexpecting your first time out of the box; turning your recruiting faucet on and off; failing to gain support of recruiting internally; and arrogance. See Chapter 9.

Q8: We're losing many of our recent MBA hires, what should we be looking at/doing?

A8: The top reasons we hear from our and other MBA alumni are: (1) a bad boss, (2) unkept promises (more options, new responsibilities after a certain amount of time), and (3) the company is doing poorly (lack of funding, a not-so-good executive team, not meeting earnings expectations, not profitable, new entrants to the space, a nonworking business model). First you'll need to find out why—don't retaliate and don't be defensive about what you hear. Find out why these MBA hires are leaving. Don't be afraid to ask and then have the openness to listen to what they're saying. You can then decide what you do or don't want to do about why they are telling you they are leaving. Many things can be fixed. A bad boss can be coached. Developmental opportunities can be addressed. Unkept promises are sometimes just a matter of misunderstanding or communication. If it's stuff like funding or profitability, you may not be able to fix it, but at least you can address this honestly and help people get through it. If it's on one person's mind, it's bound to be on others so you can proactively talk about these issues and what you are doing.

Q9: Are there some really effective things you've seen companies do to keep their people?

A9: There are 7Cs: live your core values and culture; connect and interact frequently; communicate like you mean it; create continuous learning opportunities; care about career development; commit managers to people and make sure there's accountability; compensate with tangibles and intangibles. Refer to Chapters 15 and 16 on developing and keeping great talent. You'll glimpse valuable lessons from some exceptional managers in start-ups and global, mature companies who share what's working for them.

Q10: The major business school rankings—*Financial Times, Business Week, U.S. News and World Report*—are all different. For example, in a few recent surveys, Wharton, Harvard, and Stanford each took the top spot or tied, with wide variations on those that followed. How do I choose what business schools at which to recruit?

A10: There are many excellent MBA programs available, and the best advice is to choose to recruit at the ones that are best for you—those that best fit your needs regarding kinds and numbers of talent, the resources you have to dedicate to MBA recruiting, your location, how quickly you can build visibility or tap into the schools' other options for accessing their students. The rankings are one data point in your overall research and evaluation to get a feel for top-tier business schools in general and how they differ across dimensions.

The main reason that each ranking is different is that they each evaluate different criteria in different methodologies. For example, *U.S. News and World Report* looks at the educational aspects of the schools and includes input from business school deans about their peer schools. *Financial Times* assesses the international aspects of the business schools and the value of the MBA. *Business Week* focuses on who it considers customers of the schools, surveying a subset of recruiters who hire MBAs and the schools' students. Rankings are one data point in your overall evaluation and research on the schools.

Fast Track to Recruiting on the Fly

IDEAS AND RESOURCES FOR MBAs AND BEYOND

The preceding chapters discussed ideas when there is time for planning your MBA recruiting, and when there is a critical mass of job openings for MBA talent for which you would want to expend your resources for recruiting on campus and building relationships with the schools.

For many of you, there is *no* time. You need just to jump in there and do it, perhaps recruiting on and off at various points within the MBA cycle, and/or broadening beyond MBAs to finding sources for other great talent.

If you need to fast track your recruiting, here are nine ideas and resources for recruiting MBAs and other great talent on the fly—when there's no time for a strategic, integrated program. The first seven ideas are MBA focused. The last two are geared to your overall recruiting needs.

#1. Participate in Already-Planned School-Sponsored Events and Programs

In any one year, there are usually many school-sponsored events offered, such as career fairs, conferences, study trips, treks, and speaking opportunities. Taking advantage of these school events is an efficient option for tapping into the student talent, especially when you have only a few jobs, limited time or money, or are at a location disadvantage, far from the schools in which you are most interested.

The best sources for finding out what events and programs the schools are offering are by calling the career center staff to point you in the right direction or checking out their Web sites. Refer to Chapter 2, which lists the sites for thirty top MBA programs, and Chapter 10, in which twenty career center directors tell what options they offer beyond on-campus recruiting.

Where you will look on the sites will vary, but, typically, find an event calendar or go to the information on ways to recruit the students.

Events are organized by the career centers, student clubs or groups, or the dean or faculty. Events are hosted either on the campuses or off site in cities around the world as part of the schools' outreach, to make their students more accessible to companies, but also to provide students with exposure to different regions as part of the educational experience.

Events usually fall into two categories, recruiting or education, although often they encompass both. Examples of events include Stanford's Growth Company Career Forum, a Cool Products Expo for manufacturing companies, and Entrepreneurs Conference; Harvard's Latin American and Venture Capital Conferences; and Wharton's European, Health Care, Investment Management, and Media and Entertainment Conferences.

Chicago, Duke, and Columbia organize treks to Silicon Valley, among other places. These involve students visiting a number of companies each day, hearing from executives to learn more about their businesses and companies, a job fair or opportunities for interviews, and social events such as a reception with the area alumni. Kellogg offers classes which focus on various regions, and then students travel there during spring break to visit companies. On a similar note, Stanford students lead study trips to places such as Brazil, India, and Australia. For these types of events, if you would like to invite the students to visit you while in your area, contact the organizers, the earlier on the better.

In addition to events, schools offer programs for companies' involvement. Kellogg invites employers to conduct specialized workshops for students and to critique résumés as part of their Resumania program. At Stanford the dean hosts a distinguished speaker series called "View from the Top," annually inviting around twelve CEOs on campus to speak.

While these are not recruiting events per se, participation in them raises the profile of the company appreciably. Such visibility can prove valuable in creating a company presence and may be leveraged at that time or later, to give a boost to informal recruiting activities, such as contacting students directly about job openings or hosting a lunch for a group of students after a talk.

#2. Send a Job Listing

Most career centers provide job listings as an alternative to on-campus recruiting for those companies with limited resources or few openings. These are also known as job postings or correspondence opportunities. Basically, you send a job description along with information on how a candidate should apply, and any plans and timing for interviews. Interviews could be conducted first by videoconferencing or by telephone, then followed up with an in-person interview for the finalists. The career center then makes the postings available to the students.

Before you go this route, find out how far along students are in their job search, so you can gauge how many are still available and actively search- ing. Also, ascertain what to expect in response to your job listing. Sometimes companies are flooded by student interest, while at other times there is no response at all. The job listing manager in the career center will be able to help with this information.

Job listings by themselves are highly *ineffective,* because this is the least resource intensive means of recruiting for companies and therefore the most passive. You need to do something to break out from the clutter. There are several ways to make your listings attention-getting:

- Send a supplemental e-mail to the students—en masse to a class if you can, or to those you target from the résumé book, career center referrals, or other means.
- Send a more personalized e-mail to select student club leaders and ask them to help you get the word out.
- Place a small ad in the student newspaper.
- Generate some interest by offering a giveaway or some other hook to grab attention.
- Send a few flyers or posters to the career center if they will post them.

#3. Ask for Referrals from Career Management Staff

This is easy and quick. Call the center and find out who could best help you. Let them know what jobs you have available and the types of backgrounds you need. Send any company or job information to them in advance of your call or after to follow up. Contact these referred students with an e-mail, package to their home, or a call.

#4. Target Students from the Résumé Books

The career center Web site, recruiter guide, or a call to the staff will inform you when the class résumé books are available, their cost (usually between $350 and $800 for a set covering both classes), and how to order them. Almost all schools have résumé/CV books, which include individual student résumés for each class—those in the first year of their programs interested in summer internships and those who will graduate and are seeking career positions.

To supplement the hard-copy résumé books, many schools offer Web versions, which allow multiple access to the résumés by your company (especially good when in diverse locations) and give you the functionality to search for students who fit your desired candidate profile.

You can search for students based on your specific criteria, such as career interest or prior work experience, foreign language skills, or location preference, then use your search results to contact those students directly, by e-mail or telephone, to invite them to an open house or to meet with you the next time you're in the area.

#5. Connect Directly with Student Clubs

To add to the idea already touched on above, determine if there's a particular intriguing executive who could speak at a club event. Contact student club leaders; find out what they have planned that could benefit from a dynamic, knowledgeable speaker or what they could add to their program/event schedule given the opportunity. Bounce around ideas on current student interests and how those can intersect with intriguing topics on which executives in your organization could speak or host a session in coordination with a student club. To contact student clubs, you'll need to look for a list on the school Web site or call the career center and ask for one.

Although clubs are inundated with offers from companies to do this, if you hit on something that works, you would build visibility quickly and combine a recruiting event along with the speaking. For example, after the event your speaker could host a reception or lunch or bring a few other executives along who could host a larger dinner for interested students.

Another way to connect with students directly is the old-fashioned way, sending snail mail to their home. The personal touch still works. Consider sending a letter introducing your company and job opportunities, along with recruitment materials, and perhaps a handwritten note and small gift. Follow up with a telephone call or e-mail. To make the most of your time, target students through résumé books or career center referrals first.

#6. Tap into the School's Alumni Career Services

Most schools offer some kind of alumni career services. The career center or a separate alumni relations group usually handles these. Look on the school Web site or call the career center. The types of services usually offered for companies are (1) sending job listings to their alumni, via hard copy or online; (2) organizing alumni networking events for companies to participate in, for example, by sending a speaker to a workshop (these are hidden opportunities you will need to ask about) or participating in a networking reception; or (3) hosting e-mail distribution groups that allow an alumnus of the school in your company to send a job posting to alumni groups organized by industry, interests, class, or location.

Schools also frequently have on staff career strategists or advisers who work with alumni on job changes or career resources. Introduce yourself and get to know them. Tell them about your company, what jobs you have, and ask them how you can work together.

#7. Leverage Online Resources

Tap into a select number of employment Web sites that focus on MBA and/or high-caliber candidates. Chapter 14 lists a cache of thirty employment Web sites that were researched and selected from the more than 2,500 available. It is worth noting here three leading resources that focus on MBAs and companies that wish to recruit them. *Cruel World* works with start-ups to the largest global enterprises and 285,000 MBA alumni and students worldwide for middle to executive level management. *Global Workplace* is a portal for global jobs based out of London, which has relationships with 1,200 companies, twenty-four schools in thirteen countries for $100k jobs and above. I will overview their (1) contact information; (2) background on the companies; (3) what they offer employers; (4) kinds of companies with whom they work, focus of jobs, and demographics of the MBA candidates; and (5) fees. The third leading resource of note, *WetFeet.com,* provides Web-based recruitment technology products, marketing services, and strategic research.

I interviewed all three of the co-founders of these enterprises. What follows are highlights of interviews with Jeff Hyman, former CEO for Cruel World, and Steve Zales, president and CEO, Spencer Stuart Talent Network, Geraldine Kilbride, co-founder and principal of Global Workplace, and Gary Alpert, CEO of WetFeet.com.

Cruel World, Inc. (www.cruelworld.com)

Background: Founded in 1996, as MBA Central, Cruel World uses unique JobCast™ technology to quickly and inexpensively match qualified business professionals and software developers with hiring managers. In December 2000, Spencer Stuart, a leading executive search firm, acquired Cruel World to create a full-service, Internet-enhanced recruitment solution and leadership development Web site. Targeting passive job seekers, Cruel World does all the searching and filtering for a company.

Services for employers: Within five business days, the company receives résumés from interview-ready candidates. Recruiting search consultants work with companies to develop detailed search criteria that match job specifications.

Kinds of Positions/Companies/Candidates

Companies: Cruel World serves the newest start-ups and the largest global enterprises. A sampling includes Amazon.com, Amgen, Applied Materials, Bank of America, Black & Decker, Cisco Systems, CitySearch, Continental Airlines, Frito-Lay, Gap, Home Depot, NBC, Nestlé, Nike, Patagonia, PepsiCo, Pixar, Starbucks, Summit Partners, Time, Toyota, and Visa.

Positions: (1) Business Professionals: Consulting, Marketing, Finance, Sales, Product Management, Public Relations, Business Development, Operations, Planning, and more. (2) Software Professionals: Software Engineers, Programmers, Systems Analysts, Development Managers, Application Developers, and others. Key Area of Focus: Middle to Executive Management.

Position Levels: Manager, Director, VP, CFO, CMO, and COO.

Candidates: members are spread evenly across the United States; have significant education and work experience, for example, 53 percent have post-graduate degrees, 77 percent of which are MBAs; 60 percent have more than five years of functional work experience with an average of 7.4 years' work experience in their functional specialty; 60 percent have management responsibility; 50 percent have manager titles or above. Candidates work for all kinds and sizes of companies.

Most are employed and not between jobs—they're passively looking for that next opportunity.

Cruel World notes that it has "the largest group of high-caliber MBA alumni and students in the world." Its MBA membership is quite diverse. It currently (2/2001) exceeds 125,000 unique members and continues to grow at a fast pace. They have relationships as well with alumni and career development offices at the nation's top 50 business schools. Thirty percent of Cruel World's MBA members went to a top ten program, 42 percent to a top twenty, and 60 percent come from a top fifty program. Top five areas of experience: technology, professional services, financial services, consulting, and consumer products.

Top four areas of functional experience: marketing, consulting, finance, and business development.

Fees: $3950 for ten business résumés from interested and qualified candidates and $1995 for three technical résumés from interested and qualified candidates.

Global Workplace (GWP; www.global-workplace.com)

Background: Founded in August 1999, it came out of an initiative started at London Business School in 1997. GWP now works directly with companies as well as co-branding services with top MBA programs' alumni relations as partners. They brand themselves as the network of premier business schools worldwide and are vigilant in protecting that exclusivity. GWP seeks to work as the outsourced recruitment arm of each school's alumni relations dept. Its site is co-branded with that of the partner school and they ask for exclusivity in the arena of online alumni recruitment for that school. For their North American partner schools, that exclusivity only extends to international recruitment.

Services offered to employers: Global Workplace takes up to two weeks to identify suitable candidates for a position. Once a job has been listed, they conduct an automatic search against their listed profiles and automatically e-mail alumni who match the criteria. Those candidates are then free to apply for the position or not, as they choose.

Kinds of Positions/Companies/Candidates

Companies: Currently they have 1,200 registered companies, 85 percent of which would be company recruiters (not recruitment intermediaries) and list between 200 and 300 jobs per month, with a minimum salary of $100k. On the school side, they work with twenty-five schools in fourteen countries and have access to 130,000 alumni.

Companies include: Deloitte and Touche, Booz Allen and Hamilton, GE Capital Services, Coca Cola, and so forth, and an array of e-startup companies looking to recruit their management teams. Partner schools include Kellogg, Tuck, Darden, Chicago Graduate School of Business, and schools in Europe as well as Japan, Singapore, Australia, and Hong Kong.

Positions: Diversity of positions with a minimum salary of $100,000. Job titles include European Marketing Director for FMCG; principal level of various strategy consultancies; CEO of a variety of start-ups.

Candidates: Their database includes 130,000 MBAs who are alumni of partner schools. The most active candidates are those in their mid-thirties, who are most comfortable with the use of the technology to enhance their careers.

Fees: They list companies' job openings free of charge and earn fees on successful placement of candidates. They also offer an MBA shortlist service, whereby GWP will screen candidates and work with the employer until the position is successfully filled; they charge a fee of 20 percent of first year's salary. A new service has recently been added which offers a full search service for interested company recruiters, at a fee of only 30 percent of the first year's compensation.

WetFeet.com: Your Internet Recruiting Partner

WetFeet.com Inc. extends a valuable mix of offerings to companies and MBAs, as a leading provider of Web-based recruitment technology products, marketing services, and strategic research to Fortune 1000 and high-growth companies. Customers include enterprise clients such as Merrill Lynch, Cisco Systems, and Procter & Gamble and high-growth firms such as Draft Worldwide and Bravida Corporation who deploy WetFeet's integrated suite of services and applications to power the corporation's recruitment Web site, build the corporation's recruitment brand, enable talent sourcing across the Web, and benchmark the performance of the firm's human capital management strategies against other leading corporations. Additionally, WetFeet operates WetFeet.com and InternshipPrograms.com, two of the Web's career sites connecting top talent to top companies, and provides career research at over fifty major Internet sites and over 100 leading universities worldwide.

Founded in 1994, WetFeet.com offers resources for job search candidates, recruiters, and career centers, and is both a research and job listing site. For job searchers, WetFeet.com provides research reports on companies, careers, industries, locations, and salaries; advice on diverse career topics; and a searchable database of over 32,000 job and internship listings. For companies, WetFeet.com provides research on recruiting trends and best practices, technology for recruiting candidate management, and marketing services to build company recruitment Web sites, and a job posting service.

#8. Sponsor an Open House

Open houses loosely defined are organized gatherings for attracting potential candidates for specific jobs or for all of your openings. Candidates are invited to meet and mingle with your hiring managers or HR recruiters. You can host an open house at your headquarters, various regional locations, or even consort with other companies, even competitors, to use their venue when you are trying to strengthen the interest in your industry and lure nontraditional talent to talk with you.

Open houses are a great way to increase your company's visibility, attract a broader-than-usual group of candidates, and target the event to your openings and your needs. At a public career fair you're competing among potentially hundreds of companies. By hosting open houses you can make any hires at relatively lower cost than through other sources. They work well to fill exempt, hourly, and even independent contractor employee needs.

The basic elements of an open house include:

- Refreshments and an executive speaker.
- Brief remarks on the company, why people are important, the kinds of opportunities available.
- Introductions of the people in your company representing the areas that are hiring, so that candidates note their faces and can seek them out. You may let these representatives each say a few words about their groups and jobs, then position them in specific signed sections of the room (e.g., the four corners of the room) so candidates can easily find them.
- Distribute handouts: a company recruitment brochure or annual report; one-page handouts with pertinent job descriptions and contact information on how to apply; hard-copy employment applications or online versions.

Ideally, open houses last about 3 hours, allow an up-close view of your company and people, give a feel for your products and services, and generate excitement about working with you. Advertising in the Sunday career section of the paper is the best way to advertise an open house, although novel ways have also been effective: a billboard on a heavily trafficked freeway, movie screens, and a radio spot targeting commuters.

Suggestions for advertising in the newspaper include:

- Be straightforward and simple in your message.
- Give the day, date, time, and location of the open house
- Direct candidates to more information about you on your job-specific Web site
- Three to five bullet points on you or your strengths
- Areas hiring and sample job titles
- Address, brief directions, RSVP specifics if any
- Your contact information: person to send résumé via fax or Web site

#9. Create an Employee Referral Program

These programs can yield remarkable results for bringing in new employees and also for strengthening ties with your current ones. Programs can make your current employees feel like an important part of growing the company by helping to bring in key talent. The programs can engender loyalty and excitement from your employees, and keep them feeling good about working with you, since, after all, the employees are recommending the company to others. Concurrently, referral programs can turn up high-quality candidates, because your talented employees presumably know other talented people.

There are three main steps to designing and launching an employee referral program: (1) Select the jobs for which you could use extra help or candidates, for example, just the hard-to-fill ones, all open requisitions, or by certain classifications. (2) Advertise and communicate internally to generate awareness and interest. Flyers, posters, a simple brochure, and a special page on your Web site all work. You want to build excitement, support, and visibility. (3) Develop financial or other incentives. Offering different tiers or levels is best. For example, you may offer different cash awards if a referred candidate gets an interview, gets an offer, accepts, or stays beyond one year. You don't have to offer anything elaborate; however, they should be tangible rewards that your employees would want: food baskets, inclusion in a drawing for a trip to Hawaii, movie or dinner certificates, or days off. (For more ideas, see the tchotchkes section in Chapter 3.)

Leveraging Your Web Site and Other Internet Resources

IN AN INTERVIEW, HEATHER KILLEN, senior VP of international operations at Yahoo!, shared her eclectic insights on the power of the Internet for recruiting globally. She also gave her thinking on her interviewing approach as part of building a great organization (Chapter 6).

Killen articulates that how you use the Internet in your recruiting processes depends on who you are. Your strategy needs to be customized to who your audience/customers are. She says that for Yahoo!, "given the kind of footprint we have and the broad audience that we attract," the company can do a lot of recruiting through its network of sites: jobs@yahoo.com. The Internet "is a good source of résumés and potential candidates. We post all of our jobs on the site and are really serious about the resources dedicated to make sure it's done well." The Web site alone doesn't take the place of "the old jungle telegraph and employee referrals" (in which Yahoo! is also very successful), "but recruiting online represents an effective tool for us." Although Yahoo!'s Web site annually receives more than 100,000 unsolicited résumés, the Internet plays a small part in a much larger, integrated strategic staffing pipeline that Yahoo! uses. Kirk Froggatt, Yahoo!'s VP of HR, shares his insights on this pipeline in Chapter 11.

Gary Alpert, CEO of WetFeet.com, adds this about using the Internet for recruiting:

The Internet has very quickly become the single most important and cost-effective channel for recruiting top candidates. From the job seeker's perspective, it is the number one resource for learning about an employer's business, competitive differentiators, career paths, and workplace culture and lifestyle. With the Web, candidates are able to evaluate the "keep attractiveness" of multiple companies without even having to make contact with them—and they do. In fact, 26 percent of candidates rule out applying to a company based on its Web site alone. What that means for employers is that they need to make sure that they are putting their best foot forward on their own Web sites, with the understanding that top talent is constantly using the information there, in conjunction with information that they are gathering from a variety of other sources (career centers, friends and family, and third-party career sites), to make decisions about where to work. From the company's perspective, the Internet offers two substantial opportunities: first, to reach out to a broad and diverse applicant pool through a relatively inexpensive recruitment marketing program; and, second, to capture and manage those candidates through Internet-based sourcing, screening, and tracking systems. A company that understands these three things—how candidates are using the Web, how companies can market to talent through the Web, and how companies can increase the efficiency of their organization through Internet tools—will have a substantial advantage on the hiring front.

Companies that have an edge over others leverage the Internet in two key ways. They create their own winning Web sites that are sure to get their share of sticky eyeballs. This chapter notes ten rules for creating a Web site that helps you better your chances for attracting the kinds of quality candidates you are seeking and building positive visibility for your company that sets you apart from the pack. The second part of the chapter is your very own cache of thirty of the top employment Web sites from the approximately 2,500 sites available today. These have been researched and short profiles on each are provided.

STICKINESS FOR YOUR WEB SITE

As Alpert notes, MBAs and candidates view a company's Web site not only for the job listings but as a primary way to research the company and to get a general impression of what it would be like to work there. Many of our alumni, ten to fifteen years out after being recruited for senior roles at dot-coms, say that the Web site is one of the first places they look after they've been contacted about a job. Your company Web site speaks volumes about you, and there are many exceptional ones out there, all vying for mind share, attention, and those all important sticky eyeballs. To stand out from the pack, you don't have to use gimmicks or spend a lot of money. Here are ten recommendations to develop a winning Web site:

1. Have a vision for your Web site; know its objectives with regard to reputation/recruiting.
2. Develop an eye-catching headline, visual, or compelling home page that overviews the site.
3. Make your site easy to navigate and intuitive to use (use radio buttons or icons to click on, frames, flows from a user's perspective, headlines or titles that convey precisely and concisely information you'll find there).
4. Make your site interactive and update it frequently. Ensure that links are not broken or outdated.
5. Use design, look and feel, style, and color that catch the viewer's attention but that are in sync with the culture of the company.
6. Include to-the-point content on your company mission and vision; job openings (what kinds of talent you are looking for; job locations; benefits, including any special perks); company culture; an online application; testimonials, or profiles by/on current employees or customers; a search engine; event listings; and company history or background. Some of the more complex sites incorporate career advice and how-to-interview tips; a representative day or week on the job; interviews with employees (background and career moves to date); remarks by the CEO or senior manager on streaming video; and contests or fun quizzes.
7. Make the text easy to read (broken into chunks) and visually appealing to bring the words to life.
8. Treat all visitors to the site as you would a valuable customer or word-of-mouth referral, thanking them for stopping by. Provide clear yet flexible information on what will happen next. Indicate whether you have lots or a limited number of openings. Indicate you will contact and follow up if there is a fit.
9. Integrate your print advertising with your online advertising, that is, common headlines or tag lines in both, pointing to each other.

10. Call on the right mix of talent in your company for the Web site development—for the content, look and feel, and technical aspects. These usually require different people, who need to work together: someone in HR who is a recruiting expert; someone in IT who can build the site and discuss cutting-edge possibilities; and for input on the look and feel perhaps a marketing or PR person who understands the company image and positioning.

Content and Style

In many companies the hiring managers and HR leave the Web site development to the IT people. They delegate and ultimately relegate their Web sites to those who may not be as knowledgeable or current on the recruiting picture and how to leverage the Web site strategically to attract and inform the kinds of candidates the company needs. Although IT or Web developers need to play an integral role in building your recruiting Web site, it is imperative that hiring managers and your HR experts stay intently involved all through its creation and evolution.

It's also best when those who are recruiting, typically in HR, work actively on the site's content and are very involved with the IT people or Web master, if you're lucky enough to have one, on developing and upgrading the Web site. HR can in turn work directly with the hiring managers of the groups to flesh out content that is relevant and deep enough about what that group does and its openings. The value add of the IT staff and programmers assigned or Web master lies in making the technical aspects, such as creating the search engine or online forms, navigation tools, and organizing the site or doing a site map, amazing. The expertise and perspectives of HR, the hiring managers, and IT need to be blended so that there's a holistic approach to your Web site as part of your overall recruiting strategy.

Your Cache of Thirty Web Sites to Bookmark

There are more than 2,500 career-related Web sites at last count. The Internet can be a powerful tool for recruiting. However, the caveat is that this way of recruiting can be nondiscriminating—more broadcast and shotgun than nuanced and targeted. The Internet gives online job hunters and employers another option for connecting, but it doesn't take the place of good old-fashioned offline alternatives.

Specifically, MBAs and other top talent may not be on the market. They may not be pursuing opportunities, and in fact may be happily employed. The best ways to reach them are still proactive, strategic ways, such as formal MBA recruiting at top schools, tapping into their alumni network, employee referrals, select use of executive search firms, and targeted newspaper ads.

To reach MBAs and other top talent, here is a cache of thirty sites that are very effective for making the types of impressions and attracting the kind of quality candidates you want. These sites are good for helping you cast your net wider for all kinds of talented candidates, while the focus of these sites is on managerial and executive roles. These sites are the ones we hear about most often from companies that recruit MBAs and other managerial and executive talent. They also include many that my colleague career center directors say they find most useful for their MBAs. Many thanks to Fran Noble and Becky Scott, who researched each of these sites. The descriptions for the sites are in shorthand, not in complete sentences, to allow for quick review.

Bloomberg.com (www.bloomberg.com/careers/): Excellent site for financial jobs. Part of the CareerBuilder Network. More than 136 million page views per month and 4.8 million monthly unique visitors: professionals in financial markets, accounting, consulting, management, computer services, telecommunications, marketing, and sales. No résumé bank. Candidates e-mail résumés directly. Recruiters can receive, sort, score, and route résumés.

BrassRing, Inc. (also CareerExpo.com; www.brassring.com *or* www.careerexpo.com): A comprehensive leading technology-based information and career portal. Through partners Westech and Career Expo and *High-Technology Careers* magazine offers over ninety expos where high-tech professionals can meet with companies in twenty-eight major U.S. high-tech markets.

Over 70,000 jobs at 1,600+ companies and 1,700,000 visitors per month; 10,000 résumés sent from candidates to recruiters daily and 380,000 active résumés in the database.

CareerBuilder (merged with CareerPath.com; www.careerbuilder.com): For employers, the CareerBuilder network offers exclusive exposure on more than sixty of the best branded career centers on the Internet through a single point of contact such as MSN and USAToday.com, Bloomberg, and more than thirty-five localized news sites such as chicagotribune.com and BayArea. com. Delivers strong national and local market reach for online employment.

CareerJournal.com (www.careerjournal.com): Focuses on executives. Sample positions: senior and general management, sales, marketing, finance, technology, and a range of related fields. Job hunters can also research publicly traded companies that post their jobs with one-click access to WSJ. com's Briefing Books. Strategic alliances with Futurestep, Exec-U-Net, Job-Star, FreeAgent.com. and others.

Chief Monster (www.chiefmonster.com): Top employers, executive search firms, and VCs offer senior-level opportunities and gain access to exclusive membership. An excellent resource for senior executives.

Cruel World, Inc. (www.cruelworld.com): Unlike job posting boards or résumé databases, uses unique technology to match qualified candidates to hiring managers. Sends résumés within five business days. Targets passive job seeker; A-list companies as clients; 125,000 members and growing.

Datum (www.datumeurope.com; www.datum-usa.com; www.datum-asiapacific.com): Network for global jobs. Focuses currently on United Kingdom/Europe. Companies list 5000 new U.K. and European jobs posted every week. Candidates may search by country, city, and key word. The European site is offered in English, German, French, and Italian. Asian site is under construction.

eProNet (www.epronet.com): MindSteps merged with University ProNet, started in 1990. Exclusive online recruiting and career management network for alumni of twenty top U.S. universities. Proprietary database of over 100,000 highly accomplished and well-educated candidates who are rarely found on other recruiting sites. Serves employers, from the Fortune

500 to start-ups, and alumni job seekers. Database of talent includes alumni with experience in the fields of engineering, business, and science.

ExecuNet (www.execunet.com): Executive network and membership organization for those making $100,000+. Twelve years old. Provides job listings, career information, and the ability to network with other members.

First Tuesday (www.firsttuesday.com): A global meeting place and marketplace for start-ups. Founded in October 1998 in London, it hosts events in more than 100 cities across the globe, has helped entrepreneurs to raise $150+ million seed capital with 100,000+ members. More than 500 entrepreneurs, business angels, and venture capitalists have addressed First Tuesday audiences—hundreds of start-ups have received financing and senior management hires. Some 6,000+ venture capitalists, business angels, and private investors have attended First Tuesday "Matchmaking" events around the world, and 25,000+ people attend events worldwide each month.

Futurestep (www.futurestep.com): Started in 1997. Executive search service for management professionals from Korn/Ferry International, the world's largest executive search firm, and *The Wall Street Journal*. Offers access to exclusive opportunities with companies worldwide. Fosters long-term career management relationship, including assessment tool and feedback on best fits for industries and companies. Members scan jobs and send their own résumés to companies.

Global Workplace (GWP; www.global-workplace.com): Works with companies and co-brands its services with top MBA program alumni relations groups. 1200 registered companies. Range of top clients. Works with twenty-five schools in fourteen countries. Minimum salary for jobs is $100,000. Some 130,000 MBAs worldwide on database.

Golden Parachute (www.GoldenParachute.com): A free online networking community exclusively for alumni of the top 150 worldwide universities and colleges enabling these alumni to network on business, career, and social levels in a private, secure environment.

Headhunter.net (merged with CareerMosaic; www.headhunter.net): A powerful online recruiting site. Notes more than 6 million job seekers, 1,100,000 résumés, and 250,000 job postings that represent more than 10,000 of the nation's employers. Positions itself as top site for mid-to-senior level executives.

HotJobs.com, Ltd (www.hotjobs.com): Has seven regional offices in major markets across the United States and offices in Canada, Australia, and the United Kingdom. Member companies enjoy access to a database of highly qualified professionals, Web-based recruiting, and award-winning applicant tracking system.

JobAsia (www.jobasia.com): Launched in 1997. Positioned as pioneering and leading interactive recruitment service for Asia. Helped over 3,000 companies, from Hong Kong to New York and London, to recruit employees. One of Asia's largest databases of registered candidates—330,000 as of September 2000. Job ads are classified into thirty-four job areas, twenty-six job titles, and eighty-seven industries. Applicants search on seven criteria, then apply to the companies directly via contact links.

Job Safari (www.jobsafari.com): Features fresh links to the jobs/employment information pages of leading companies, categorized by alphabet and location. Provides extensive and useful index of companies with employment information on the Internet.

JobStar California (www.jobstar.org): Offers job information and community resources for the following California areas: San Francisco, Los Angeles, Sacramento, San Diego. Provides extensive area job listings—searchable database of 30,000 + middle- to senior-level positions that is updated daily from newspapers and Internet, hotlines, fairs. Daily, 17,000 visitors are provided special mix of local and national job search information.

JOBTRAK Corporation (www.jobtrak.com): A dominant player in the college job listing and résumé markets. The company has formed partnerships with and provides private-label, co-branded job listing and résumé databases for more than 1,000 college and university career centers, alumni associations, and MBA programs nationwide. Used by 500,000 + to target

college students and alumni for internships, full-time and part-time employment. Some 50,000 + access site daily.

LatPro.com (www.latpro.com): Launched in 1997. Leading source for
Spanish and Portuguese jobs, connecting recruiters and employers. Offers
employers and recruiters free and effective recruiting solutions, including
free job postings and instant résumé searching for thousands of high-quality
professionals. The fifteen most active countries accessing include the United
States, Mexico, Brazil, Canada, Colombia, Argentina, United Kingdom, and
Chile.

MBA CAREERS.com (www.mbacareers.com): This site offers a job
bank, résumé bank, MBA resources and news, a business school directory,
and more. Provides information/profiles directed strictly toward MBAs—on
recruiting companies and business schools with MBA resource links, a job
bank, and résumé posting.

MBA-Exchange (www.mba-exchange.com; e-mail: webmaster@mba
exchange.com): MBA-Exchange offers career management and networking
for students and alumni of top business schools. Working relationships with
European and U.S. business schools. Allows companies to post jobs to the
students/alumni of a selection of schools and automatically alert MBAs who
may be interested in the posting. Will screen candidates on behalf of the
recruiter, by request.

MBA FreeAgents.com (www.MBAFreeAgents.com): Combines elements of executive recruitment. Almost 10,000 MBAs throughout the
world. MBAs submit a career profile, a cover letter, and have access to job
listings internationally. Opportunities that match a candidate's background
and profile will be automatically delivered to their e-mail account. Within
five business days, companies receive at least five top candidates for any job
posting.

MBA Job (www.mbajob.com): Comprehensive resource for MBAs and
corporate recruiters. MBA recruiters may use the site to advertise job openings or to pinpoint MBAs who meet specific hiring criteria. Candidates re-

ceive e-mail job notification and details on which companies are looking at their résumés and when.

Monster.com (www.monster.com): Seven million job-seeker accounts, over 15.2 million visits per month, and extensive résumé database online of 464,000+ job postings. Job posting life of sixty days. Network consists of sites in the United States, Canada, United Kingdom, Belgium, Australia, Germany, Singapore, Spain, and others. For employers, offers real-time job postings, complete company profiles, and résumé screening, routing, and searching.

Mercurycenter.com (www.mercurycenter.com/careerpath *or* www. careers.bayarea.com): Part of careerbuilder.com. The former mercurycenter. com, now bayarea.com specializes in the Bay area, but allows access to a U.S.-wide search via the CareerBuilder network of posting jobs that are advertised in newspapers on-line. Provides advanced job search and application features.

NETSHARE (www.netshare.com): Confidential membership service developed for executives. Currently serves over 2,000 highly experienced senior executives from a variety of industries around the country. Focuses on positions with salaries of $100,000 and up.

Riley Guide: International Job Opportunities (www.dbm.com/job guide/internat.html): Provides a directory of employment and career information sources and services on the Internet for job searching outside the United States. Links to resources and online job banks for Africa and the Middle East, Asia/Pacific Rim, Canada, Europe, and Latin America. No résumé posting or job listing search feature, but does provide descriptions of and links to sites that do.

Startup/Network.com, Inc. (www.startupnetwork.com; e-mail: info@ startupnetwork.com): High-quality candidates and career opportunities for high-tech start-ups. Offers two complimentary services: Job Exchange, which allows hiring managers to source candidates for midlevel management and technical positions, and Founder's Forum, an executive search and networking service that helps speed formation of senior management teams and advisory boards for high-tech start-ups.

WetFeet.com (www.wetfeet.com): Offers valuable mix of offerings to companies and MBAs as a leading provider of recruitment technology products, marketing services, and strategic research. Fortune 1000 and high-growth companies.

Chapter 15

Developing and Keeping
Your Talent

WILLIAM F. MEEHAN III, DIRECTOR and chairman of the West Coast practice, McKinsey and Company, Inc., and lecturer in strategic management, Stanford University Graduate School of Business, offers these wise words:

> *It turns out that we have learned again that employees are as important as customers. And just like customers, it turns out that it's far more economic to retain a really good one than to go hire or acquire a new one. And, in the end, employee retention is about aligning the company's interests with the employees. Now that we have moved away from the era of expecting a twenty-five-year career with one organization, a company must be able to communicate and deliver against the proposition that staying with their organization will maximize the professional development and personal opportunity for that employee as an individual. In other words, the person should stay, yes, of course, because this is a great company—but, more to the point, because this is the best place for you as an individual and here are three specific reasons why.*

McKinsey's "War for Talent 2000," a survey of 6,900 executives and managers in fifty-six companies, found that only 9 percent strongly agreed with the statement: "We are confident that our current actions will lead to a stronger talent pool in the next three years." Indeed, not only finding, but also keeping great talent in organizations is a foremost challenge and opportunity for companies today and in the foreseeable future. The war for talent rages on, even with the cooling economy. Why? Great employees are always in high demand and have many options. This is nothing new, but it does create tremendous potential for all kinds of leaders to make a significant impact to their organizations through a strategic focus on retaining great talent.

THE GOOD, THE BAD, AND THE UGLY

So you've recruited successfully. That's good. The people you wanted, those talented candidates, have said yes and agreed to a start date. How do you help your new employees get up to speed as quickly as possible so they can begin to contribute? Looking at an employee life cycle, how do you keep them on track from the time they are recruited, to their getting up to speed and contributing in their roles, to their continuing to develop and learn and be inspired? How do you keep them *in* the organization and not tempted to leave, much less from actually walking out the door? If you buy into the thinking that human resources, the employees, are valuable, that human capital is a competitive advantage, and that hiring and keeping talented people are critical to business success, then concerted efforts for developing and keeping your top talent are just as important as recruiting them.

The bad news we keep being bombarded with are stories about employers across all industries who say that they are still experiencing difficulty in attracting new employees and that they have trouble keeping them.

Some of the not-so-pretty, *ugly* stories I hear that cause me the most grief, as someone who cares about people, organizations, and great matches between the two, are about new hires leaving a company after a short time, in just 1 month, 2 months, or even within a year. Among HR circles, you hear it's not just MBAs who are leaving after short stints in their companies, it could be IT professionals, those in start-ups, and high potentials in general who have a repertoire of marketable skills and experience that are always in demand.

Over the years, coaching career management to employees when I was in industry, and now to our MBA alumni who are interested in changing jobs, I've heard a myriad of reasons why the talent walks out the door: They didn't like the boss or didn't feel appreciated. The company's vision or culture changed and it was no longer a good fit, or it wasn't the job they signed on for. The list goes on: better opportunity elsewhere; promises weren't kept; not enough developing or learning; company was just not growing or doing as well as they had hoped. The good thing is that all of these reasons for leaving can be counteracted, so that your valued human resources feel motivated to do great work and consciously choose to remain with you.

HOW GOOD IS YOUR WORKPLACE?

Let's start with a reality check: How good is your workplace? What's your climate like? How would you answer these questions?

- Are you clear with your employees about their role and responsibilities, about what's expected of them?
- Do they have ownership over their work and the ability to do it to the best of their abilities?
- Do they know the company's priorities and how they fit in?
- Do they receive feedback on their performance, and support and resources to do their jobs, and to further their career management?
- Do your employees seem happy? Are there smiling and engaged people when you walk about?
- Do your employees know that you care about them, collectively and individually?
- Do you listen to what they have to say?

These are the list of questions I've used over the years. What others do you have? How would you rate your company?

Other ways to get a read on how good your workplace is include:

- What is your turn (turnover rate)? Is it trending up or down? Concentrated in certain groups? Why?
- What are the exit interviews telling you? Are there recurring themes in the feedback from your employees when they leave the organization?
- What's your churn (churnover rate), which takes into account internal

moves, including developmental moves and promotions? How do you compare within your industry?

- What's your absenteeism like? What about your return-to-work rate, when people are on maternity or other leaves, including sabbaticals?
- How are the sales in your employee store? Brisk or sluggish? A former boss of mine who sits on many boards and is a finance guru told me that a company he works with finds a positive correlation between how employee store sales are doing and employee morale and satisfaction. This isn't obvious, but it makes sense that an employee who feels part of the company and is proud of it would want to buy company branded products and support the store.

If you don't know the answers to these questions or need to benchmark, helpful resources can be found by consulting your local professional associations or networking groups; a knowledgeable colleague; the Society of Human Resource Management; or such experts as the Saratoga Institute. Since 1977, the Saratoga Institute has provided thousands of clients worldwide with the means to evaluate, structure, position, and benchmark the contributions that people make to a business. By supplying and also interpreting human capital data, it helps human resource professionals become stategic partners with the senior management in their organizations. Saratoga Institute's research and methodology focus on arming human resource professionals with the data they need to determine how their people, and policies regarding those people, can affect the bottom line. Two information-packed resources are books by Jac Fitz-enz: *The ROI of Human Capital* (AMACOM, 2000) and *How to Measure Human Resources Management* (2d ed., McGraw-Hill, 1995).

Qualitatively, just do a gut-level check. Do you seem to be losing the people you want to keep? Is this a problem for you? How much of one? What are you willing to do to address it? What is your timeframe?

SEVEN REMARKABLE MANAGERS

In this section, seven remarkable managers share how they've managed to develop and keep their people motivated and productive.

Strategies and Stories

Gert Stuerzebecher, vice president, corporate management development, Bertelsmann, New York. Stuerzebecher is a strong proponent of a company committing to and developing its people, and he lauds chairman and CEO Thomas Middelhoff's leadership in this area. As Middlehoff said in a recent speech to Bertelsmann top management, "We have to be the most attractive employer for management talent. We must make top talent with a passion for the media business enthusiastic about us. Bertelsmann must be the most powerful magnet in the market for personnel: from apprentice to skilled workers to management talent." And from the "Bertelsmann Essentials," he quotes, "We dedicate significant resources to the development of our employees and offer equal opportunities based on individual potential and performance. We promote careers across functions, countries, and product lines."

Stuerzebecher adds to this, "Recruiting and development is a key ingredient of our way of doing business, and Thomas Middelhoff spends a great deal of time on forming our future top management team."

Bertelsman puts strong emphasis not only on recruiting but also on developing talent. Says Stuerzebecher, "We schedule several congresses, seminars, and intensive trainings every year for top, middle, and junior management, such as the well-known Bertelsmann University events." In addition to career development and continuous learning, the firm values the importance of communication, on which Stuerzebecher shared this: "We think it is of especially high importance to create powerful networks within our decentralized organization, and have developed many different formats and platforms to improve our internal communication flow, create knowledge, and increase access to both people and information."

David Stuart, VP of operations, Computer Motion, and formerly director of materials at Quantum. Having spent the last twenty-one years managing people, Stuart is by all accounts an extraordinary motivator and leader of people, while relentless in his high expectations and in developing high-achieving teams who are able to accomplish exceptional results. David is currently responsible for manufacturing, materials, new product introduction, reliability, sustaining engineering, and business development. In an interview, he shared seven valuable lessons learned for developing and keeping great employees:

- "Fix problems, not blame. Look forward at solutions and do not look back to place blame. Understand the root cause of a failure in terms of the work content and not in terms of personalities or skills. Problems are always solved, or could have been avoided, by doing things differently. Concentrate on understanding what different things can be done moving forward. Always reward failure. Anyone who had anything to do with a failure has a lot to be proud of. They tried, they failed, and they want to win next time more than anyone else. It is never the personal fault of a person that a failure occurred. Failures are complex events involving contributions from many people, and much can be learned and enjoyed from them.

- "Make everything *fun.* Do not allow doom and gloom or negative thoughts to permeate the work environment. Laugh at failures, smile, and cheerlead to the next success.

- "Connect all groups to the company goals. Share resources between groups. Let everyone feel like they are pulling on the same rope in the same direction. Do not allow undermining of individuals by individuals. Discourage judgmental thinking and opinions. Focus on work content.

- "Establish relationships with your employees: encourage a healthy relationship-based environment for the entire company. Lead by providing clear objectives, listen to co-worker opinions and problems, always lend a helping hand and reward progress. Show that you *trust* them, believe in them, need their ideas, and treat them with great respect. Pay homage to all of your employees frequently, good deed by good deed. Treat everyone equally, never allowing favoritism, hierarchy, or cliques to develop. Do not allow people to divide the culture with bias in favor of longer-term employees. Convince (or teach) the longest-term employees to show appreciation toward the newer employees for believing in the company cause and to show thanks for their willingness to join in. Get away from employee-boss thinking. Encourage all employees to think of one another like colleagues of equal value in different ways dedicated to one common cause. If executives and senior managers behave in this way, then employees will believe in this behavior and practice it also.

- "Communicate high-level business plans and results to date. Offer this information in very regular and consistent time frames. Use this as a chance to rally excitement for the next set of short-term goals. Keep important short-term goals in clear and present view of all employees. Goals that are large and long will never be met on time, because there are too many unknown factors. Understand long-term goals, set short-term achievable objectives.

- "Organize by projects. Keep the focus on completing those projects. Always have the next project staged ahead of time so all employees know what it is. Let them think about that next challenge, but *do not* let them work on it until this project is done. The moment a project is complete, have an official release/completion celebration marked with the official beginning of the next project, as well as an official announcement of the next staged project that they cannot work on. Plans can always change, but think ahead, keep projects small (30–90 days), and deliver the rewards and next challenges consistently.

- "Make decisions. Do not ponder or vacillate on topics for too long. Allow all employees impacted by a decision the opportunity to share their opinion on a topic, so that they can feel as though they participated in the decision in a constructive way. Do *not* break down decisions in black and white polls and then take a vote. Establish a feedback gathering technique that makes everyone a part of building on an idea that leads to a logical conclusion with a decision made by you. Most people will not feel that *they needed* to get an equal vote. Rather, they need to know you understood their perspective and that it broadened your viewpoint."

Elizabeth Murphy, VP of HR and director of information management and recruiting, Goldman Sachs. Murphy says that her firm "focuses on creating an environment that fosters long and interesting careers. The firm utilizes dimensions like compensation and career development, which shows in the level of commitment their people in turn exhibit to the firm. We offer a competitive compensation structure as well as world-class amenities such as our concierge services, health and wellness center, and backup child-care facilities. We offer our people the opportunity to move ahead more rapidly than is possible at most other places. We allow our professionals freedom to change divisions as they advance through the firm, and we provide a variety of opportunities for global mobility." Murphy goes on to say that "the dedication of our people to the firm and the intense effort they give their jobs are greater than one finds in most other organizations. We think that this is key to our success."

Karin Porticos, supply chain manager, Hewlett-Packard. This manager understands the needs and what's important to the people that work with her. Consistent with the winning H-P culture, Porticos and her colleague managers make some commonsense ideas translate to success in retaining key talent: "We offer jobs for managers and individual contributors. A common schedule is three ten-hour days for both job share partners, with Wednesday as the transition day when both people are at work. The downside for the company is that a job share can take up to 1.5 FTEs (full-time equivalents) to do one job. However, job shares are a competitive advantage to retention. They build company loyalty and two people in one job with complementary expertise and skill sets can make a strong team. Two heads are better than one. We also allow individuals to do a 4- to 6-month rotation in another function to gain new expertise and explore if they would like to move into a role in that new function. We give people as much responsibility as they can handle, as quickly as they can handle it. Generally, people feel empowered by this and enjoy having the opportunity for continuous learning. Lastly, we allow flexible schedules such as four 10-hour days. People can also work from home as long as they can be effective working remotely. Most people work 10 to 25 hours at home and the rest in the office. These are seemingly small things that make a big difference in retaining talent."

Louis Amory, partner, Bain & Company. According to Amory, there is "nothing magic" to retaining talent, and he follows with these additional insights:

> *People are primarily concerned about their learning environment. They like you to be demanding, tough, and honest when giving feedback; they care about being on the right path, and managers must demonstrate that they take a personal interest in their associates' development and careers, and take the time to discuss their futures. Managers also need to be aware of what's going on and be proactive to avoid event-driven defection.*

Terry Krivan, director of individual giving, The Tech Museum of Innovation, shares his view about his company's motivation and productivity efforts:

> *CEO Peter Giles and the entire VP leadership team lead the way by living and modeling our values for Learning, Innovation, Integrity, Inclusion, and Teamwork. We are truly focused and live by these values at The Tech, which makes it a wonderful place to work.*
>
> *[The] greatest asset for both attracting and keeping talent is our mis-*

sion driven business environment. Many people see nonprofit work as the pathway to meaningful work.

Krivan and other managers at the museum do a few things that make a real impact on keeping their talented people. These include:

. . . recognizing people for their extra effort. We have a Wow award given monthly to a staff member nominated by other staff. The leadership team selects the winner based on the nominator's remarks. The award is a day off and $100 in cash. We also have various incentive programs that reward people for going above and beyond. HR also does some kind of quarterly staff party after work at The Tech with good food, a DJ, drawing prizes, and so forth.

In our development department, we put a lot of effort into small but meaningful recognition and support of each other, for example, birthdays, special needs, recognizing successes (big and small) at our department meetings or on e-mail—all things that help people feel we are family and build commitment to one another and our work. All of these are really powerful tools that people resonate with.

K. G. Ouye, San Mateo City chief librarian. As Ouye says:

The best incentive for keeping your top talent if you have hired the right people is to keep them engaged and challenged, then have a barometer— meaning, observe, ask, and listen to how they are doing. I am concerned that people feel good in their jobs, that they share a sense of accomplishment, have fun, and enjoy change. But fun and change are my energizers and are not shared by all, even the high achievers. Learn to let people feel as comfortable as they need to be with their own motivation and drivers.

SETTING UP NEW HIRES

As a hiring manager, you'll want to set up your new hires for success. A good manager helps to provide a strong foundation from which to start out. Retaining your talent is moot if they've crashed and burned or derailed early on. You've heard the old adage about starting off on the right foot. Anecdotally, you probably can recall in your own organization individuals who have come in and, for whatever reasons, gotten up to speed quickly, acclimated to the culture, and gone on to do exceedingly well. They are probably still in your organization or on to bigger and better things elsewhere but with positive recollections for what they learned in your company.

On the flip side, you've also probably witnessed individuals who come into your organization with anticipated promise and stellar credentials, who can never quite get off the ground. They remain fledglings, never fulfilling their potential, and most of these people end up leaving or being asked to leave.

These are extreme examples, but the takeaway here is that the first 90 days of a new hire's entry into the organization can make a substantial difference to future success or failure. Of course, the individual employee owns his or her career and is responsible for it. As a hiring manager, you can perform a vital role in the initial entry into the company. During the first 90 days, initial impressions are formed about the new employee's abilities; relationships and alliances start coalescing (or not); and missteps—such as unintentional violations of company culture or how people communicate, or not understanding the context of job responsibilities—while recoverable, can derail the new hire fast.

You as a hiring manager or someone coaching or mentoring can make a significant difference in ensuring that new hires are set up for success. You can help them build a strong foundation.

HIRING MANAGER'S CHECKLIST
- Let your recruiting team know when the new hire will join, and thank them for any involvement they had in recruitment and selection. Ask for their support in helping the new hire get up to speed quickly.
- Communicate, based on company norms, about the new hire: start date, background, and key responsibilities. Invite your community to join in welcoming the new employee and implicitly supporting the new arrival's integration into the organization.
- Schedule a time for an orientation beyond what the HR group provides. Include any other key people you want the new hire to meet with early on and ask them to hold time on their calendars. In addition to what HR covers for new employees, such as company mission, organizational structure, performance review process, benefits, and career development resources, discuss job specific information.

- Prepare for your orientation. The purpose is to take off where HR has left off to give your new hire a foundation and the knowledge to perform his or her role and responsibilities, while integrating into the team and company. Components would include:
  - Your group's mission and priorities and how they fit with the company's.
  - Expectations for priorities over the next twelve months.
  - Your management style, the employee's style; including preferred style of communication, how you give and like to receive feedback, whether you are hands on or hands off.
  - Context: your view of the culture, key groups and people with whom the employee will work, and roles and responsibilities on your team.
  - Competencies: the skills and abilities required to be effective; suggestions for resources and where to go to get help; and criteria of evaluation.
  - Start setting aside information in a folder for your new hire as e-mail or hard copy. Examples of what to include are relevant information on company goings on, staff meeting notes, an invitation to an upcoming team celebration, analyst research about new entrants to the market and competitors, an updated company directory, press releases about new product launches or interviews with the CEO.
  - Make sure that as many of the up-front administrative details are handled, so the first few days are smooth: Did HR sent the offer letter? Ask your administrator to find out the new hire's preference for name on the business cards and order them. Figure out the office space situation and have someone make sure there's a working phone and e-mail account, ready for the first day of work.

Over the next 30, 60, and 90 days:

- Sometime after your orientation, do a walkabout. Introduce the new hire to others.
- Agree on standing meetings to touch base, so you can both set time aside for them on your schedules; at least 30 minutes every week or so for the first 3 months will do.

- Touch base regularly outside of your weekly meetings—informally check in to see how things are going, get and give feedback. Make yourself available as a resource and coach.
- At the end of 90 days, whether your company requires one or not, give a performance review. Schedule a time to sit down and talk. Write up something, even a page review. Provide an abbreviated version of any annual or midyear formal performance review you do companywide. Listen to feedback about how the new hire thinks he or she is doing, and which areas still need to be worked on, how your relationship is working, and what both of you can do better.

Setting up your new hire for success, especially during the first 90 days, will go a long way, but it's still not happily ever after from here. Employee and employer relationships are like wonderful marriages. They need continuous attention and care. The next chapter discusses in detail the seven Cs of keeping your great talent now that you have it. Your mission, should you decide to accept it, is to motivate, energize, and develop. May the force be with you.

Chapter 16

Retention Tool Kit

AFTER THE INITIAL ENTRY INTO an organization and the honey-moon period is over, the kinds of retention tools and strategies you use will influence whether your great new hires stay or go. Over the years I've developed what I call the seven Cs. Whether you have thirty people or 30,000, these can be effective influences on keeping the talent you want and keeping them motivated, happy, and developing. These overlap, interplay, and intersect. Optimally, these seven Cs are pervasive in a company's daily management practices and philosophies.

THE SEVEN Cs

1. Core Values and Culture

When I asked Paul DiNardo, managing director of the High Technology Group, Investment Banking Division at Goldman Sachs, how his firm creates a culture that keeps people there and high performing, he said most eloquently:

The most important aspect of any corporate culture is the behavior it fosters. At Goldman Sachs, this is embodied within our core business principles, the first of which is, Our client's interests always come first. Everything else derives from that unambiguous commitment. Within that context, we strive daily to create and maintain an environment of teamwork and mutual respect, not merely because we believe that it is appropriate, but because we believe that in the increasingly complex and global investment banking industry, it is the most effective way to serve our clients. This combination of a supportive work environment and unwavering client commitment enables our professionals to best serve their clients and maximizes the opportunity for both professional success and personal enjoyment in their jobs.

Core values and culture are inextricably linked. Simplistically, values are the foundation of what you or your company holds dear and are the underlying principles that guide you. Culture is a system of shared values and norms that define appropriate attitudes and behaviors for its members.*

Whether you're an established company and have defined core values and culture, or a start-up that's beginning the dialogue, either bottom up or top down, knowing your values and culture and living them authentically will create resilient bonds among people and with the company. It also serves a purpose in attracting and screening candidates. Values and culture are incredibly powerful levers not only for attracting the people you want but also for keeping them moving together and feeling a sense of community and belonging with the company and their colleagues.

Over time, the core values don't change markedly, although they may evolve. They are guideposts through the tsunamis and sea changes along the way.

2. CONNECT AND INTERACT FREQUENTLY

Connecting people to people, and people with the company, at its best is planned happenstance. Connections happen because of all sorts of reasons, for example, because the company goes out of its way through its communication or rewards system to help its employees feel part of a higher purpose, part of building a great company. They happen because an employee enjoys and finds fellow workers interesting. Connections result from open lines of

*Tushman and O'Reilly, *Winning Through Innovation,* Harvard Business School Press, 1997.

communication—people know what's going on and therefore can connect what they are doing to the bigger picture. A powerful influencer connecting people to each other and the company is frequent interaction, across levels, groups, and locations.

Structured and unplanned interactions can build common ground and purpose; generate excitement, enthusiasm, and energy about coming to work; keep people feeling a part of something bigger; and keep employees updated on business wins, challenges, problems, and how things are going. You're also sending an implicit message that you care about people as human beings, collectively but also individually.

People can feel connected to each other, to their team, to the company, to its products or services, to its vision of where it wants to go, and to a higher purpose. People who are connected to each other are more likely to take each other into consideration when they make decisions. They are more likely to stick it out even if the going gets rough, because they don't want to let their friends down. They are more likely to give every ounce of energy to help the company win because they feel a part of the company's direction and goals. Sometimes, through sheer brute force, they can pull off something astounding—something no one else has done or thought they could do—because they feel connected to their team and their CEO and manager.

Interactions take place formally and informally through activities, gestures, events, and communication. We've read about the lengths to which companies go to connect senior executives and employees and to create common goals. There are coffee and wine tastings, orientations with senior managers in dunk tanks, open mike programs, company clubs and sports teams, inspirational speakers, book clubs, and money set aside for each employee to spend on items for themselves or colleagues to enjoy—such as foosball tables, wind chimes for the lobby, rafting trips, and charitable causes.

In my current role at Stanford, I host a fun day once a quarter where we may see a movie, go for ice cream, or have a BBQ at my home. At the end of one year and before developing plans for the next, we do a retreat where we celebrate successes, talk critically about the past year-in-review, and brainstorm plans for the future. We connect on many levels. When working in marketing for Dole Packaged Foods, as we were introducing new frozen desserts we enlisted the help of colleagues through impromptu taste testing. We laughed together, dripped our desserts together, and debated what we liked and didn't about each texture and flavor. We connected and helped produce a better product.

These are activities, gestures, and events that help connect people to people—one person at a time—and connect people with the company. Communication is such an important interaction that it deserves its own focus.

3. COMMUNICATE LIKE YOU MEAN IT

Beyond activities, gestures, and events, companies facilitate connectedness through communication. Companywide internal communication initiatives such as an employee intranet or newsletter have worked over the years and still do. Beyond these, personal communication by managers to their staffs and by the company executives to employees not only keeps people connected, it keeps them informed, productive, and happy: They feel like they are insiders, know where the company is going, and have the information they need to do their jobs as best they can. Examples of effective high-touch communication are all-hands meetings, weekly conference calls with direct reports, or customized e-mail distribution lists to share information or solicit input.

Most employees really want to hear about their company's vision, strategy, short- and long-term priorities, and how the company is doing. They are invested in the company; they are engaged, giving their time, talent, and, sometimes it seems, much of their lives to work. People have an innate need to hear from their leaders about what's on their minds, and to ask, Do they walk their talk (do their words and deeds match?), are they genuine, do they care about me as a person, are they real, and do I believe in their ability to lead the company? This is not only at the CEO level but from their boss's boss on up to any senior manager that is going to influence the direction and performance of the company (Figure 16-1).

As a side note, I've coached incredibly capable executives over the years who failed to fulfill their potential of greatness because they were ineffective communicators. Communication is a learned skill, but its genesis must be the belief that it's important and the authenticity to say it because you mean it.

Beyond the executives, the company as a whole needs to communicate like it cares. Usually there is an internal communications or HR group that

Figure 16-1. The Seven Cs.

Culture and Core Values

Connectedness

Commitment to People

Communication

Career Development

Continous Learning

Compensation

Integrated, these seven principles can help you
develop and keep your talent
in good times and challenging ones.

handles this responsibility. In a start-up, perhaps it's the "keeper of the culture," the CEO. Traditional means of internal communication initiatives that still work effectively today are HR manuals, newsletters, quarterly meetings, copies of the CEO's or executives' speeches, suggestion boxes, nominations for appreciation awards, and remarks on the state of the company at an event such as a picnic or a holiday party.

New ideas we're seeing include town hall meetings, suggestion or appreciation boxes, culture or strategy summits, radio hours (presentations supplemented with open discussion on live issues between company leaders and employees), weekly online chats with a different senior manager each time, and employee rap sessions. There are also outstanding examples of companies' imaginative employee Web sites and corporate portals.

The better intranets are effective because they provide the basics, such as information on upcoming events, the company stock price, welcomes to new employees, benefits forms, press releases, HR policy manuals, a company directory, and job listings, among others. As important, they are also interactive, always changing, easy to navigate, and a favorite destination that employees want to check out. They keep content fresh, relevant, and interesting.

Companies like PricewaterhouseCoopers and CEO Express's EnterpriseExpress are experts in the arena of intranets, extranets, and company portals:

- PricewaterhouseCoopers (www.pwcglobal.com): Its extensive range of offerings includes audit, assurance and business advisory services, business process outsourcing, corporate finance and recovery services, global HR solutions, management consulting services, and global tax services. The firm works with clients to select and implement the components that will further your e-business initiatives, from Web site development to the design of Web applications that are fully integrated with your existing systems.
- CEO Express (www.ceoexpress.com *or* www.ceoexpress.com/html/inexintraextra.htm): Enterprise Express provides private-label intranet and extranet products for companies wanting to communicate with employees and clients. Its corporate portal product provides a unique software and service hybrid that incorporates technology and human intellect. With their business content on the Web and a simple yet powerful development and administration interface that virtually anyone in your organization can use, you can launch a great site quickly. Features include launching a site—templates, multiple editing levels, and so on; updating and managing a site—multistate options, revision tracking and control, automatic content release, and so on; organizational considerations—multiple platform deliver, single site as intranet, Web site, and extranet, hosted ASP or behind-the firewall solution, and so on.

4. CREATE CONTINUOUS LEARNING OPPORTUNITIES

There are numerous books and resources that delve into the gamut of learning organizations, training, company universities and campuses, business simulation tools to help people acquire new skills and knowledge quickly, mentoring programs, and distance learning. I discuss here why it is important to create continuous learning opportunities and a few suggestions of how that might look.

Great companies use continuous learning as a retention tool—keeping their employees' development on the front burner—but they also know pragmatically that employees who continuously learn use that new learning in their jobs on behalf of the company.

Talented employees want the opportunity to keep on learning, to feel like they are growing and developing, and enriching themselves personally and professionally. They want both the developmental opportunities and the one-to-one learning, for example, their manager giving feedback on performance. They may also need some structured development, additional learning in soft and hard skills so that they can do their jobs better and become more competent. A soft skill, for example, is public speaking. A hard skill may be learning how to do develop a marketing plan or a budget.

I keep saying learning versus training because, bluntly, dogs are trained, people learn. You're probably also beginning to see the title *chief learning officer* for the top HR executive in training and organizational development.

Continuous learning is a basic human need and although not a deal-breaker—the reason someone would leave the company—it is a high-impact retention tool. It's also a two-way deal. The company can provide opportunities for learning but ultimately it takes initiative and commitment from the employee—the motivation and energy to learn. The better companies I've worked with offer the tools and resources to support the employee's development, then let the employee do his or her part. This could be in both informal and formal ways. Some proven ideas that work well are:

- A learning center open 24/7 and a manager on site during regular office hours. The center would offer books, workbooks, videos, audiotapes; bookmarked and linked Web sites and other online materials for gaining new skills or knowledge.
- A company university. Industry experts, leading academicians, and company stars are used to teach courses. There's a curriculum, books, tests, classroom participation, a certificate or celebratory event upon graduating or completion of the course or set of courses, as in school.

Courses include one-time workshops and short courses lasting a few days to extensive ones lasting several weeks.

- Noontime workshops facilitated by an expert or interesting speaker on a particular topic such as performance management, project management, high-performance teams, work-life balance.
- Executive education courses at top business schools. Almost all of the top-tier schools offer nondegree courses for managers. Their school Web sites would have application information, schedules, and program descriptions. You could selectively choose to send high potential managers to offerings ranging from strategic HR to supply chain management, finance for nonfinance managers to longer "mini" MBA type programs that are residential and last for 3-6 weeks.

Two standout resources are Ninth House Network (www.ninthhouse. com), an e-learning company that simulates everyday situations that come up in work—kind of like going to business school but you can learn while on your PC. Ninth House Network is designing, developing, and deploying a comprehensive e-learning solution for today's leading businesses. They effectively integrate cutting-edge content, technology, and services into a comprehensive learning solution that addresses today's critical business issues. Solutions include instant advice, eSeries, measuring results, technology, services, and learning channels that focus on business solutions.

Pensare (www.pensare.com) is a leading e-learning company that creates business knowledge communities which offer content from renowned business and academic thought leaders. Within the communities, professionals share best practices, leverage practical tools, and engage in strategic discussions to solve critical business problems. Currently Pensare offers business content from top-tier business schools and industry experts in such program areas as e-commerce, finance, marketing, information management and operations, management, strategy, leadership, entrepreneurship, customer relationship management, and global business.

Beyond structured learning opportunities, employees learn perhaps best by hands-on experiences:

- Filling in for a colleague in a different job who is on maternity leave or sabbatical.
- Serving on a task force, for example, an engineer contributes on the HR

policy committee, a director of finance sits on the social committee, an HR manager is on the new technology integration team.

- Handling an in-place assignment. This involves the employee staying in place but picking up additional responsibilities within the group, such as media interviews or doing some recruiting or mentoring. The old-fashioned term for this is cross-training. It is good because it gives you backup if someone is out.

Through all of these learning opportunities, employees tackle new challenges, and continue to add new skills, abilities, and knowledge to their repertoires. This all impacts how they feel about the company and their work, which in turn affects whether they stay or they go. These sorts of things also build up credits (versus debits) for you so that an employee is more likely to stick through tough times with you and not be tempted to talk to the next headhunter who calls.

5. CARE ABOUT CAREER DEVELOPMENT

Continuous learning gives employees more confidence and a broader, deeper repertoire of skills, abilities, and knowledge. Ideally, the employees then use their newfound learning to perform better in their current jobs or make a career-enhancing move within the company. Career enhancing because gone are the days of the pyramid—top talent moving up, up, up, vertically. Career enhancing or broadening is commonplace today and for the foreseeable future. This means people experiencing a diversity of functions and areas, like a portfolio of jobs and responsibilities, throughout one's career.

Career development engenders employees who are more committed, loyal, and productive. In the best-case scenario, the employee owns his or her career, but the company provides resources and support to move it along. A helpful resource is Careerdiscovery.com, founded by Tim Butler and James Waldrop of the Harvard Business School. Among their respected body of work, they have identified some character traits that get in the way of success. Their BCII (business competencies and interests inventory) is used at many business schools to help MBAs in their own career and self-assessment.

6. COMMIT MANAGERS TO PEOPLE AND MAKE SURE THERE'S ACCOUNTABILITY

If people are a priority, managers up to the CEO need to believe it, embrace it, and show it. From the top down, managers who show their commitment to people and are accountable for it make a significant impact on motivating and energizing their workforce. Many companies include in their managers' objectives core people issues and challenges such as recruiting, developing, and retaining. They put teeth into the objectives by making a commitment to people issues as part of their performance evaluations. They unequivocally convey that people are important. People issues like managing performance, building morale, and listening to employees are par for the course and are absolutely expected. And they allow their managers the time to spend on it; it's not just work on top of everything else they have to do; it is valued work.

Using 360-degree feedback is also useful. We see 360-degree feedback happen when you solicit feedback from a person's boss, staff, and peers. A manager who consistently falls short, especially to his or her staff, needs coaching. If HR is doing exit interviews with employees and there are themes emerging for a particular manager, that manager needs the feedback and the action items and resources for changing. The company needs to make the manager accountable for results.

7. COMPENSATE WITH TANGIBLES AND INTANGIBLES

Total compensation in the broadest sense is the sum total of everything that an employee receives from the company, the job, the environment, colleagues, and so forth. Along this line of thinking, all six of the retention tools discussed here are part of compensation—both tangibles and intangibles. For a refresher, Chapter 8 covers compensation fundamentals and talks about the importance of the intangibles that really mean a lot to people these days. If you're doing the above, you're already a long way on the intangibles—living your core values and culture, giving people opportunities to learn and develop in their careers.

Worth noting here are some of the best ways that companies use compensation in the more traditional sense, and beyond base pay, to keep great talent: incentives like stock options and bonuses; perks such as on-site child care or exercise facilities; telecommuting; flexible hours; job shares, sabbaticals; job content; job titles; and good, old-fashioned recognition and praise like a note or an acknowledgment in a staff meeting.

Words of Wisdom

John Helding, former senior director for Worldwide Recruiting at Booz, Allen and Hamilton, sums up the gist of this chapter with his insights on how companies can keep their talent:

The key is to treat all employees as customers rather than as a resource (one of the reasons I think HR is a misnomer). In today's marketplace for talent, any company, new or old economy, is offering a product—a career or some part of a career. Candidates are consumers shopping for the best career offering. They are not some static resource like oil or silicon.

They make decisions and choose the career opportunity that best meets their needs at the moment. As such, you need to analyze your career "product" in the same way you'd analyze any product offering. What do they really want?

How can your organization best supply that and do it better or differently than anyone else?

Keeping top talent is clearly in part a matter of being competitive financially, but beyond that it's being exceptional across the full set of employee needs or desires. Things such as a sense of community and belonging, purpose beyond a P&L, pride in the organization, professional challenges and growth, some control over one's destiny. It's the overall offering that's critical in having any chance of keeping at least some of your top talent. A fixation on compensation alone just reinforces that as a deciding factor, not to mention attracts the gold seekers to your firm in the first place. Hiring more broadly and serving a broader set of needs not only builds stronger professionals, but also encourages a stronger and more lasting sense of commitment and loyalty. Sounds old fashioned, but then again, the dot-coms once sounded invincible.

Career Development/Employee Retention

First, Break All the Rules: What the World's Greatest Managers Do Differently, Marcus Buckingham and Curt Coffman, Simon and Schuster, 1999.

"A Market-Driven Approach to Retaining Talent," Peter Campelli, *Harvard Business Review,* January–February 2000.

Love 'Em or Lose 'Em: Getting Good People to Stay, Beverly Kaye and Sharon Jordan-Evans, Berrett-Koehler Publishers, 1999.

Employment Web Sites

Career X Roads: Where Talent and Opportunity Connect on the Internet, Gerry Crispin and Mark Mehler, MMC Group, 2000.

WEDDLE's *Recruiter's Guide to Employment Web Sites 2001,* AMACOM.

Strategic Human Resources

Competitive Advantage Through People, Jeffrey Pfeffer, Harvard Business School Press, 1994.

The Human Equation: Building Profits by Putting People First, Jeffrey Pfeffer, Harvard Business School Press, 1998.

Hidden Value: How Great Companies Achieve Extraordinary Results with Ordinary People, Jeffrey Pfeffer and Charles A. O'Reilly III, Harvard Business School Press, 2000.

Winning Through Innovation: A Practical Guide to Leading Organizational Change and Renewal, Charles A. O'Reilly III, Harvard Business School Press, 1997.

Harvard Management Update, hbsp.Harvard.edu, 800-668-6705
Harvard Business School Publishing: Manager's bookshelf, 800-668-6780
www.hbsp.harvard.edu
www.hbsp.harvard.edu/ideasatwork/managersite

Society for Human Resource Management

1800 Duke Street
Alexandria, VA 22314 USA
Ph: (703) 548-3440   Fax: (703) 535-6490
E-mail: shrm@shrm.org

The Society for Human Resource Management (SHRM) is the leading voice of the human resource profession. Providing education and information services, conferences and seminars, government and media representation, on-line services and publications, SHRM has more than 145,000 professional and student members worldwide. The Society is the world's largest human resource management association.

Workforce Week
www.workforce.com

Thousands of articles, tips, forms, bulletin boards, and product listings. A respected source of work-force management information.

MBA Recruiting Cost per Hire (CPH)

MBA COST PER HIRE = Total Costs/# of Hires

Total Costs =

- Recruiting Staff Salaries
- Image/Branding Strategy
  - Collateral Materials, e.g., Recruitment Brochures, Event Invitations, Flyers, Banners, Posters, Direct Mail, etc.
  - Campus Newspaper Ads
  - Sponsorship of School Events
  - Focus Groups
  - Career Fair Booth or Upgrades to Existing
  - Giveaways, e.g., Career Fairs, Info Sessions, Thank Yous
- Internet Strategies
  - MBA-Dedicated Web Site
  - Job Posting Sites
  - Résumé Database
  - Banner Ads
- Travel and Entertainment
  - Employer Information Session

- • Day-on-the-Job
- • Second-Round Program
- • Sell Weekend Program
- • Staff Travel, e.g., Campus Visits, Pre-Recruitment, On-Campus Interviews
- • Candidate Travel, e.g., Second Rounds, Sell Weekend
- • Relocation Costs
- • Incentives/Signing Bonuses

Note: There are many variations of cost per hire. Some include indirect costs, such as interviewer cost of time allocated. The most straightforward cost per hire is all program costs including HR staff dedicated to MBA recruiting plus other direct costs.

FACTORS AND GENERAL BENCHMARKS IN CPH

Cost per hire (CPH) varies widely across industries and companies. If you further calculate CPH by individual school, the variances could be dramatic. There are no comprehensive reports on industry-specific CPH, and individual company information is proprietary. Anecdotally, here are some observations.

Factors

CPH depends on factors such as where you are in your MBA recruiting life cycle—a start-up stage or a mature, fine-tuned phase; your company location in proximity to your target campuses; the competitive demand and level of aggressiveness for your desired candidates; how elaborate or basic your recruiting plans; how effective you are.

A Benchmark

A good benchmark is how your MBA CPH compares on a relative basis to your other recruitment sources for managerial/exempt talent. In general, you are doing well if your MBA CPH is even with or lower than other sources, for example, executive recruiter fees, employer referral finder's fees, print or online advertising, Web site job postings, career fair participation.

Average Range

Most companies will have MBA CPHs between $5,000 and 25,000. The bottom of the range may be a popular high-technology company; midrange would be a consumer products company; top of range may be a consulting firm.

Low/High

The total range of CPH I've seen is $1000–60,000. The low was a sexy local Net start-up; the high was an investment bank.

Other MBA Recruiting Metrics

Second-Round Interview Ratio $=$	$\dfrac{\text{# On-Campus Interviews (OCI)}}{\text{# Second-Round Interviews (SRI)}}$	Call back 25–20%
OCI to Hire Ratio $=$	$\dfrac{\text{# On-Campus Interviews}}{\text{# Hires}}$	12–14 Interviewed to 1 Hire
SRI to Hire Ratio $=$	$\dfrac{\text{# Second-Round Interviews}}{\text{# Hires}}$	4–6 Call backs to 1 Hire
Offer Rate $=$	$\dfrac{\text{# Offers}}{\text{# Second-Round Interviews}}$	25–50%
Yield $=$	$\dfrac{\text{# Hires}}{\text{# Offers}}$	25–50%*

*0–25% yield is subpar
26–50% yield is good
51–75% yield is excellent
76–100% yield is superb

BERTELSMANN

Joining Bertelsmann as an MBA

Bertelsmann is a complex, multifaceted organization. On the one hand, it is an established, professional media company with leading positions in almost every field of media. But Bertelsmann is also highly decentralized in structure, composed of many hundreds of independent businesses that, taken together, form a network of opportunity for the entrepreneurially minded MBA. In short, Bertelsmann combines the feel of unlimited possibilities that a start-up can offer with the proven standards of a globally active, powerful corporate structure.

Your new colleagues and our entry-level programs for MBAs reflect Bertelsmann's diversity. We employ individuals with high potential who display a very specific pattern of talents and interests. They come from various backgrounds, for example, the media and Internet industry, professional-services firms including consultants and investment banks, or entrepreneurial businesses they have created themselves.

In order to help these people achieve their career goals and ambitions, we tailor our developmental activities to the individual as much as possible. Here are two examples of the many ways MBAs can join Bertelsmann:

Our Global Junior Executive Group

Every year up to ten people with strong entrepreneurial potential and various educational, personal, and professional backgrounds are accepted into our Global Junior Executive Program. The program has an international scope—members will have a home base either in New York or in Europe and have the opportunity to work in many different business environments.

You will work on projects, gain both operational and strategic experience, and learn how we do things—and how we became one of the world's most admired companies (*Fortune,* 1999)—from both the creative and business side. You will enjoy hands-on responsibility, from strategy and design all the way to the concrete implementation of ideas and projects. You will develop a network across the entire Bertelsmann organization. After you have completed the program, you will find yourself prepared to soon assume responsibility for a business operation.

The program is under the aegis of Dr. Thomas Middelhoff, CEO and Chairman of the Board of Bertelsmann AG. You will meet with him and other members of the executive board regularly to discuss developmental issues—your own development as well as that of the Bertelsmann group.

The foremost prerequisite is your entrepreneurial spirit: If your academic track record, your professional experience, and your personality point clearly toward a career in management and leave no doubt that you will quickly rise to the top of one of our companies or divisions, then please contact us.

Corporate and Business Development

Corporate Development at Bertelsmann means developing future opportunities, preparing strategic decisions, and coordinating initiatives across the businesses and divisions. You will quickly get a feel for the media world—and the broad picture. This is the place where many important corporate policy initiatives originate and are later put into practice, and where strategic alliances are forged and ideas for new businesses are developed. You will directly help to shape the future of Bertelsmann.

Working in Corporate Development means being a part of an international, dynamic, fast, and flexible team. Currently, Bertelsmann offers such positions on a corporate level in New York and in Germany, as well as on a divisional level in Munich and New York (Bertelsmann Book Group, Random House, BMG Entertainment), Luxembourg and London (CLT-UFA), Hamburg and Paris (Gruner+Jahr Newspaper and Magazine Business, BeCG—Bertelsmann eCommerce Group), and Guetersloh (New Media).

As the ideal candidate, in addition to an advanced degree from a leading business school, you will also have a distinctive "consulting" profile with the relevant experience and mindset. Your analytical skills, as well as your communicative abilities, must be outstanding. And—in order to help us build new businesses—you are highly creative.

Training

We believe in the principle of "learning by doing." You will work with an extremely high level of autonomy from the very first day. Learning at Bertelsmann means autonomy and responsibility, access to successful role models and meritocracy. Custom-designed development programs (organized both internally and externally with some of the leading business schools, including Harvard and MIT from the United States and INSEAD or IMD from Europe) and other intensive training opportunities are offered to help you develop your leadership skills and to become totally familiar with the Bertelsmann structure and culture.

Networking events with many of our most senior executives at Bertelsmann take place every year and include all MBAs in the strategic discussions of the firm.

How to contact us: www.zm.bertelsmann.de/en

CHARLES SCHWAB & CO., INC.

Management Associate Program

The Management Associate Program is a seven- to ten-month development and matriculation program designed to provide functionally directed exposure to Charles Schwab & Co. The Management Associate participates in one 6-month headquarters-based project that offers project management responsibilities, leadership development, business analysis training, and technology skill building.

An optional 3-month rotation is also available to provide additional exposure to a different enterprise. The associate will have an opportunity to work with longstanding Schwab employees, leaders, and senior management. In addition, participants receive structured training throughout the program. At the end of the program, the goal is for participants to move into managerial positions throughout the company.

Qualifications

- Master's Degree: emphasis in finance, marketing, systems, operations, or human resources desirable
- Five plus years of business experience, with at least two years' experience working in a fast-paced environment
- Demonstrated project management capability emphasizing teamwork, strategic thinking, and results-driven implementation
- Excellent quantitative/analytical capabilities, superior communication skills, and PC aptitude
- Interest in financial service industry
- Strong customer service skills
- Foreign language fluency a plus

L'ORÉAL USA

Marketing Assistant

Job Profile

The Marketing Assistant will be hired and placed in a New York headquarters brand marketing assignment with L'Oréal USA. The Marketing Assistant will be assigned to a specific division of L'Oréal, which may be within the Hair Color, Hair Care, Styling, Treatment, Fragrance, Cosmetics, or Sun Care Category.

Key Brand Marketing Responsibilities

Promotion
- Tracks and analyzes past activities, competitive programs.
- Executes selected projects.

- Tracks spending.
- Proofs all bluelines/mechanicals/promo order forms/sell-sheets/pricing sheets.

Advertising Media
- Tracks and reconciles spending.
- Routes and reconciles estimates.
- Prepares monthly budget reconciliation for Finance.
- Tracks competitive spending.
- Participates in evaluation of promotional advertising.
- Participates in meetings with Agencies.

Sales
- Develops understanding of sales function, marketplace, and trade via sales training, in-market experience.
- Tracks account performance.

Market Research
- Analyzes data (Nielsen).
- Coordinates project material preparation with Creative Services, Labs, etc.

Finance/Forecasting
- Drafts monthly brand forecasts.
- Prepares monthly budget reconciliation for Finance.

Manufacturing
- Traffics all documentation that relates to cost estimates, etc.
- Coordinates projects feasibility.
- Manages key dates schedules.

Packaging
- Traffics all packaging-related materials.
- Proofs bluelines, mechanicals.

Language Skills
- Foreign language skills a plus.

Computer skills required: Microsoft Office Package

Interested candidates should send résumé with cover letter to:

Corporate Human Resources
575 Fifth Avenue
34th Floor
New York, NY 10017

Candidate Evaluation Worksheet

School: _____ Date: _____

Interviewer: _____ Extension: _____

Position: _____ Career ☐ Summer ☐

	Poor				Excellent
Company-Specific Criteria					
Leadership/Management Potential	1	2	3	4	5
Intellectual/Analytical Horsepower	1	2	3	4	5
Interpersonal/Communication Skills	1	2	3	4	5
Job-Specific Criteria					
Relevant Work Experience	1	2	3	4	5
Technical Abilities	1	2	3	4	5
Fit with Team	1	2	3	4	5

Recommend: ☐ Invite Back ☐ Refer to Other Dept: _____
             ☐ Hold for Now ☐ Don't Pursue

Comments:

Final Status:
☐ Follow-up Interview Date: _____ ☐ Group/Job: _____
☐ Offer ☐ No Offer   ☐ Accept ☐ Decline/Why?

SHERRIE GONG TAGUCHI EARNED HER MBA from Stanford in 1989 and has 16 years of HR, recruiting, and marketing experience as VP of university relations for Bank of America and as director of corporate HR at Dole Packaged Foods and Mervyn's Department Stores. For seven years, Taguchi has been assistant dean and director for the MBA Career Management Center at the Stanford Graduate School of Business. She also heads the business school's Management Communication Program. Taguchi's areas of expertise include MBA and college recruitment, career development, executive coaching, succession planning, change initiatives and turnarounds, new product and service launches, and building high-performance teams. She lives in the San Francisco Bay Area with her husband, Mark, a senior manager at Openware Systems. Her most recent speaking engagements include the International Telecom Conference in São Paulo, the International Placement Directors Conference in Paris, the Merrill Lynch Global Executive Forum, the Stanford Business School Alumni Women's Conference, and the Professional Business Women of California May 2001 Conference. Taguchi may be reached at staguchi@onebox.com.